T0178385

Communications
in Computer and Information Science 1960

Rationale

The CCIS series is devoted to the publication of proceedings of computer science conferences. Its aim is to efficiently disseminate original research results in informatics in printed and electronic form. While the focus is on publication of peer-reviewed full papers presenting mature work, inclusion of reviewed short papers reporting on work in progress is welcome, too. Besides globally relevant meetings with internationally representative program committees guaranteeing a strict peer-reviewing and paper selection process, conferences run by societies or of high regional or national relevance are also considered for publication.

Topics

The topical scope of CCIS spans the entire spectrum of informatics ranging from foundational topics in the theory of computing to information and communications science and technology and a broad variety of interdisciplinary application fields.

Information for Volume Editors and Authors

Publication in CCIS is free of charge. No royalties are paid, however, we offer registered conference participants temporary free access to the online version of the conference proceedings on SpringerLink (http://link.springer.com) by means of an http referrer from the conference website and/or a number of complimentary printed copies, as specified in the official acceptance email of the event.

CCIS proceedings can be published in time for distribution at conferences or as post-proceedings, and delivered in the form of printed books and/or electronically as USBs and/or e-content licenses for accessing proceedings at SpringerLink. Furthermore, CCIS proceedings are included in the CCIS electronic book series hosted in the SpringerLink digital library at http://link.springer.com/bookseries/7899. Conferences publishing in CCIS are allowed to use Online Conference Service (OCS) for managing the whole proceedings lifecycle (from submission and reviewing to preparing for publication) free of charge.

Publication process

The language of publication is exclusively English. Authors publishing in CCIS have to sign the Springer CCIS copyright transfer form, however, they are free to use their material published in CCIS for substantially changed, more elaborate subsequent publications elsewhere. For the preparation of the camera-ready papers/files, authors have to strictly adhere to the Springer CCIS Authors' Instructions and are strongly encouraged to use the CCIS LaTeX style files or templates.

Abstracting/Indexing

CCIS is abstracted/indexed in DBLP, Google Scholar, EI-Compendex, Mathematical Reviews, SCImago, Scopus. CCIS volumes are also submitted for the inclusion in ISI Proceedings.

How to start

To start the evaluation of your proposal for inclusion in the CCIS series, please send an e-mail to ccis@springer.com.

Min Zhang · Bin Xu · Fuyuan Hu · Junyu Lin ·
Xianhua Song · Zeguang Lu

Editors

Computer Applications

38th CCF Conference of Computer Applications, CCF NCCA 2023
Suzhou, China, July 16–20, 2023
Proceedings, Part II

 Springer

Editors
Min Zhang
Suzhou University
Suzhou, China

Bin Xu
Tsinghua University
Beijing, China

Fuyuan Hu
Suzhou University of Science
and Technology
Suzhou, China

Junyu Lin
Institute of Information Engineering, CAS
Beijing, China

Zeguang Lu
National Academy of Guo Ding Institute
of Data Science
Beijing, China

Xianhua Song
Harbin University of Science and Technology
Harbin, China

ISSN 1865-0929   ISSN 1865-0937 (electronic)
Communications in Computer and Information Science
ISBN 978-981-99-8760-3   ISBN 978-981-99-8761-0 (eBook)
https://doi.org/10.1007/978-981-99-8761-0

This Springer imprint is published by the registered company Springer Nature Singapore Pte Ltd.
The registered company address is: 152 Beach Road, #21-01/04 Gateway East, Singapore 189721, Singapore

Paper in this product is recyclable.

Preface

As the chairs of the 38th CCF National Conference of Computer Applications (CCF NCCA 2023), it is our great pleasure to welcome you to the conference proceedings. NCCA 2023 was held in Suzhou, China, during July 16–20, 2023, and hosted by the China Computer Federation (CCF), organized by the CCF Computer Applications Professional Committee, and co-organized by Suzhou University, Suzhou University of Science and Technology, Jiangnan University, Nanjing University, Nanjing University of Science and Technology, Wuxi University, Nanjing University of Aeronautics and Astronautics, Nanjing University of Posts and Telecommunications, etc., supported by Jiangsu Computer Society, Guangdong Computer Society, Heilongjiang Computer Society, Jilin Computer Society, Shenzhen Computer Society, Shenyang Computer Society, Dalian Computer Society, CCF Suzhou Member Activity Center, CCF Wuxi Member Activity Center, and other academic associations.

This year's conference attracted 197 paper submissions. After the hard work of the Program Committee, 39 papers were accepted to appear in the conference proceedings, with an acceptance rate of 19.8%. The major topic of this conference was artificial intelligence and its applications. The accepted papers cover a wide range of areas related to basic theory and techniques for artificial intelligence and its applications including artificial intelligence and its applications, pattern recognition and machine learning, data science and technology, network communication and security, and frontier and comprehensive applications.

We would like to thank all the Program Committee members, a total of 267 people from 46 different institutes or companies, for their hard work in completing the review tasks. There were at least 3 reviewers for each article, and each reviewer reviewed no more than 5 articles. Their collective efforts made it possible to attain quality reviews for all the submissions within a few weeks. Their diverse expertise in each research area helped us to create an exciting program for the conference. Their comments and advice helped the authors to improve the quality of their papers and gain deeper insights.

We thank the team at Springer, whose professional assistance was invaluable in the production of the proceedings. A big thank you also goes to the authors and participants for their tremendous support in making the conference a success.

Besides the technical program, this year NCCA offered different experiences to the participants. We hope you enjoyed the conference.

July 2023

Min Zhang
Bin Xu
Fuyuan Hu
Junyu Lin

Organization

Honorary Chair

Weimin Zheng   Tsinghua University, China

General Chairs

Min Zhang   Suzhou University, China
Bin Xu   Tsinghua University, China

General Vice Co-chairs

Xuebin Chen   North China University of Science and
                                Technology, China
Junhui Zhao   Beijing Jiaotong University, China
Shaoliang Peng   Hunan University, China

Secretary General

Zeguang Lu   National Academy of Guo Ding Institute of Data
                                Science, China

Vice Secretary General

Jing Liu   Hebei University of Technology, China

Program Chairs

Fuyuan Hu   Suzhou University of Science and Technology,
                                China
Junyu Lin   Chinese Academy of Sciences, China

Secretary General of the Steering Committee

Peng Liu   Changchun University of Science and
           Technology, China

Domain Chairs of Procedural Committee

Guanghui Yan   Lanzhou Jiaotong University, China
Biqing Zeng   South China Normal University, China
Weipeng Jing   Northeast Forestry University, China
Jing Liu   Hebei University of Technology, China
Zhaowen Qiu   Northeast Forestry University, China
Xuebin Chen   North China University of Science and
           Technology, China
Bing Xia   Zhongyuan University of Technology, China
Jianquan Ouyang   Xiangtan University, China
Youxi Wu   Hebei University of Technology, China

Organization Chair

Lan Huang   Jilin University, China

Secretary General of the Organizational Committee

Tian Bai   Jilin University, China

Award Committee Chair

Zumin Wang   Dalian University, China

Secretary General of the Award Committee

Bing Xia   Zhongyuan University of Technology, China

Award Committee Members

Jing Liu	Hebei University of Technology, China
Lan Huang	Jilin University, China
Mei Li	China University of Geosciences, China
Guanghui Yan	Lanzhou Jiaotong University, China
Biqing Zeng	South China Normal University, China

Competition Committee Chair

Bin Xu	Tsinghua University, China

Competition Committee Vice Chairs

Bo Lin	Weiye Xuanran Education Technology (Beijing) Co., Ltd., China
Xinbo Wang	Chengxiang Training School Co., Ltd., China

Propaganda Committee Chairs

Aibin Chen	Central South University of Forestry and Technology, China
Zhongchan Sun	National Academy of Guo Ding Institute of Data Science, China

Industrial Applications and Exhibition Chairs

Jing Liu	Hebei University of Technology, China
Zhaowen Qiu	Northeast Forestry University, China

Contents – Part II

Network Communication and Security

Frontier and Comprehensive Applications

Contents – Part I

Data Science and Technology

Efficient Medical Image Data Management Based on a Lightweight Sharding Blockchain

Fuan Xiao[1] (ID), Zhengfei Wang[1,2] (ID), and Jiaming Hong[1,2(✉)] (ID)

[1] School of Medical Information Engineering, Guangzhou University of Chinese Medicine, Guangzhou, China
{wzf,hjm}@gzucm.edu.cn

[2] Intelligent Chinese Medicine Research Institute, Guangzhou University of Chinese Medicine, Guangzhou, China

Abstract. Medical images play an important role in clinical diagnosis. However, the management of medical images has fallen into the dilemma of information islands. Blockchain technology is proposed to solve the problem of medical images' information islands due to its decentralization, transparency, openness, autonomy, anonymity, and information tampering. However, each node needs to maintain the complete blockchain, and with the amount of medical image data rapidly increasing, the performance limitations of blockchain are emerging, such as poor performance in effectively querying and storing medical image data. Sharding technology is proposed to address the above limitations. In this paper, we propose an efficient management architecture based on a lightweight sharding blockchain for medical image management (EASBM). Our architecture consists of four layers: sharding blockchain layer, distributed storage layer, cache layer, and application layer. The sharding blockchain layer splits each block into head and body and divides each participant into corresponding shards, implementing a lightweight blockchain framework. The distributed storage layer saves the raw data and hash values of medical images, reducing the storage burden of blockchain and implementing off-chain storage. Our empirical evaluations suggest that the time spent querying a record is less than 4 ms in our proposed architecture, which contains a network of 1024 participating nodes.

Keywords: Blockchain · Sharding · Medical Image Management · Distributed Storage · Off-chain Storage

1 Introduction

In today's healthcare system, medical images play a significant role in diagnosing diseases, such as computer tomography (CT), magnetic resonance imaging (MRI), and ultrasound, which are crucial in assisting disease diagnosis [1]. In biomedical research, medical images provide an important source of anatomical and functional information. However, in the current medical system, medical image data for disease examination cannot be shared. The medical image data of a patient's disease examination in a hospital can only be carried by the patient themselves when they change hospitals for treatment.

M. Zhang et al. (Eds.): CCF NCCA 2023, CCIS 1960, pp. 3–9, 2024.
https://doi.org/10.1007/978-981-99-8761-0_1

The inability to share medical image data has led to unnecessarily repeated examinations by patients, increasing their burden [2]. Medical image data sharing can solve the problem of medical image data for patient disease examination not being interconnected among different hospitals [3]. The development of blockchain technology provides technical support for medical image data sharing [4, 5]. Blockchain has the characteristics of transparency, openness, anonymity, and tamper resistance. Blockchain technology is widely used in data sharing systems [6].

In medical image management systems, blockchain technology can not only preserve patient privacy but also solve data storage problems. Chen et al. [7] propose a complete medical information system model based on blockchain technology, which utilizes cloud servers and proxy re-encryption algorithms to ensure the storage and security of medical data. Patel [8] proposes a framework for the cross-domain sharing of medical images based on blockchain consensus algorithms. This framework ensures the security of medical image data without the involvement of third-party certification agencies and establishes a classification ledger for radiation research and patient-defined access permissions. Seo et al. [9] propose a medical image sharing system based on the Hyperledger Fabric blockchain, which can solve the problem of expensive repeated examinations caused by patients seeking medical treatment in different hospitals. Examination image data in one hospital can be shared among different hospitals. Sultana et al. [10] propose a medical image sharing system based on zero trust rules and blockchain technology, which can resist attacks on medical data and enable secure access and storage of medical images between different hospitals. The above research works only propose blockchain-based medical data sharing solutions, but with the explosive growth of blockchain data, the scalability of blockchain storage performance in these solutions is poor, and the throughput is small. Sharding technology can solve the problem of blockchain performance expansion. Kokoris-Kogias et al. [11] proposed the OmniLedger model, which can maintain the long-term security of sharding blockchains. It also proposed a cross-shard submission protocol, which can handle transactions between multiple shards at the atomic level. It also optimizes blockchain performance through transaction processing between multiple shards and ledger pruning through collective signature status blocks. Zamani et al. [12] propose RapidChain, which can resist Byzantine errors of one-third of participating nodes, achieve high transaction throughput and secure reconfiguration mechanism through block channel cross-shard consensus algorithm to ensure the robustness of blockchain, as well as effective cross-shard transaction authentication technology. OmniLedger and RapidChain both propose using sharding technology to extend the performance of blockchain, but when it is necessary to reassign the sharding of nodes at the beginning of each EPOCH, the performance consumption is significant. This paper adopts lightweight sharding, which determines the number of shards when the system starts and splits a block into head and body. Each shard stores a type of medical image data to avoid consumption caused by redistribution.

In this paper, we propose a more effective blockchain architecture for medical image data management via lightweight sharding and off-chain distributed storage. Our contribution is to design a new lightweight sharding mechanism that combines blockchain and block splitting to support faster and more convenient medical image data management requirements, such as uploading, querying, and downloading.

2 Architecture

This section presents the architecture of the EASBM system, which includes the sharding blockchain layer, distributed storage layer, application layer, and cache layer. The system architecture is shown in Fig. 1. The sharding blockchain layer and the distributed storage layer are the main components. The sharding blockchain layer is used as the tamper-proof underlying database to shard the blockchain that stores medical image data and saves the hash code of each medical image data. One shard stores a classification of medical image data. The distributed storage layer uses a distributed database as the underlying database that stores the raw data and related attributes of each medical image data and employs key-value to store. To meet the operation requirements of the medical image data management system, we employ the cache layer and the application layer in our architecture. The cache layer uses key values to cache commonly used queries. The Application layer provides various medical data upload and query services.

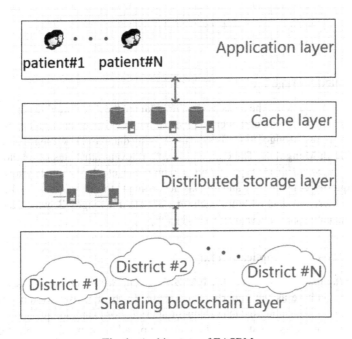

Fig. 1. Architecture of EASBM

2.1 Sharding the Blockchain Layer

Blockchain is used as the underlying database of the medical image management system for storing the hash code of each medical image data. The hash code can be used as proof of tamper-proof. To scale the performance of blockchain, we employ sharding technology. In the initialization phase of the system, we divide the whole blockchain into multiple shards according to the medical image data type. This system can handle N shards and N (N <= 32) classifications. Each classification of medical image is mapped to each shard. Each participating node is divided into its own shard according to the classification of the medical image data. The communication between different shards adopts cross-shard transactions. Participating nodes in the same shard communicate through intrashard transactions. To improve system performance, we split each block into a head and body on the sharding blockchain (see Fig. 2).

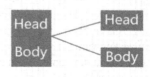

Fig. 2. Block Splitting

2.2 Distributed Storage Layer

In this subsection, we detail the process of saving data in the distributed storage layer and then describe how to upload and query a piece of medical image data. In the distributed storage layer, we use MongoDB [13] as the underlying database. Each shard corresponds to a data table in MongoDB. The data table saves relevant attributes of medical image data, such as the ShardID, the type of data, patient name, etc. In the underlying database, data can be queried conveniently and quickly according to the attributes of medical image data because there is a data table for each type of data in MongoDB, which records the correspondence between the ShardID and data types.

2.3 Cache Layer and Application Layer

To facilitate the patients' access to the EASBM system, we set up a cache layer, which uses a cache database as the underlying database. In the EASBM system, the cache database employs key-value to cache frequent queries. For example, querying the medical image data of a classification. If the patient uploads new medical image data, the system stores the new data in the cache layer first. The application layer provides users with querying, uploading, and downloading operations. For example, if a patient wants to add an attribute of medical data, it needs to send a request at the application layer.

3 Results

We implement the EASBM system based on Ethereum [14] open source code by using the Golang language. The hardware environment is mainly an Apple computer, Intel Core i7 processor, 32 GB memory, and 1 T hard disk space. To test the performance of the EASBM system, 256 nodes, 512 nodes, and 1024 nodes were deployed in the frameworks participating in the comparison. We perform experiments on an open-access benchmark dataset: BRATS2021 [15]. All subjects underwent four modalities of MRI scans, i.e., T1-weighted (T1), contrast-enhanced T1-weighted (T1c), T2-weighted (T2), and fluid attenuated inversion recovery (Flair). Therefore, there are only four types of medical image data classification we tested. That is, the number of blockchain shards is 4. Although there are only 4 types of medical image data, we set the number of blockchain shards to 4 during the test. However, our proposed architecture can handle N(N <= 32) kinds of medical image data classification. We evaluate two indicators, uploading a new data time and the time of a block query. Since RapidChain [12] has the function of sharding, we compare it with our architecture in the test experiment.

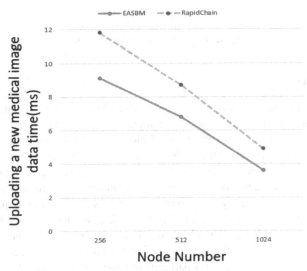

Fig. 3. The time of uploading a new medical image data item

3.1 Uploading Medical Image Data

The EASBM system supports uploading new medical image data at the application layer. To evaluate the performance of uploading, we counted the time taken to upload medical image data. We compare our architecture with RapidChain [12] in terms of uploading data. We deployed 256 nodes, 512 nodes, and 1024 nodes in the systems to compare the performance of uploading medical image data. The number of shards is 4, that is, the types of medical image data. As illustrated in Fig. 3, when the system contains the same number of shards, the more participating nodes the system contains, the less time it takes to upload data. When there are fewer participating nodes in the system, more time is required to find the target node storing data. When the system contains 1024 participating nodes, our architecture takes 3.6 ms to upload medical image data, but RapidChain takes 4.9 ms to upload medical image data.

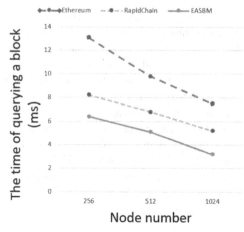

Fig. 4. The time of querying a block

3.2 Block Query

In the EASBM system, a block contains many transactions, which record the evidence of data uploaded and queried by patients. We compare the EASBM system with Ethereum [5] and RapidChain in terms of the time of block query. Ethereum has no sharding function. Therefore, when querying a block in Ethereum, the system must traverse all blocks on the chain, which is time-consuming. We compared the time spent querying a block in the case of different participating nodes. The number of shards is 4. As illustrated in Fig. 4, the more participating nodes there are, the less time it takes to query a block. Because we store the hash code of a block in MongoDB, when querying a block, we do not need to traverse all blocks. We only need to query the target node where the data are saved and then query a block through the field of the hash code in the MongoDB data table. When the system contains 1024 participating nodes and 4 shards, to query a block, our architecture takes 3.2 ms, RapidChain takes 5.2 ms, and Ethereum takes 7.5 ms.

4 Conclusion

In this paper, we present EASBM, the application of lightweight sharding blockchain technology and off-chain distributed storage to medical image data management. The EASBM system can not only ensure integrity, trustworthiness, traceability, and immutability but also support convenient access and storage of data. To scale the performance of the blockchain, we employ lightweight sharding technology and an off-chain distributed storage layer to save medical image data. In the application layer, we can customize the query of medical image data. Finally, our empirical evaluation shows that the EASBM system can improve the speed of querying medical image data and can also effectively reduce the storage requirements based on lightweight sharding for each node.

Acknowledgements. This work was partially supported by the Undergraduate Higher Education Teaching Quality and Teaching Reform Engineering Project of Guangdong Province (2022, No.

489), the Educational Research Project of the 14th Five-Year Plan for National Higher Education of Traditional Chinese Medicine in 2023 (Project No. YB-23–13), the Social Science Project of Guangzhou University of Chinese Medicine (Grant No. 2021SKYB01), the Opening Project of Guangdong Province Key Laboratory of Big Data Analysis and Processing at Sun Yat-sen University (Grant No. 202202), and the National Natural Science Foundation of China (82174527).

References

1. Panayides, A.S., et al.: AI in medical imaging informatics: current challenges and future directions. IEEE J. Biomed. Health Informatics **24**(7), 1837–1857 (2020)
2. Siyal, A., Junejo, A., Zawish, M., Ahmed, K., Khalil, A., Soursou, G.: Applications of blockchain technology in medicine and healthcare: challenges and future perspectives. Cryptography **3**(1), 3 (2019)
3. Prather, J.C., Lobach, D.F., Goodwin, L.K., Hales, J.W., Hage, M.L., Hammond, W.E.: Medical data mining: knowledge discovery in a clinical data warehouse. In: Proceedings of the AMIA annual fall symposium, pp. 101–105. American Medical Informatics Association, Washington DC, USA (1997)
4. Bahga, A., Madisetti, V.K.: A cloud-based approach for interoperable electronic health records (EHRs). IEEE J. Biomed. Health Inform. **17**(5), 894–906 (2013). https://doi.org/10.1109/JBHI.2013.2257818
5. Wong, D.R., Bhattacharya, S., Butte, A.J.: Prototype of running clinical trials in an untrustworthy environment using blockchain. Nat. Commun. **10**(1), 917 (2019)
6. Liu, J., Li, X., Ye, L., Zhang, H., Du, X., Guizani, M.: BPDS: a blockchain based privacy-preserving data sharing for electronic medical records. In: 2018 IEEE Global Communications Conference, pp. 1–6. IEEE, Abu Dhabi, United Arab Emirates (2018)
7. Chen, Z., Xu, W., Wang, B., Yu, H.: A blockchain-based preserving and sharing system for medical data privacy. Futur. Gener. Comput. Syst. **124**, 338–350 (2021)
8. Patel, V.: A framework for secure and decentralized sharing of medical imaging data via blockchain consensus. Health Informatics J. **25**(4), 1398–1411 (2019)
9. Seo, J., Cho, Y.: Medical image sharing system using hyperledger fabric blockchain. In: 2020 22nd International Conference on Advanced Communication Technology (ICACT), pp. 62–64. IEEE, Phoenix Park, Korea (South) (2020)
10. Sultana, M., Hossain, A., Laila, F., Taher, K.A., Islam, M.N.: Towards developing a secure medical image sharing system based on zero trust principles and blockchain technology. BMC Med. Inform. Decis. Mak. **20**(1), 1–10 (2020)
11. Kokoris-Kogias, E., Jovanovic, P., Gasser, L., Gailly, N., Syta, E., Ford, B.: Omniledger: a secure, scale-out, decentralized ledger via sharding. In: 2018 IEEE Symposium on Security and Privacy, pp. 583–598. IEEE, San Francisco, CA, USA (2018)
12. Zamani, M., Movahedi, M., Raykova, M.: Rapidchain: scaling blockchain via full sharding. In: Proceedings of the 2018 ACM SIGSAC Conference on Computer and Communications Security, pp. 931–948. Association for Computing Machinery, New York, NY, USA (2018)
13. MongoDB Tutorials. https://docs.mongodb.com/manual/tutorial. Accessed 10 Mar 2022
14. Ethereum: a secure decentralized generalized transaction ledger. https://ethereum.github.io/yellowpaper/paper.pdf. Accessed 10 Mar 2022
15. Menze, B.H., et al.: The multimodal brain tumor image segmentation benchmark (BRATS). IEEE Trans. Med. Imaging **34**(10), 1993–2024 (2015)

Research and Application
of an Incremental Extraction Scheme
for Monitoring Power Equipment Data

Dan Lu, Shuang Zhang, Yingnan Zhao[✉], and Qilong Han

Harbin Engineering University, Harbin 150001, China
zhaoyingnan@hrbeu.edu.cn

Abstract. The monitoring data of power equipment exhibit characteristics of multiple sources, a large amount of data, and high real-time
performance. To effectively extract information from these data, it is
imperative to extract monitoring data from various equipment and subject it to a series of processing steps. Data extraction is a crucial stage
in the ETL (extraction, transformation, loading) process. In this paper,
we conduct a comprehensive analysis of various incremental extraction
capture mechanisms, highlighting their respective advantages and disadvantages and applicable conditions. We then select CDC technology,
which involves analysing the database's log to identify changed data and
using the incremental extraction method to extract the monitoring data
of power equipment. Our analysis and experimental results demonstrate
that the proposed method ensures the accuracy and integrity of data to a
significant extent compared to other incremental extraction mechanisms.
Furthermore, it addresses the incremental extraction challenges between
databases in the power equipment monitoring environment and improves
the efficiency and performance of data extraction.

Keywords: ETL · Data extraction · Incremental extraction · CDC ·
Equipment monitoring data

1 Introduction

With the continuous development of science and technology, information construction in the industrial field is rapidly advancing and applying. Especially
in the monitoring of power equipment, a large amount of data with different
structures and different sources is generated every day, and with continuous
production and operation, these data will also increase geometrically. These
vast amounts of data contain significant value that can be leveraged for better decision-making through mining and analysing them. However, the sorting
and analysis of such data and information presents a challenge. ETL serves as a
major technical solution to this problem, with the key aspect being the extraction of data from various sources into a unified data warehouse to ensure data

Supported by the National Key R&D Program of China under Grant No.
2020YFB1710200.

integrity and facilitate data sharing [1]. Therefore, it is crucial to identify an efficient and reliable data capture method that can continuously extract changing data from each data source system and build an incremental data warehouse to enable data sharing and analysis across heterogeneous systems.

Data extraction is the initial stage of the ETL process and the data input part of the ETL process, which has important significance. This paper mainly studies and solves this issue in detail. During the data extraction phase, it is imperative to accurately capture and extract only the relevant data from the source database based on the subject of the target database [2]. The primary objective of data extraction is to efficiently capture the changed data in a certain period of time. When the data in the source database conforming to the subject of the target database change, the changed data can be captured in a timely manner to the target database according to the capture method adopted, which is the process of data extraction.

Data extraction can be categorized into full data extraction and incremental data extraction. Full data extraction involves extracting data directly from the source repository without altering the data in the tables or views and converting it into a format that can be recognized by the user ETL tool. This method is suitable for the initial extraction but is not recommended for large data sources because it can result in unnecessary overhead when loading data into a data warehouse [3]. Additionally, the increase in time and the increase in the amount of source data will have a certain impact on the number of datasets generated during the extraction process, which will have a ripple effect on the overall performance of the ETL process. Incremental data extraction extracts the changing data in the source system, which is widely used and helps to optimize the whole ETL process [4]. However, an important problem with incremental extraction is how to capture data that have changed since the last extraction, which is often done during the later maintenance phase.

The rest of this paper is organized as follows: The second section provides an overview of the related work on ETL and data extraction. Later, the third section presents a discussion on the common incremental extraction mechanisms and their associated challenges. Next, in the fourth section, a comprehensive analysis and comparison of the incremental data capture mechanisms are presented. The fifth section verifies the application of the incremental extraction model in monitoring power equipment data using CDC technology. Finally, the paper concludes with a summary of the incremental data extraction work and a prospectus for future research.

2   Related Work

In the current era of big data, the study of ETLs has gained significant importance. ETL serves as a crucial means to develop novel techniques that can address the mounting challenges of data integration in organizations. It enables the acquisition and analysis of vast amounts of data from diverse sources. However, this task is not straightforward, as the data are often heterogeneous at both logical and structural levels. Moreover, individuals require continuously updated data to make informed decisions [5]. The ETL process comprises three primary stages, namely, extraction, transformation, and loading. Extraction involves identifying and retrieving all pertinent data from the source. Transformation aims to clean up the data and integrate different schemas into the schemas defined in the data warehouse [6]. Loading involves physically transferring data from the operating system to the data warehouse. Currently, popular ETL tools include DataStage, SQL Server Integration Service, Oracle Data Integrator, Talend, Pantlo Kertle, Howk, lormi PowerCene, and DataStage, among others [7].

Existing methods of incremental data extraction can be roughly divided into trigger methods, timestamp methods, full table comparison methods, log table methods, and system log analysis methods according to their different ways of capturing changing data. [8] controls the extraction of time stamps by setting a time window, which can effectively improve the robustness of the system and effectively reduce the influence of system anomalies on the extraction results. [9] studied the real-time extraction method based on database log analysis to minimize the structural changes in the database. [10] proposes an automatic incremental update method based on timestamp and CDC. [11] gives a test case of trigger-based data extraction applied to a drug data warehouse. [12] proposes the trigger and identification table method, which stores incremental data while updating the source data table, but it will increase the load of the database. [13] proposes a general model of incremental data detection and net effect processing based on log analysis, but the reliability of this model is not high.

The purpose of this paper is to study the existing commonly used incremental data extraction and capture mechanisms through the analysis of different capture mechanisms, an in-depth study of their advantages and disadvantages, and exploration of a suitable method for incremental extraction of power equipment monitoring data.

3 Analysis of Commonly Used Incremental Extraction Methods

The incremental data extraction method needs to accurately and quickly capture the changing data in the source database according to a specific method, and at the same time, it cannot cause pressure on the current business system. From the demand point of view, the incremental data extraction method has higher demand than the full data extraction method, and the implementation process is more complicated [14]. The commonly used methods of capturing change data in incremental data extraction include the trigger method, timestamp method, full table comparison method, log table method and system log analysis method.

3.1   Trigger-Based Method

The main idea of this method is to automatically capture the incremental data and execute the stored procedure of the trigger by setting the corresponding trigger to a specified data table. To implement this method, it is necessary to add three triggers, namely, insert, modify, and delete, into the source database table and establish an incremental data table. Upon modification of the source table, the trigger is activated, and the changed data are recorded in the incremental table. During incremental extraction, only the incremental data from the incremental data table need to be extracted without accessing the source table. The advantage of this method is that data capture can be completed automatically after configuration, with high data capture performance and no need to modify the basic structure of tables in the source databases [15]. The downside is the need to configure triggers for each type of action for all database table entries, which can affect database performance when there are many data table entries.

3.2   Timestamp Method

The core idea of this approach is to capture records that have changed using timestamp updates. To implement this method of data capture, it is imperative to append a timestamp field to the source table. When the data of a record change, the timestamp field of the record needs to be updated to the current time [16]. In the extraction process, the data that have been manipulated can be obtained by comparing the last obtained time with the timestamp field recorded in the source table.

The advantage of this method is that it is simple and easy to implement. The downside is that the addition of a timestamp field can have a significant impact on the source databases, especially for databases that do not support automatic timestamp updates and require manual updates to the timestamp field while the data completes certain operations. This can affect the accuracy and is insufficient in the completeness of data extraction, and the method cannot capture deletion operations.

3.3   Full Table Comparison Method

During the incremental extraction process, the ETL procedure conducts a comparative analysis of records from the source and target tables on a one-by-one basis to identify new and modified records [17]. To optimize the incremental extraction process, the MD5 checksum can be utilized. Initially, a temporary table with a similar structure is created in the source table to record the primary key of the source table and the MD5 check codes for all fields. During each data extraction, the check codes of the two tables are compared to determine the changed data in the source table and update the check codes. If the primary key does not exist in the target table, the insert operation is executed. Furthermore, delete primary keys that no longer exist in the source table but remain in the target table.

The advantage of the full table comparison method is that it has less inclination to the source system. However, its drawback lies in its passive comparison of complete table data, which results in suboptimal performance. Furthermore, the accuracy of this method is compromised when the table lacks a primary key or unique column and contains duplicate records.

3.4 Method Based on Log Table

It is necessary to create a business log table in the database to record the change in specific business data. During incremental extraction, it is only necessary to read the data in the business log table to capture the changed data and corresponding operations. In this way, the update and maintenance of the business log table need to be completed by the code of the business system program [18].

This method has the advantages of simple extraction rules and backup. The downside of this approach is that the database opening mode puts pressure on the disks of the source system database, increases storage costs and is detrimental to performance.

3.5 System Log Analysis Method

This method is primarily through the analysis of the database itself log, judging the changed data, to achieve the purpose of accurate data extraction. Relational database systems store all DML operations in log files to enable database backup, recovery, and other functions. During incremental data extraction, the logs of the database are analysed, and the operations on the relevant source table are extracted after the specified time to determine the changes in the data since the last extraction. Incremental data extraction is then achieved through this process.

This method has the advantages of being nonintrusive to the source system, having little impact on various performance of the database, the short delay time of data acquisition, and high efficiency of data synchronization, but it needs additional log parsing work.

4 Comparison and Analysis

When ETL performs incremental extraction, there are several options mentioned above. Table 1 analyses the advantages and disadvantages of these mechanisms from five aspects: completeness, extraction performance, performance impact, invasiveness, and difficulty. It is evident that the current general incremental data extraction methods possess both strengths and weaknesses across all aspects. Therefore, when extracting heterogeneous incremental data from multiple sources, the pros and cons should be weighed according to the actual needs, and the appropriate extraction method should be selected to improve the extraction performance.

Table 1. Comparison Table of Advantages and Disadvantages of Common Incremental Extraction Mechanisms.

Incremental Extraction Mechanisms	Completeness	Extraction Performance	Performance Impact	Invasive	Difficulty
Trigger-based Method	High	Excellent	Great	General	Easy
Timestamp Method	Low	Good	Little	Great	Easy
Full Table Comparison Method	High	Bad	Small	General	General
Method based on Log Table	High	Excellent	Small	Big	Easy
System log analysis method	High	Excellent	Little	Big	Difficult

5   Case Study

Power equipment monitoring data are a prime example of multisource heterogeneous data. The monitoring data are complex, the monitoring duration is long, the data accumulation is large, and the data have high real-time performance and are distributed in different databases. To solve these problems, this paper uses an incremental extraction method based on system log analysis to extract power equipment monitoring data.

5.1   Dataset

This paper uses a dataset from a solar power plant located in India, which contains monitored power generation data and weather data. These data are stored in the generationData and weatherSensorData tables, which are further stored in two separate databases, namely, the generation and weatherSensor databases.

5.2   Changed Data Capture

The experiment utilizes SQL Server as the database of choice due to its comprehensive data solutions, which encompass data storage, integration, and mining. Specifically, the mechanism of changed data capture (CDC) was employed, which is a well-established technology in log comparison. CDC operates asynchronously by reading and analysing transaction logs from the selected database, thereby obtaining real-time updates on changes made to the database tables. Once CDC is activated, any changes made to the source table, whether through insertion, update, or deletion, are captured and stored in the database log. These captured data can then be accessed in a controlled manner via the database view, and functions are available to query the changing table for changes over a specified time range and return the captured data as a result set.

CDC makes data integration more efficient, especially during the extraction phase of the ETL process. At the same time, this method can also reduce the delay between the source system and the business users in the data warehouse available to the same change and is a high reliability, low latency change data capture technology. Figure 1 is a log-based change data capture framework.

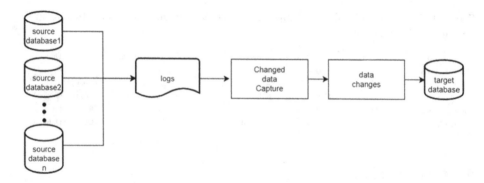

Fig. 1. Log-based Change Data Capture Framework.

The steps of change data capture through SQL Server CDC technology are as follows:

Step 1. Enable database-level CDC for both databases separately.

Listing 2.1.

```
1  USE generation;
2  GO
3  EXECUTE sys.sp_cdc_enable_db
4  GO
```

Step 2. Enable table-level CDC on the tables that store data in each of the two databases.

Listing 2.2.

```
1  EXECUTE sys.sp_cdc_enable_table
2      @source_schema = N'dbo',
3      @source_name = N'generationData',
4      @role_name = N'cdc_Admin',
5      @supports_net_changes = 1
6  GO
```

schemaname_tablename_CT is automatically created under the database system table. When the actual data are modified to the generationData and weatherSensorData tables, a table named cdc.schemaname_tablename_CT is automatically created. One row is added for deletion, and two rows are added for update before and after the update. The _$ operation field is added to distinguish the type of operation. According to the different values of the field, the type of operation can be distinguished: 1 = delete, 2 = insert, 3 = update (old value), and 4 = update (new value). The table containing this information can provide the most recent list of changes.

Step 3. Test inserting, updating, and deleting data operations on two tables. After executing DML, the recorded data can be visually displayed through cdc.dbo_generationData_CT and cdc.dbo_weatherSensorData_CT, with the change data capture illustrated in Fig. 2 and Fig. 3. For insert/delete operations, there is one row, and for the update, there are two rows.

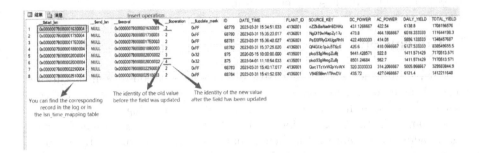

Fig. 2. dbo.generationData has changed data records.

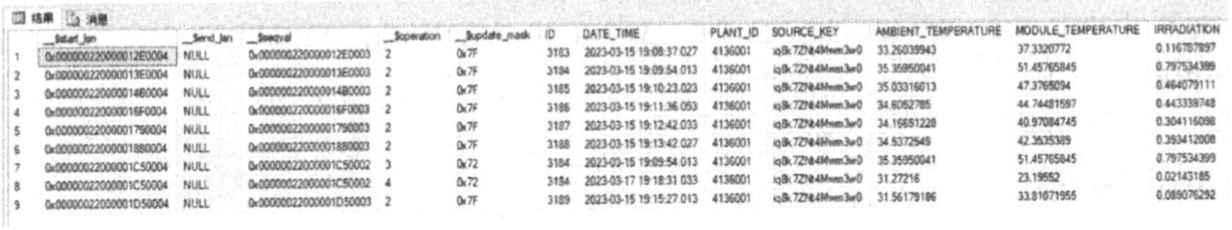

Fig. 3. dbo.weatherSensorData has changed data records.

Step 4. In the peak period of information collection, the amount of data in the changed data table becomes very large in a very short time, which also affects the query speed and performance of the table. Therefore, it is necessary to periodically clean the changed data in the table that has been loaded into the data warehouse. In the CDC mechanism, when CDC is enabled on the tables in the specified database generation and weatherSensor, two jobs are created in the database server agent. The first job focuses on reading and analysing the transaction logs in the database to retrieve the modified data. The second operation is to clear the modified data regularly. The default data clearing cycle is once a day. Therefore, it is obviously not enough to improve the query speed when the system data scale increases rapidly. For this reason, the following stored procedure is called to set the regular data cleaning time of cdc.generation_capture and cdc.weatherSensor_capture jobs in CDC.

Listing 2.3.

```
1  EXECUTE sys . sp_cdc_add_job
2       @job_type = N'cleanup',
```

```
3       @retention = 2
4   GO
```

Therefore, for cdc.dbo_generationData_CT and cdc.dbo_weatherSensorData_CT, the data cleaning time is set to every 2 min.

6   Conclusion

This paper provides a comprehensive discussion of various common capture mechanisms used in incremental extraction. The study reveals that each mechanism has inherent limitations and value. After conducting a comprehensive tradeoff analysis, the CDC mechanism based on reading and analysing database logs is adopted to capture the change data of the monitoring data of power equipment. The experimental results demonstrate that this method can effectively meet the requirements of constantly changing data extraction without interfering with the source system's database transactions due to excessive real-time updated data. Additionally, it can provide crucial information support for strategic and tactical decision-making, management, and other aspects of power enterprises. Future research can focus on exploring ways to further enhance the speed of data incremental extraction without negatively impacting the source database.

References

1. Jörg, T., Dessloch, S.: Formalizing ETL jobs for incremental loading of data warehouses, Datenbanksysteme in Business, Technologie und Web (BTW)-13. Fachtagung des GI-Fachbereichs "Datenbanken und Informationssysteme" (DBIS) (2009)
2. Kakish, K., Kraft, T.A.: ETL evolution for real-time data warehousing. In: Proceedings of the Conference on Information Systems Applied Research ISSN, vol. 2167, p. 1508 (2012)
3. Gorhe, S.: ETL in near-real-time environment: a review of challenges and possible solutions (2020)
4. El-Sappagh, S.H.A., Hendawi, A.M.A., El Bastawissy, A.H.: A proposed model for data warehouse ETL processes. J. King Saud Univ.-Comput. Inf. Sci. **23**, 91–104 (2011)
5. Chandra, H.: Analysis of change data capture method in heterogeneous data sources to support RTDW. In: 2018 4th International Conference on Computer and Information Sciences (ICCOINS), pp. 1–6. IEEE (2018)
6. Wijaya, R., Pudjoatmodjo, B.: An overview and implementation of extraction-transformation-loading (ETL) process in data warehouse (case study: department of agriculture). In: 2015 3rd International Conference on Information and Communication Technology (ICoICT), pp. 70–74. IEEE (2015)
7. Sreemathy, J., Brindha, R., Nagalakshmi, M.S., Suvekha, N., Ragul, N.K., Praveennandha, M.: Overview of ETL tools and talend-data integration. In: 2021 7th International Conference on Advanced Computing and Communication Systems (ICACCS), vol. 1, pp. 1650–1654. IEEE (2021)

8. Jia, W., Xu, Y., Liu, J., Wang, G.: VTWM: an incremental data extraction model based on variable time-windows. EAI Endorsed Trans. Collab. Comput. e1 (2020)

9. Shi, J., Bao, Y., Leng, F., Yu, G.: Study on log-based change data capture and handling mechanism in real-time data warehouse. In: 2008 International Conference on Computer Science and Software Engineering, vol. 4, pp. 478–481. IEEE (2008)

10. Thulasiram, S., Ramaiah, N.: Real time data warehouse updates through extraction-transformation-loading process using change data capture method. In: Smys, S., Senjyu, T., Lafata, P. (eds.) ICCNCT 2019. LNDECT, vol. 44, pp. 552–560. Springer, Cham (2020). https://doi.org/10.1007/978-3-030-37051-0_62

11. Ping, H., GuoJun, H.: Research and design of the incremental updates of drug data warehouse. In: 2010 International Conference on Computer Application and System Modeling (ICCASM 2010), vol. 4, pp. V4-628. IEEE (2010)

12. Hu, Q., Gan, Z., Zhang, B.: Design and implementation of oracle database incremental data capture based on trigger and identification table. In: Journal of Physics: Conference Series, vol. 1237, p. 022161. IOP Publishing (2019)

13. Peng Yuanhao, P.J.: Study on incremental data capturing method based on log analysis. Comput. Eng. **41**, 56–60 (2015)

14. Biswas, N., Sarkar, A., Mondal, K.C.: Efficient incremental loading in ETL processing for real-time data integration. Innov. Syst. Softw. Eng. **16**, 53–61 (2020)

15. Valêncio, C.R., Marioto, M.H., Zafalon, G.F.D., Machado, J.M., Momente, J.C.: Real time delta extraction based on triggers to support data warehousing. In: 2013 International Conference on Parallel and Distributed Computing, Applications and Technologies, pp. 293–297. IEEE (2013)

16. Sun, Y.-Y.: Research and implementation of an efficient incremental synchronization method based on timestamp. In: 2022 3rd International Conference on Computing, Networks and Internet of Things (CNIOT), pp. 158–162. IEEE (2022)

17. Bin, Z., Shuai, S., Zhi-chun, G., Jian-feng, H.: Design and implementation of incremental data capturing in wireless network planning based on log mining. In: 2021 IEEE 5th Advanced Information Technology, Electronic and Automation Control Conference (IAEAC), vol. 5, pp. 2757–2761. IEEE (2021)

18. Dai, H., Yang, B.: Researches on mechanics of incremental data extraction in ETL. Comput. Eng. Des. **30**, 5552–5555 (2009)

Paint Price Prediction Using a Triplet Network-Multimodal Network-LSTM Combined Deep Learning Approach

Yuan Ni[1] , Meng Zou[2]([✉]) , Feixing Dong[2] , and Jian Zhang[1]

[1] School of Economics and Management, Beijing Information Science and Technology University, Beijing 100192, China
{niyuan,zhangjian}@bistu.edu.cn
[2] Computer School, Beijing Information Science and Technology University, Beijing 100192, China
{zoumeng,feixingdong}@bistu.edu.cn

Abstract. Painting prices fluctuate over time, as does the performance of the art market. Obtaining an accurate art price prediction by exploring the dynamic change pattern of artwork painting prices remains a challenge. We propose a paint price prediction using a triplet network-multimodal network-LSTM combined deep learning approach for dynamically predicting paint prices. By using triplet sets of paintings classified by similar transaction prices, our painting price classification model can be adjusted to identify paintings with similar prices over time. After that, we use the multimodal painting price prediction model to predict the set of paintings with similar prices within specified time intervals and to determine the raw simulated painting transaction prices within those intervals. By time sorting the simulated prices of the paintings, the simulated time series data of the paintings can then be obtained, and from this, a model of long short-term memory networks is used to predict the dynamic predicted prices of the paintings. The results of this experiment demonstrate that the designed model had a 5.7% and 10.3% decrease in RMSE and MAE for 110 paintings compared to the prediction case using the model based on image and numerical information. Thus, the method is more effective at predicting painting prices and can reveal better dynamic patterns in painting prices.

Keywords: Art painting price evaluation · long short-term memory neural network · triple loss function · time series analysis · multimodal learning · convolutional neural network

1 Introduction

With art being a leading global industry, the art auction market (online and offline) has continued to grow steadily over the past several years. Art auction turnover fluctuates, as do art painting prices, which fluctuate, fall, and rise over time. According to economists [1], paintings, such as financial and real estate assets [2, 3], have a similar pattern in terms of price indexes and consumption scale, with a certain positive and negative correlation between them. It has more applications in the fields of stocks and real estate and allows us to consider the combination of time series as a form of data for price forecasting. On the subject of artwork valuation, there have been related studies using the time series ARIMA model to predict the price trend for the overall artwork painting and calligraphy price index, but the study of what is used is based on the overall price index time series, which cannot achieve the purpose of predicting the price trend for the individual painting artwork. Moreover, the research indicates that art paintings for time series analysis face the following problems: a) a painting artwork may encounter very limited or even no repeat sales records that constitute a historical price time series, thus lacking sufficient information to make such an analysis possible; b) the method for the generation of a stable historical price time series and the method for analysing the generated historical price time series need to be developed.

To solve the problem of scarce repeat sales records for the construction of historical paintings, inspired by some researchers, consider a method for predicting painting prices from current paintings through deep learning, such as that developed by Worth [4], who calculated painting similarity to create a mapping model of features to price. Thus, a model for painting price prediction based on a multi-input model is presented, which can be used to forecast the possible auction prices of paintings to be bid at the time of similar historically traded paintings and thereby simulate repeat transactions. To further improve the accuracy of the prediction results, the simulated repeat transaction records are arranged according to time tags to derive the time series of prices. We further propose using a long- and short-term memory neural network (LSTM) model to construct a painting artwork historical price time series model using the previously generated painting artwork historical price time series to study the change pattern of artwork painting price time series and to achieve the dynamic prediction of artwork painting price. This study aims to examine the changes in the time series of artwork prices and predict their future prices dynamically.

This paper examines the proposed paint price prediction using a triplet network-multimodal network-LSTM combined deep learning approach, which includes four parts: related work, model design, experimental analysis, and conclusion. The first element is related work, which summarizes existing typical artwork valuation methods, compares the related research methods involved in this paper, identifies existing research deficiencies, and determines new research directions. Next, the model design is presented, which introduces the proposed method in general and then in detail and explains its practical implementation. In the third part, specific experiments are conducted, and the results are analysed. The fourth part of this paper summarizes the overall research and identifies limitations and future research directions.

2 Related Work

2.1 Artwork Valuation Methods

Please note that the first paragraph of a section or subsection is not indented. The first paragraphs that follows a table, figure, equation etc. does not have an indent, either.

Subsequent paragraphs, however, are indented. In fact, art appraisers have evolved over a long period of time, starting with traditional economic methods, such as the like-for-like comparison method, the dual sale method, and the average price method. Comparing a piece of artwork with another piece of artwork of similar quality that has already been sold in the market and calculating its current price based on sales records is called the "like-for-like" comparison. As the name implies, the dual sales method uses repeat sales data, combined with the continuous compound interest rate of return formula, to generate price returns during the interval of sales of artwork. This method is compared to the "like-for-like" comparison since it employs the same art sales data for comparison, and the predicted price is more realistic; however, the reliability of this method needs to be examined, especially given the limited number of repeat sales data and the very large interval between sales. Furthermore, owing to the special nature of artwork price assessments, most artwork price assessments use similar methods of comparison for forecasting, but they cannot consider the heterogeneity of artwork assessments and the complexity of the forecasting process; for example, it is impossible to achieve a certain level of differentiation in the needs of forecasting different artworks at different points in time.

Later approaches to artwork valuation focused on artwork feature mining to identify the variables relevant to artwork valuation and then quantify their degree of association. By applying multifactor statistical methods, including gray correlation and hedonic regression, to the assessment of artwork prices, Renneboog [5] and others used hedonic models to predict trends in artwork prices. Even so, this method of incorporating artwork value factors into regression models to predict prices does not appear to be effective, most likely because dynamic relationships between artists, colors, and other dimensions and how they affect pricing are difficult to capture by simple regression models such as hedonic regression. In other words, traditional multifactor statistical equations may be a good fit for certain linear problems but are difficult to use when considering nonlinear phenomena such as art prices.

A growing number of scholars are considering the use of machine learning and deep learning to enhance artwork value prediction methods since machine learning models avoid many of the systematic biases found in human appraisals, which cause a failure to sufficiently reduce the predicted value of artwork price estimates when faced with relevant negative information about declining market sales prices. In a study conducted by Ayub et al. [6]. CNN models are applied to determine the relationship between the visual characteristics of the artwork itself and its auction price, assisting people who do not possess a background in art to determine the market value of the work. When appraisers were not able to avoid the influence of past auction prices when valuing artworks for resale, models trained using actual auction prices as well as numerical data performed much better than models involving only images, suggesting that the characteristics of a painting's image are not as important as one might believe when trying to predict the painting's selling price. According to the corresponding study, researchers found that convolutional neural networks performed least well in predicting art prices in their own auctions, that models based on numerical data performed better than models based only on images and that machine learning models performed well when trained on numerical data (including artist, year of creation, material, and size) by Aubry et al. [7]. On the same data, they trained hedonic regression models and found that their machine learning model produced more accurate results than training hedonic regression models. Other studies have explored more varied concepts, such as Powell [8], who used machine learning techniques (such as k-nearest neighbors, support vector machines, and random forest classifiers) to examine descriptions of artwork and information about the artist biographical to see if the number of words is indicative of their selling price. There is a consensus that the above techniques, such as machine learning and deep learning, are most concerned with examining historical transaction data from the past to make predictions of artwork values and then mining patterns from the past to make future predictions. This paper also presents an analysis of the use of deep learning techniques for evaluating artwork values.

2.2 Classification Model of Paintings Based on the Triplet Loss Function

To calculate the similarity metric for images, mainstream methods extract features such as the histogram of orientation gradient (HOG), scale invariant feature transformation (SIFT), local binary pattern, and other methods of feature extraction. Using these extracted features, we calculate the similarity between them. Then, deep learning models are used to identify the query image, and the common L1 parametric (Manhattan distance) and L2 parametric (Euclidean distance) are important methods to measure the similarity between images in deep learning. To estimate fine-grained image similarity, a triplet loss function [9] is used, which produces a triple of fine-grained image similarity relationships. A neural network based on the triplet loss function can reduce the gap between anchor samples and positive samples and increase the gap between anchor samples and negative samples to achieve the classification of images with small differences in details and similar inputs and cope well with the multiclassification problem, which meets the objectives of this study.

2.3 Long and Short-Term Memory Model (LSTM Model)

A time series is a set of numbers with time indexes sorted by time to form a series. Time series is a common form of data that is widely used in nonstationary data such as the economy, weather, stock prices and retail sales. Time series analysis is built on the data form of time series, which is expected to predict future results by mining the rise and fall pattern of historical time series data. The common modelling methods include linear regression models, traditional time series models such as ARMA/ARIMA, and feature engineering models such as XGBoost and LSTM convolutional networks.

The value of the same artist's work over a large span of time may exhibit large differences; only in the price range of a more uniform distribution of artists or to assess the price of an artist's artwork for a certain period is the method more applicable. Therefore, temporal data models such as the long short-term memory network (LSTM) [10] are taken into consideration.

3 Design of Paint Price Prediction Using a Triplet Network-Multimodal Network-LSTM Combined Deep Learning Approach

3.1 Architecture of the Model

Please note that the first paragraph of a section or subsection is not indented. The first paragraphs that follows a table, figure, equation etc. does not have an indent, either.

Subsequent paragraphs, however, are indented. As part of our work, we analyse historical artwork painting data to generate time-series data, which need to be comprised of timestamps and simulated transaction prices for artwork paintings under each timestamp. To achieve such purposes, it is necessary to find similar artworks that have been sold in the market under each timestamp node and determine their relationship with the paintings to be predicted to simulate historical transaction records. The entire experimental process consists of a classification model for paintings with similar prices, a painting price prediction model based on visual and numerical data, and a dynamic painting price prediction model based on a long- and short-term memory network model. A diagram depicting the structure of the entire prediction process is shown in Fig. 1.

These are the steps involved in the painting price time series prediction model based on long- and short-term memory networks.

1. Classify the historical transaction data from the training set by price range $[P_1, P_2, \ldots, P_n]$ and train the similar-price painting classification model based on the triplet loss function so that the model will be able to identify the value range of a given artwork painting;
2. The historical transaction data are grouped by transaction time $[T_1, T_2, \ldots, T_n]$, , the sample (anchor) to be predicted and split transaction data set in each time group $T_x (x = 1 \ldots n)$ is put into the triplet loss-based painting classification model. By computing the cosine similarity of the feature vector between the sample (anchor) to be predicted and split transaction data set, the set of similar paintings corresponding to the samples to be predicted (anchor) with time tags $[T_1, T_2, \ldots, T_n]$ can be derived;
3. Putting the images and numerical data of the similar painting sets grouped by $[T_1, T_2, \ldots, T_n]$ into the multi-input painting price prediction model, each group can calculate one simulated trading record, and after N groups calculate, we can obtain multiple sets of simulated trading records of paintings with time tags $[T_1, T_2, \ldots, T_n]$;
4. The simulated transaction records of paintings are sorted by timestamps $[T_1, T_2, \ldots, T_n]$ $[T_1, T_2]$ to obtain simulated painting time series data, which are then put into a dynamic price prediction model based on the long short-term memory network model to determine predicted painting prices;

3.2 Similar Price Painting Classification Model Based on the Triplet Loss Function

Subsequent paragraphs, however, are indented. We need to take into account the characteristics of the painting data itself when developing a classification model. First, it is generally necessary to consider the paintings that have a fine gap between each image

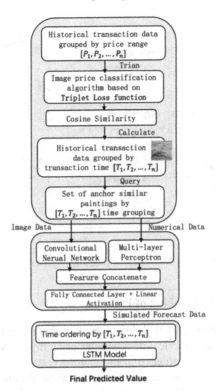

Fig. 1. Framework of paint price prediction using a triplet network-multimodal network-LSTM combined deep learning approach.

of paintings, and the classification of these images is usually complex, regardless of the consideration of genre, author, price range, etc. It is not possible to avoid the problem of multiple classification with a great number of art classification categories.

This triplet network is appropriately adapted to the abovementioned situation by feeding each element of the ternary group into a network D with shared parameters to achieve the characteristics of the output three images, $D(p)$, $D(a)$ and $D(n)$, respectively, with $D(p) - D(a)$ being the distance between the anchor and the positive sample and $D(n)$-$D(a)$ being the distance of negative samples from the anchor.

With successive learning, the distance between anchor and positive samples will become as small as possible, and the distance between negative samples and anchor will become as large as possible, so that positive pictures are more similar to query pictures than negative pictures, and this is reflected in the loss function of the whole painting similarity calculation model, as follows:

$$L(a, p, n) = max\{0, [D(p) - D(a)] - [D(n) - D(a)]\} \qquad (1)$$

Our training set $[P_1, P_2, \ldots, P_n]$ is used to classify the historical transaction data by price range, and from such data, the painting classification model with the triplet loss function can classify paintings of similar price ranges into one category. The framework structure of the model is presented as follows:

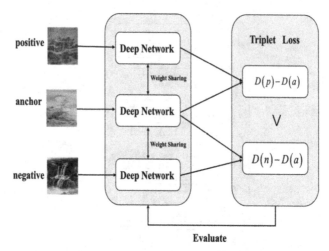

Fig. 2. Classification model for paintings based on triplet loss.

3.3 The Price Similarity Ranking of Paintings

To ensure the reliability and reproducibility of the painting price prediction model developed based on image and numerical data, similar price images should be selected for training and prediction. After processing the feature vectors by the triplet loss-based painting classification model, the cosine similarity method is used to determine how similar the prices of the two different painted features are. The following is a formula for calculating the cosine similarity (see Fig. 2).

$$Similarity\left(V_{anchor}, V_{(T_x,i)}\right) = \frac{\sum_{j=1}^{z} V_{anchor} \times V_{(T_x,i)}}{\sqrt{\sum_{j=1}^{z} (V_{anchor})^2 \times \sum_{j=1}^{z} \left(V_{(T_x,i)}\right)^2}} \qquad (2)$$

V_{paint} represents the classification feature vector of the painting, Z represents the vector length of V_x, and (V_x, i) represents the paintings in the T_x grouping (where x ranges from 1 to n and i represents the number of paintings within T_x). Based on the cosine similarity between all (T_x, i) and the classification feature vector of the anchor paintings to be predicted, the ranking of painting similarity can be derived by ranking all their calculated results.

3.4 The Multimodal Painting Price Prediction Model

Please note that the first paragraph of a section or subsection is not indented. The first paragraphs that follows a table, figure, equation etc. does not have an indent, either.

Subsequent paragraphs, however, are indented. The above painting price similarity ranking enables us to select a group of paintings, which are selected from each painting grouping in different T time periods, corresponding to the set of similar paintings $Similarity_{T_x} (x = 1 \ldots n)$. We decide to utilize the characteristics of image data and numerical data on the painting artwork to make a more accurate price prediction. In the painting price prediction model based on image and numerical data, the image data are processed using the convolutional neural network (CNN) model to identify the features in the image, and simple multilayer perceptron (MLP) processing is used to obtain numerical features. Common features of numerical and image features are then stitched together by fully connected layers to create a final multi-input model for training a model to predict artwork prices. Through the multi-input model, the four most representative paintings in $Similarity_{T_x}$ (the image to be predicted, the most similar image, the image with the largest value, and the image with the smallest value) are used as image features. The corresponding numerical features of paintings (such as the largest price of paintings sold, the smallest price of paintings sold, the average price of paintings sold, etc.) are stitched together. Then, through the fully connected layer, the model learns the relationship between the combined features and painting prices.

The following equation allows us to calculate the average price of similar paintings at different time groups $T_x(x = 1 \dots n)$, which is used as the historical price of the simulated painting to be predicted and as the target value for model learning.

$$Y = \frac{1}{n}\left(y_{sim_{T_1}} + \dots + y_{sim_{T_n}}\right) \qquad (3)$$

where Y is the historical painting transaction price generated by the simulation, and $y_{sim_x}(x = 1 \dots n)$ is the historical transaction price of similar paintings.

It consists of simulating the generation of representative artwork transaction records of the target anchor painting under each $[T_1, T_2, \dots, T_n]$ group, concatenating the corresponding time indexes, and then resampling and interpolating the data into equally time interval observations to generate a painting historical price time series.

4 Experiments and Results

Subsequent paragraphs, however, are indented. This paper is primarily based on public auction results on the website of Artron (https://auction.artron.net/). Artron's Chinese art auction database is one of the most comprehensive and encompassing databases in China, covering a wide range of influences and a large amount of auction data. Based on a crawl of the data, the research object was identified as Chinese paintings and calligraphy works.

The paintings with special painting type descriptions, such as three pairs and two frames, were also eliminated by subword processing of the artwork painting names, so that the painting research object focused on traditional flat paintings. A total of 44,996 pieces of Chinese paintings and calligraphy-type valid paintings were obtained, and these paintings were divided into 88 groups according to the date of auction. The price range of artwork was between 100¥ and 156,800¥, and the time span of artwork was April 16, 2000, through April 19, 2022, as shown in Table 1.

Table 1. Auction painting data set.

Field	Type of field
Name of the painting	Text
Author	Text
Image of the painting	Image
Length of the painting	Number
Width of the painting	Number
Auction price of the painting	Number
Painting auction time	Number

4.1 Preprocessing and Paint Price Series Data Generation

Our data need to be processed to remove missing values and outliers, to eliminate outliers in the auction value when counting the amount frequency, and to perform other processing that can improve the model. This can include screening the authors to ensure that each has enough paintings to be trained in the model and that there are sufficient training samples. To train the similar-price painting classification model based on the triplet loss function. An additional 2,000 paintings were crawled, categorized based on the quantile of the overall sale price and entered into the model for training. In the next step, more than 40,000 paintings will be grouped according to their auction date. Since auction companies usually hold 1–2 auctions per season, the paintings will be divided into groups every three months. Based on the previously trained similar-price painting classification model, we can identify target similar priced paintings for each season time grouping by using the model. By utilizing this found similar painting information, the image- and numerical-based painting price prediction model can calculate simulated painting transaction prices for target paints every three months. When generating the original prices after forming the price time series, there may be missing values due to an insufficient number of artworks, and when filling the empty segments, backfilling or forward filling may be used. To obtain the final predicted price, we used a long- and short-term memory neural network to simulate the time series of 110 paintings sold between March 2022 and May 2022. This study uses a painting of the "landscape axis" by Lu YanShao as a representative subject, and its simulated historical price time series is calculated as follows:

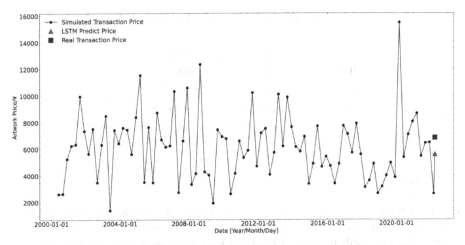

Fig. 3. Simulated historical price time series of the painting "Landscape Axis".

4.2 Model Comparison

The evaluation metric used for model prediction is a combination of root mean square error (RMSE) and mean absolute error (MAE), which is one of the most commonly used metrics in evaluation (see Fig. 3).

$$RMSE = \sqrt{\frac{1}{2} \sum_{i=1}^{n} (\overleftarrow{y} - y_i)^2} \tag{4}$$

$$MAE = \frac{1}{n} \sum_{i=1}^{n} \left| \overleftarrow{y} - y_i \right| \tag{5}$$

where y_i is the predicted price of the i-th artwork painting and y_i is the true price of the i-th artwork.

Multilayer perceptrons (MLPs) are selected as predictions in this study, as well as support vector machines (SVRs), which are often applied to nontime series models. Recurrent neural networks (RNNs), gated recurrent units (GRUs), and long- and short-term memory (LSTM) recurrent neural networks are typically used for time series models. Based on the table below, the results of the model related to time series predictions are better, while it is also evident that the price prediction model based on the LSTM model for painting time-series data produces better results (Table 2).

Table 2. Auction painting data set

Model	RMSE	MAE
MLP	25534.34	18844.25
SVR	24729.52	17614.92
LSTM	22840.69	16486.32
GRU	23025.18	16441.98

5 Discussion

To achieve the goal of being able to predict the price of artwork paintings within a good error range, an image classification model is used to classify artwork paintings in a range of price intervals to cluster like-priced paintings together into the next painting prediction model based on both image and numerical data. In the next step, the model for predicting painting prices based on image and numerical data is used to make further accurate predictions in a fixed price interval, and finally, the price is dynamically adjusted by combining the time series data. To predict painting prices for the same batch of artwork at the same point in time, a painting price time series prediction model based on the LSTM model and an algorithm that takes into account both images and numerical values are used. The following figure illustrates that paint price prediction using a triplet network-multimodal network-LSTM combined deep learning approach can increase the accuracy of the prediction when compared to the painting price prediction algorithm based on visual and numerical data. This section may be divided by subheadings. It should provide a concise and precise description of the experimental results, their interpretation as well as the experimental conclusions that can be drawn (Table 3).

Table 3. Comparison of prediction results of paintings

Model	RMSE	MAE
Painting price prediction model based on image and numerical data	22840.69	16486.32
OUR	24213.44	18384.74

6 Conclusion

As opposed to traditional methods of estimating the price of artwork paintings, traditional methods can only make static predictions for artwork paintings, and their predicted prices will not fundamentally change if the artwork attributes remain unchanged. This paper describes the development of paint price prediction using a triplet network-multimodal network-LSTM combined deep learning approach that solves the problem of missing enough sales records in dynamic pricing calculations. This paper begins by applying the image classification model with the triplet loss function to similar price painting classification to create a similar price painting image similarity calculation model, followed by creating a painting price prediction model based on image and numerical data. We simulated and generated historical transaction records of artwork paintings to address the problem of missing data series required for dynamic price prediction of paintings based on LSTM models. As a final step, a long short-term memory neural network method is employed to predict the painting price time series, with the aim of achieving the objective of dynamic pricing calculations and improving the accuracy of artwork painting valuation.

Further work should consider the value of artwork text data mining, including the possibility of developing a painting image classification model using triplet loss functions of the merged image and text data, as well as natural language processing methods to process information such as the text description of artwork paintings, which can be added to the painting price prediction model based on visual and numerical data to enhance the value of the prediction. Moreover, more maturity time-series data prediction models can find a more accurate dynamic price prediction model for paintings based on time-series data.

Acknowledgements. This paper is supported by the China National Key R&D Program for Young Scientists, China Ministry of Science and Technology (Nos. 2021YFF0900200).

References

1. Juan, H.: Economic significance of product markets. China Auction **6**, 38–41 (2014)
2. Mehtab, S., Sen, J., Dutta, A.: Stock price prediction using machine learning and LSTM-based deep learning models. In: Thampi, S.M., Piramuthu, S., Li, KC., Berretti, S., Wozniak, M., Singh, D. (eds.) Machine Learning and Metaheuristics Algorithms, and Applications. Communications in Computer and Information Science, vol. 1366, pp. 88–106. Springer, Singapore (2021). https://doi.org/10.1007/978-981-16-0419-5_8
3. Wang, F., Zou, Y., Zhang, H., Shi, H.: House price prediction approach based on deep learning and ARIMA model. In: 2019 IEEE 7th International Conference on Computer Science and Network Technology (ICCSNT), pp. 303–307. IEEE (2019)
4. Worth, T.: Painting2auction: art price prediction with a siamese CNN and ISTM (2020)
5. Renneboog, L., Spaenjers, C.: Buying beauty: on prices and returns in the art market. Manage. Sci. **59**(1), 36–53 (2013)
6. Ayub, R., Orban, C., Mukund, V.: Art appraisal using convolutional neural networks. Unpublished Stanford University (2017)
7. Aubry, M., et al.: Machines and masterpieces: predicting prices in the art auction market. J. Finan., Forthcom. (2019)
8. Powell, L., Gelich, A., Ras, Z.W.: Developing artwork pricing models for online art sales using text analytics. In: Mihálydeák, T., et al. (eds.) Rough Sets. IJCRS 2019. Lecture Notes in Computer Science(), vol. 11499, pp. 480–494. Springer, Cham (2019). https://doi.org/10.1007/978-3-030-22815-6_37
9. Schroff, F., Kalenichenko, D., Philbin, J.: FaceNet: a unified embedding for face recognition and clustering. In: Proceedings of the IEE Conference on Computer Vision and Pattern Recognition, pp. 815–823 (2015)

10. Kawakami, K.: Supervised sequence labelling with recurrent neural networks. PhD thesis, Technical University of Munich (2008)
11. Pawlowski, C., Gelich, A., Ras, Z.W.: Can we build recommender system for artwork evaluation? In: Bembenik, R., Skonieczny, L., Protaziuk, G., Kryszkiewicz, M., Rybinski, H. (eds.) Intelligent Methods and Big Data in Industrial Applications. Studies in Big Data, vol. 40, pp. 41–52. Springer, Cham (2019). https://doi.org/10.1007/978-3-319-77604-0_4
12. Tang, D., Chen, H., Zhang, Z.: Research on the pricing of Chinese artwork based on unascertained measure and GM (1, N) Model. J. Phys.: Conf. Ser. **1792**, 012066 (2021)
13. Jang, D., Park, M.: Price determinant factors of artworks and prediction model based on machine learning. J. Korean Soc. Qual. Manage. **47**(4), 687–700 (2019)
14. Li, Y., Sun, W., Zhu, J.: Research on factors influencing art auction sale prices-an analysis based on HPM method and auction TV program data. Manage. Rev. **31**(10), 142 (2019)
15. Ahmed, E., Moustafa, M.: House price estimation from visual and textual features. arXiv preprint: arXiv:1609.08399 (2016)
16. Kelek, M.O., Calik, N., Yildirim, T.: Painter classification over the novel art painting data set via the latest deep neural networks. Procedia Comput. Sci. **154**, 369–376 (2019)
17. Piao, Y., Chen, A., Shang, Z.: Housing price prediction based on CNN. In: 2019 9th International Conference on Information Science and Technology (ICIST), pp. 491–495. IEEE (2019)
18. Law, S., Paige, B., Russell, C.: Take a look around: using street view and satellite images to estimate house prices. ACM Trans. Intell. Syst. Technol. (TIST) **10**(5), 1-19 (2019)

Pattern Recognition and Machine Learning

Design of Mobile Application System for Recognition and Analysis of Dynamic Running Posture

Yikun Zhao[✉] and Fen Dai

College of Electronic Engineering (College of Artificial Intelligence), South China Agriculture University, 483 Wushan Road, Tianhe District, Guangzhou 510642, China
zhaoyikun@scau.edu.cn

Abstract. Aiming at sports injuries caused by incorrect running postures, this paper designs a mobile application system based on Android for the recognition and analysis of running postures. According to the profile running video, the system extracts the frame set of the time sequence from the filtered images, using the OpenPose algorithm to achieve runners' 18 joint coordinates and calculate the corresponding eight bone vectors and four joint angles. A dynamic skeleton with four joint angle time sequences is constructed by convolutional neural network fitting and using the dynamic time wrapping (DTW) algorithm to calculate the similarity between the measured and the standard dynamic skeleton, finally identifying the time when the abnormal running position appeared and the corresponding body position. All user information is written into the MySQL database as JSON data, and the front-end interaction uses Android Studio to present visual running posture analysis data. The results show that the system can identify a variety of abnormal running postures, can better adapt to complex backgrounds, has a higher recognition accuracy and calculation rate, and provides users with scientific real-time movement guidance.

Keywords: running posture recognition · computer vision · OpenPose · convolutional neural network · dynamic time wrapping

1 Introduction

Running is an excellent aerobic exercise. However, approximately 70% of runners have problems in running posture, such as excessive body tilt, overweight swing, and other abnormal movements. Wrong running posture not only fails to achieve the ideal fitness effect but also may cause irreparable sports injury to the body [1]. Therefore, how to capture and analyse running posture has become a key difficulty in sports guidance.

At present, the motion attitude recognition system usually adopts wearable sensor devices installed in various moving parts of the human body to obtain behavioral information, such as posture and planar pressure parameters in running [2]. This method not only requires additional hardware equipment, but also may have potential injury risk. However, using the computer vision method [Wang Jianbing, Li Jun, 2019] can not

M. Zhang et al. (Eds.): CCF NCCA 2023, CCIS 1960, pp. 35–42, 2024.
https://doi.org/10.1007/978-981-99-8761-0_4

only quickly and effectively identify the body data of human posture but also provide comprehensive movement guidance according to the analysis results.

Considering the periodic movement characteristics of running as well as the difference in individual body shape, height and pace, the change in body joint angle can be used to explain the change in running posture [3]. This system uses the OpenPose algorithm [4] to identify the position of human joints and build a human dynamic skeleton based on the change in joint angle time. Through the dynamic time planning algorithm, the similarity degree between the runner and the standard dynamic skeleton is calculated. Finally, all the data are presented in the user's mobile phone program in a visual way. This system provides an idea for the recognition and analysis of periodic whole-body motion posture and can be widely used in sports and fitness, motion acquisition, 3D adaptation and other fields.

2   Running Posture Recognition and Suggestion Algorithm

2.1   OpenPose Algorithm to Extract Joint Information

In this paper, the key node extraction algorithm of OpenPose is adopted to extract the features of running pose images, including those with fuzzy images, partial occlusion, and incorrect gestures. The OpenPose algorithm is based on the human posture estimation technology of convolutional neural networks and supervised learning technology to realize the estimation of human movements, facial expression changes, finger flexion and extension movements and other gestures. It extracts confidence graphs and partial similarity domains (PAF) from images through feedforward neural networks and realizes single or multiperson image or video recognition with very good robustness [5].

Figure 1 shows the main process of the OpenPose algorithm: the input picture (Fig. 1 (a)) is turned into image features using a 10-layer VGG19 network, and image features are then divided into two branches into a deep convolution network to predict the confidence level of each key point of S (Fig. 1 (b), shows the location of the human body joint) and affinity column L (Fig. 1 (c), illustrates the connection between each key point). Then, through the greed of the confidence level of each key point S and accessibility vector L, the key point of clustering (Fig. 1 (d)) is realized, and skeleton assembly (Fig. 1 (e)) is realized.

Taking the front side running pose video with a blank background from YouTube as an input file, the system first filters noise and extracts the frame image in the time series afterwards. The data of 18 nodes of the human running pose can be calculated with the OpenPose algorithm from the frame images. A bone vector can then be constructed by connecting two adjacent nodes. In this case, there are 12 bone vectors in total. The angle between two adjacent bone vectors is the angle between the elbow or femoral joint of the human body, that is, 4 joint angles in total. For example, the RW-RL bone vector and the RL-RS bone vector constitute the joint angle RW-RL-RS. Figure 2 shows the recognition results of the OpenPose algorithm for all 18 nodes in a single step cycle, including three elements of pull up, key running pose and falling running. The corresponding 12 bone vectors and 4 joint angles are calculated according to the coordinates of each of the three adjacent joint nodes in the image.

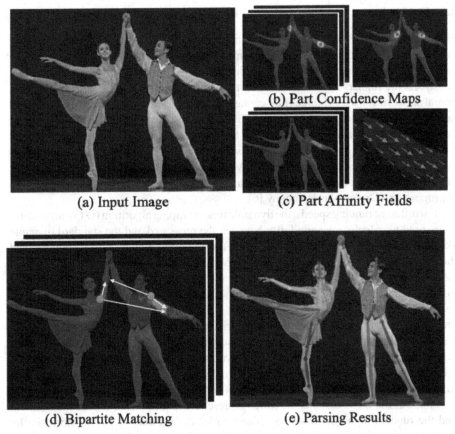

Fig. 1. The main process of the OpenPose algorithm[a]. a referenced from OpenPose [5]

Fig. 2. 18 Key points, 12 bone vectors and 4 joint angles in one running period

2.2 Establishment and Comparison of the Human Dynamic Skeleton

Since the changes in body joint angles can be used to describe the changes in running posture, the system fits the discrete sequences of the four joint angles calculated above into four periodic smooth curves with the discrete convolutional neural network and then constructs the runners' dynamic skeleton in the process of running. The convolutional neural network consists of three fully connected layers, each of which has 50, 20, and 10 neuron elements. The network adopts SIGMOD as an activation function and gradient descent as an optimization algorithm, and the learning rate is 0.01. The fitting dynamic joint angle change curve of RW-RL-RS is shown in Fig. 3, where the joint angle has been normalized in a single step period. Meanwhile, the standard dynamic skeleton is obtained from the processed demonstration video, in which the standard running posture is proposed by Dr. Nikolas Romanov [6].

For different running speeds, the dynamic time wrapping algorithm (DTW algorithm) [7] is used to calculate the similarity between the measured and the standard dynamic skeleton and finally identifies the time when the abnormal running posture appears and the corresponding body parts. The DTW algorithm is an algorithm used to calculate the similarity of two action sequences. It has great advantages in the sequence similarity of different lengths over the other traditional time-based point-to-point sequence similarity calculation algorithms. The time series of the measured and standard dynamic skeletons are set as the template sequence and comparison sequence, respectively, and their corresponding durations are n and m. Each time point in the sequence corresponds to an eigenvalue. The DTW algorithm compares and calculates the shortest distance between these two-time series by constructing an n *m matrix and stretching or contracting the time axis by the torsion method. The sum of the distances at each point on the matrix is defined as the DTW distance D, which represents the similarity between the standard and the runners' dynamic skeletons. The smaller the value of D is, the more similar the time series of the two running postures. Figure 4 is the similarity curve comparison between the measured and the standard skeleton obtained by the DTW algorithm. The abscissa in Fig. 5 represents the number of frames of the test video, and the black lines are the distance of each point.

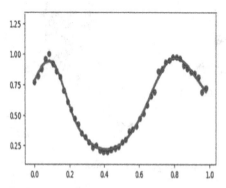

Fig. 3. The dynamic RW-RL-RS Joint angle curve

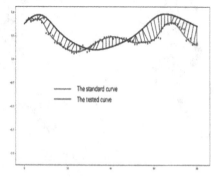

Fig. 4. The similarity curve of dynamic skeleton

3   Application Design

To visualize running posture, this paper develops a mobile application based on the Android system to score and suggest human running posture. Under the framework of the Android front-end, Tomcat server, and SSM based on Java, the system processes the side running video by building a back-end logic server. The MySQL database is used for data storage and storing user information and video information. Android Studio is used for front-end interaction to present running data to the user in a visual form.

After successful registration, users can directly upload the front running video captured by the mobile phone camera on the home page. The video duration is limited to 10–15 s, and the format is MP4, as shown in Fig. 5(a). After identifying the running form and calculating the similarity through openpose and the DTW algorithm, the system sends the pose analysis data in JSON format back to the application. When the processing is complete or incomplete, "Suggestions for Run Speed and Run Attitude Adjusted" or "Waiting for Server Processing" are displayed, as shown in Fig. 5(b). In the app, users can search for all uploaded records on the history page, browse real-time running information at any time on the information page, view the current ranking status and share their running records on the personal page.

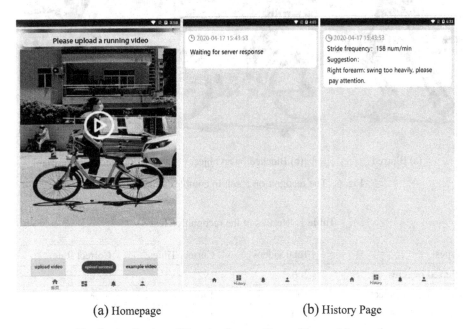

(a) Homepage   (b) History Page

Fig. 5.   Application of Running Posture Recognition and Suggestions

4   Test and Result Analysis

4.1   Analysis of Joint Recognition Testing

In view of the complex background in running video, this paper takes three situations into account, which include blurred pictures, runner blocked by objects, and runner blocked by pedestrians. Figure 6 shows OpenPose recognition results in three complex situations. The number of test videos in each of the three cases is 200, and the results of the experiment are shown in Table 1. Even if there is a situation where the runner is blurred or blocked, OpenPose can accurately localize the runner's joints. However, for the occlusion caused by pedestrians, the accuracy of OpenPose would be lower than in other situations.

(a) Blurred   (b) Blocked by an object   (c) Blocked by pedestrian

Fig. 6.   The recognition result in complex situations

Table 1.   Results of the recognition test

Types	Total videos	Correct Times	Correct Rate
Blurred pictures	200	192	96%
Occlusion by objects	200	196	98%
Occlusion by pedestrians	200	186	93%

4.2   Incorrect Gesture Recognition Testing

To verify the recognition effect of three incorrect postures, excessive forward-leaning and excessive arm or leg swing, five volunteers were required to record 200 side running test videos of incorrect posture and correct posture. The recognition results are shown in Table 2. Table 2 shows that the recognition accuracy rates in the four types of postures are 88%, 91%, 80%, and 82%.

4.3 Running Testing

The Android application size is 8.44 MB, and the running status of the system is maintained at a high response and low occupancy during the testing process. The hardware configuration of the cloud server is 10 M bandwidth and 4G memory. Table 3 shows the server test results, which show that the response time increases with the number of threads and that the system can realize a real-time response.

Table 2. Wrong posture correction test result

Types of posture	Total videos	Correct times	Correct Rate
Good Posture	200	176	88%
Excessive body lean	200	182	91%
Excessive arm swing	200	159	80%
Excessive leg swing	200	163	82%

Table 3. Server test results

Number of threads	Average response time	Median response time	Error Rate
100	3 ms	3 ms	0%
300	5 ms	4 ms	0%
500	178 ms	212 ms	0%
1000	1414 ms	1489 ms	0%

5   Conclusion

This paper introduces a mobile terminal system based on computer vision technology combined with the OpenPose algorithm, convolutional neural network and DTW algorithm for dynamic recognition and analysis of running posture. The recognition rate of the three complex situations is above 93%, and the accuracy rate of the three wrong gestures is above 80%. The test results show that the user can complete the visual analysis of running posture only through the mobile phone, and the system has high precision and stable operation.

References

1. Cong, L., Zhu, J.: Running posture and sports injuries. Athletics **06**, 62 (2016)
2. Ming, Z.: Research on Trajectory Reconstruction Method of Highway Based on Travel Time Estimation. North China University of Technology (2019)
3. Xu, Y.P., Zang, Y., Li, Q.J.: Human action recognition based on joint data. Comput. Knowl. Technol. **15**(27), 200–203 (2019)
4. Zhe, C., Gines, H.M., Tomas, S., Shih-En, W., Yaser, S.: OpenPose: realtime multi-person 2D pose estimation using part affinity fields. In: IEEE Transactions on Pattern Analysis and Machine Intelligence (2019)
5. Open Pose Demo Output [EB/OL]. https://github.com/CMU-Perceptual-Computing-Lab/openpose/blob/master/doc/output.md. Accessed 7 Nov 2018
6. Romanov, N., Brungardt, K.: Pose Method. Zhejiang People's Publishing House, China (2015)
7. Rakthanmanon, T., et al.: Searching and mining trillions of time series subsequences under dynamic time warping. In: Proceedings of the 18th ACM SIGKDD International Conference on Knowledge Discovery and Data Mining, pp. 262–270. ACM (2012)

One-Shot Municipal Solid Waste Detection via Object-Relevant Feature Enhancement and Category-Level Feature Fusion

Kun Ren[1,2,3(✉)], Furong Ren[1,2,3], and Honggui Han[1,2,3,4]

[1] Faculty of Information Technology, Beijing University of Technology, Beijing, China
renkun@bjut.edu.cn
[2] Engineering Research Center of Digital Community, Ministry of Education, Beijing, China
[3] Beijing Laboratory for Urban Mass Transit, Beijing University of Technology, Beijing, China
[4] Artificial Intelligence Institute and Beijing Laboratory for Intelligent Environmental Protection, Beijing University of Technology, Beijing, China

Abstract. Due to the significant variation of municipal solid wastes in appearance and composition, as well as the lack of abundant labeled samples, deep learning-based municipal solid waste detection is a challenging problem. This paper presents a novel one-shot municipal solid waste detection model based on Faster R-CNN and the attention mechanism to improve detection performance via object-relevant feature enhancement and category-level feature fusion. Concretely, a spatial attention-based feature enhancement module, SAFEM, is designed to enhance object-relevant information and improve object localization. Then, the channel attention-based fusion module, CAFM, is proposed and applied in two stages separately. In the first stage, CAFM uses the category-level information of the support features to help the region proposal network filter out non-support category query proposals; in the second stage, CAFM is used to enhance the classification accuracy of support category objects. The effectiveness of the proposed model is verified by experiments on the waste dataset of Huawei Cloud Competition 2020. The experimental results demonstrate that the proposed model achieves remarkable performance in one-shot municipal solid waste detection.

Keywords: Meta-learning · Faster R-CNN · Municipal Solid Waste · One-shot Object Detection

1 Introduction

As people's expectations for a high quality of life continue to rise, there has been an increase in the pace of upgrading products related to daily life. This has resulted in the emergence of various types of municipal solid wastes, which consist of items used and discarded daily, such as product packaging, furniture, clothing, bottles, food scraps, newspapers, paint, and batteries. They originate from our residences, schools, hospitals, and businesses. Hoornweg et al. projected that by 2025, global municipal solid waste (MSW) generation in major cities would reach 2.2 billion metric tons [1]. Such a massive

© The Author(s), under exclusive license to Springer Nature Singapore Pte Ltd. 2024
M. Zhang et al. (Eds.): CCF NCCA 2023, CCIS 1960, pp. 43–53, 2024.
https://doi.org/10.1007/978-981-99-8761-0_5

amount of garbage will cause environmental pollution and waste resources, which hinder the city's economic development [2, 3]. Therefore, finding an efficient method to dispose of MSW to protect the environment and reuse resources is an urgent matter on a global scale.

At present, there are three primary methods for dealing with MSW: incineration, landfill, and reuse [4]. Among these methods, reuse is the most complex and consists of three processes: sorting, recycling, and conversion. However, manual sorting, currently the mainstream method, is inefficient and costly, preventing the development of waste reuse. To address this issue, deep learning-based object detection technology has been used and has made remarkable achievements. For example, Lin et al. [5] proposed a YOLO-Green model based on YOLOv4 and achieved a mean average precision (mAP) of 78.04% on a homemade waste dataset containing 7 categories. Panwar et al. [6] proposed an AquaVision model based on RetinaNet, acquiring 81.48% mAP on the Aqua Trash dataset containing 6 categories. Ma et al. [7] designed a model based on Faster R-CNN and reached a 92% mAP on a homemade waste dataset containing 10 categories.

Despite advancements in MSW detection, deep learning models still face challenges when processing MSWs in actual applications. The same category of MSWs varies significantly in appearance and composition. Even identical objects with different contamination, damage, or deformation degrees are hardly recognized by deep-learning detectors, especially on a few labeled samples. However, collecting and labeling the MSW dataset, which includes multiple categories and massive samples of varying appearances, is extremely laborious and time-consuming. Therefore, developing detection models with good generalization ability to various MSWs with few labeled samples (i.e., few-shot detection) or even only one labeled sample (i.e., one-shot detection) is challenging and appealing to the research community.

Two main methods are commonly used to address the challenge of one-shot object detection, i.e., transfer learning and meta-learning [8]. Transfer learning aims at training a model on a source domain and then fine-tuning the model on a novel domain to make the model adaptable to novel data. However, transfer learning may not always perform well when the distribution of the novel domain data significantly differs from that of the source domain. In contrast, meta-learning involves training a model on a variety of meta-tasks without fine-tuning, enabling the model to have the ability to adapt to novel tasks. Each meta-task contains one support image and one query image, and the purpose of training is to recognize and locate the object of the support category in the query image. For example, the query image in Fig. 1 has two categories of objects: chopsticks and leftovers. When the support image category is chopsticks, the model can detect the chopstick category objects in the query image. Similarly, when the support image category is leftovers, the model can detect the leftover category object in the query image.

Meta-learning-based one-shot object detection models are commonly constructed with the two-stage detection framework Faster R-CNN [8]. The model uses convolutional feature extractors to extract query and support feature maps from query and support images, respectively. Then, by fusing these two feature maps, the merged feature maps

Fig. 1. One-shot detection with different support images.

are obtained and forwarded to the RPN and RoI (Region of Interest) layers to generate region proposals and RoI features, respectively. The RoI features are then applied to the classification and regression tasks. Different one-shot object detection methods implement aggregation in different ways, such as SiamMask [9], OSOD [10], and FOC OSOD [11], where OSCD additionally fuses the RoI features with the support features.

Inspired by OSCD and considering the characteristics of MSW images, we propose a novel one-shot MSW detector via object-relevant feature enhancement and category-level feature fusion based on spatial and channel attention mechanisms. Specifically, we first utilize the spatial attention mechanism to enhance the expression of object-relevant information in both support and query features. Second, we use the channel attention mechanism to improve the expression of category-level information of support and query features and achieve the fusion of category-level information. The effectiveness of our model is verified by ablation and comparison experiments on a homemade MSW dataset with 29 categories and 11176 images. Our main contributions are as follows:

- A spatial attention-based feature enhancement module, named SAFEM, focuses on enhancing the representation of the object-relevant features in the spatial dimension, is to improve the localization accuracy of the objects of interest.
- A channel attention-based fusion module, named CAFM, is used in both two stages of Faster R-CNN. The CAFM integrates category-level support information into query features to enhance the model's ability to identify support category objects.
- Ablation and comparison experiments are conducted on an MSW dataset of Huawei Cloud Competition 2020 to validate the efficiency of our proposed model.

2   Related Work

2.1   Object Detection

One-shot object detection aims to address the poor generalization ability of deep models caused by the lack of training samples [10, 12]. Recently, there have been advances in one-shot object detection using the two-stage detection network as a base framework. For example, the Siamese Mask R-CNN [9] based on Mask R-CNN introduces a matching module that enhances useful information in query features utilizing the similarity of the query and support images. The CoAE [13] based on Faster R-CNN uses a channel attention mechanism to weigh the channel information of both the support and query features, helping the RPN (region proposal network) generate more proposals associated with the object category. FOC OSOD [11] further refines the detection tasks to classification and localization and designs the fusion module for the classification branch to guide the model to place more importance on the information of the support category. Despite the great progress made in previous works, there are still some shortcomings, such as the inability to extract category information for fusion, which can easily mix information unrelated to the support category and affect detection accuracy. Therefore, based on previous works, we propose a novel one-shot model for MSW detection.

2.2 Attention Mechanism

When humans receive an image, they can judge the object's significance. In computer vision, attention mechanisms mimic this ability by assigning weights to input image features, enabling the model to focus on important information and ignore unimportant information according to the specific task. Channel and spatial attention are two common types of attention mechanisms [14]. Channel attention assigns weights to each channel of input features. SENet [15] enhances important channel information by weighing input features with channel attention weight. Specifically, the input features are average pooled in the spatial dimension and processed by two fully connected layers to achieve the interaction of channel information and obtain the channel attention weight. ECANet [16] improves on SENet by using a high-speed one-dimensional convolution of size K instead of full-connection layers, reducing interactions between unrelated channel information and saving computing resources. As an instance of spatial attention, self-attention [17] computes the similarity of different regions of input features to help the model identify which image regions are most relevant for the specific task. Due to the global information and correlation of input features being considered, the feature representation is improved. In general, channel attention focuses on figurative characteristics, such as color, shape, and texture; spatial attention adds location information for features, further enriching the feature information.

3   Related Work

3.1   Overall Architecture

For the characteristics of waste images, we propose a one-shot MSW detection model based on Faster R-CNN; the overall architecture is shown in Fig. 2. First, we extract feature maps from the support and query images using stacked convolution layers. Second, we design a SAFEM to enhance the spatial information of support and query feature maps to optimize the localization task. Third, we propose a CAFM to enhance specific category information in the channel dimension and fuse category-level information of support feature maps with query feature maps. Subsequently, the RPN can filter out nonsupport category proposals. We then utilize RoI Align to adjust the RoI features to the same size for further computation. Unlike RoI pooling, RoI Align can capture finer feature details [18]. To further boost category-level information in query features, we employ the CAFM to fuse the information of support and query RoI features in the channel dimension. Finally, we predict the fusion features directly.

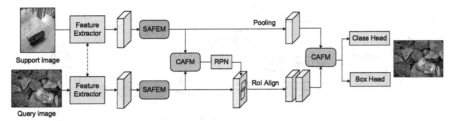

Fig. 2. Overall architecture of the one-shot MSW detection model.

3.2 Feature Extractor

We use stage 1-stage4 of ResNet50 [19] as the feature extractor, incorporating the residual structure to address the issue of overfitting that can arise from excessively deep network layers. The specific extraction process is shown in Fig. 3. The input feature is obtained from the input image prepossessing. Stage 1 consists of 7×7 convolution and max pooling processing. Stages 2–4 consist of stacked 1×1 and 3×3 convolution blocks that utilize the residual structure.

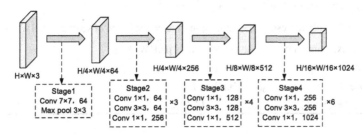

Fig. 3. Architecture of the ResNet50 feature extractor.

3.3 Spatial Attention-Based Feature Enhancement Model

We propose a spatial attention-based feature enhancement model, named SAFEM, to highlight the parts of the input feature maps related to the object. The specific structure of the SAFEM is shown in Fig. 4. The process begins with two 1×1 convolutions to reduce the computation parameters. The obtained results are then multiplied to calculate the similarity between each spatial location information and all locations of the input features. The similarity scores are then processed through softmax processing. This step is necessary to ensure that the scores add up to one and can be interpreted as weights for the importance of each spatial location. The module then uses a 1×1 convolution to process the input features and multiply them with the spatial similarity scores. This step assigns a weight to each pixel of spatial location information according to its degree of correlation with the object category. Finally, the enhanced features are processed by another 1×1 convolution and then fused with the input features. The calculation process of SAFEM is shown in Algorithm 1.

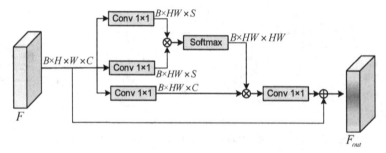

Fig. 4. The architecture of SAFEM.

Algorithm 1 Pseudocode for SAFEM

#Input: a tensor F, the shape of F is [B, HW, C], B: batchsize, H: the height of F, W: the width of F, C: the channel of F, S=256

#Output: a tensor F_{out}, the shape of F_{out} is [B,HW,C]

#Conv represents 1×1 convolution

$F_q = Conv(F)$ #shape of F_q is [B,HW,S]

$F_k = Conv(F)$ #shape of F_k is [B,HW,S]

$score = \frac{F_q^T \times F_k}{\sqrt{dim}}$ # dim represents the dimension of features, shape of score is [B,HW×HW]

score=Softmax(score, dim = 1) # shape of score is [B,HW×HW]

$F_v = Conv(F)$ # shape of F_v is [B,HW,C]

$F_{en} = score \times F_v$ # shape of F_{out} is [B,HW,C]

$F_{out} = Conv(F_{en}) + F_{en}$# shape of F_{out} is [B,HW,C]

3.4 Channel Attention-Based Fusion Module

We propose a channel attention-based fusion module (CAFM) to realize category-level interaction and fusion between support and query features. The structure of the CAFM is depicted in Fig. 5. The module first obtains the category-level information of the support and query features separately in the channel dimension using SENet. SENet obtains the compressive information by average pooling the input features in the spatial dimension and then adjusts the information by full connection to generate the attention mask. The attention mask weighs the input features to obtain enhanced features. Then, the module performs convolution calculation for enhanced query features using the vector of enhanced support features after average pooling as a convolution kernel. The convolution achieves category-level information fusion, which attenuates support-irrelevant information and improves the accuracy of classification. The calculation process of the CAFM is shown in Algorithm 2.

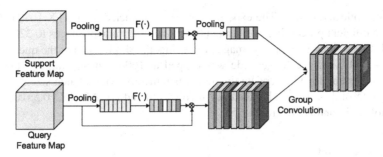

Fig. 5. The architecture of CAFM.

Algorithm 2 Pseudocode for CAFM

#Input: support feature $\mathbf{F_s}$, a tensor with shape [B,$H_S W_S$,C], query feature $\mathbf{F_q}$, a tensor with shape [B,$H_Q W_Q$,C]

#Output: fusion feature $\mathbf{F_{fusion}}$, a tensor with shape [B, $H_Q W_Q$,C]

#Avg represents avg pooling

#Group_Conv represents group convolution

#F(·)=Sequential(Linear(C,S),ReLU(),Linear(S,C),Sigmoid())

attn_s = Avg($\mathbf{F_s}$)

attn_s = F(attn_s)#shape of attn_s is [B,1,C]

$\mathbf{F_s}$ = attn_s × $\mathbf{F_s}$#[shape of $\mathbf{F_s}$ is [B,$H_S W_S$,C]

attn_q = Avg($\mathbf{F_q}$)

attn_q = F(attn_q)#shape of attn_q is [B,1,C]

$\mathbf{F_q}$ = attn_q × $\mathbf{F_q}$#shape of $\mathbf{F_q}$ is [B,$H_Q W_Q$,C]

$\mathbf{F_{fusion}}$=Group_Conv($\mathbf{F_q}$, $\mathbf{F_s}$) #shape of $\mathbf{F_{fusion}}$ is [B,$H_Q W_Q$,C]

---

4 Experiments

To assess the effectiveness of our proposed approach, we conducted comparative experiments using a Huawei Cloud dataset. Additionally, we conducted ablation experiments to analyse the individual contributions of each proposed module. Furthermore, we presented visualization results showing one-shot MSW detection, providing supplementary evidence to validate the efficacy of our proposed method.

4.1 Details of the Experimental Settings

The model is trained on base class data using massive meta-tasks and then directly tested on novel class data without fine-tuning. Each meta-task includes a single support image and a single query image, while the query image is selected in order from the corresponding dataset according to the stage of training or testing. The support images are randomly selected from a fixed support dataset, which consists of 10 samples of each class collected online. The experiments were conducted on a GTX 1080Ti GPU. To ensure efficient processing, we limited the size of the support images to 320 × 320. Similarly, for standardized query image processing, the shorter side of the query image was set to 600, and the longer side was capped at 1000. During training, the SGD algorithm was employed to update the model parameters, with a batch size of 2 and a learning rate of 1×10^{-3}. The accuracy metrics utilized are AP (IoU 0.5:0.05:0.95), AP50 (IoU 0.5), and AP75 (IoU 0.75).

4.2 Waste Dataset

The MSW dataset is selected from the Huawei Cloud dataset and consists of 29 common categories of municipal solid waste. Of these, we have selected 22 classes as the base classes, while the remaining seven classes are set as novel classes. The base classes are comprised of 10111 images, including objects such as eggshells, fruit pulp, dry batteries, fish bones, seasoning bottles, plastic toys, plug wires, shoes, ceramic utensils, metal food cans, carton boxes, expired medicines, ointments, cigarette butts, vegetables, wine bottles, pans, plastic clothes hangers, pillows, and disposable fast food boxes. On the other hand, the novel classes consist of 1065 images, covering items such as leftovers, butts, drink bottles, bags, towels, tea residue, and drink boxes.

4.3 Comparison Experiments

We conducted experiments to compare our method with the baseline. The baseline model has a two-stage detection framework as Faster R-CNN, and only in the second stage aggregates the support and query features by group convolution without feature enhancement and channel attention fusion. The experimental results are listed in Table 1. Our method has better generalization ability than the baseline, with an AP improvement of 2.8%. Furthermore, it is worth noting that our method performs significantly in the three classes: bag, butts, and towel; there are 7.6%, 5.6%, and 6.9% improvements, respectively, which provides compelling evidence of the effectiveness of our method.

Table 1. The comparison experiments on 7 novel classes of data, the evaluation metric is AP (IoU 0.5:0.05:0.95).

Model	leftover	bag	butts	drink bottle	towel	drink box	tea residue	AP
Baseline	15.2	45.0	37.3	43.9	22.8	25.4	30.0	24.4
Ours	17.9	52.6	42.9	44.0	29.7	26.6	30.0	27.2

4.4 Ablation Experiments

To prove the effectiveness of our proposed modules, we performed ablation experiments; the results are shown in Table 2. CAFM1 and CAFM2 denote the CAFM in the first and second stages, respectively. Scheme 1 is the baseline model, and Scheme 5 is our model. Firstly, comparing the experimental results of Schemes 2 and 5, the SAFEM can increase AP by 2.1%, AP50 by 0.5%, and AP75 by 1.9%. This improvement illustrates that the SAFEM can enhance the object-relevant information and facilitate object localization. Secondly, the experimental results of Schemes 3 and 5 show that CAFM1 increases AP by 1.9%, AP50 by 1.4%, and AP75 by 2.8%. The experimental results of Schemes 4 and 5 show that CAFM2 increases AP by 1.7%, AP50 by 1.2%, and AP75 by 2.4%. These results demonstrate that the CAFM can enhance the category-level information useful for object classification. Finally, the experimental results of Schemes 1 and 5 show that our model (including SAFEM, CAFM1 and CAFM2) can effectively enhance the detection performance of the baseline model: increase AP by 2.8%, AP50 by 2.1% and AP75 by 3.9%. The whole scheme has the best performance. It is noted that AP75, a more stringent metric than AP50, exhibits a 3.9% increase, surpassing the 2.1% improvement of AP50. These experimental results effectively validate each proposed module's efficacy and synergistic collaboration.

Table 2. The ablation experiment on novel class data. The evaluation metrics are average AP (IoU 0.5:0.05:0.95), AP50(IoU 0.5), and AP75(IoU 0.75).

Schemes	SAFEM	CAFM1	CAFM2	AP	AP50	AP75
1				24.4	48.9	21.4
2		✓	✓	25.1	50.5	23.4
3	✓		✓	25.3	49.6	22.5
4	✓	✓		25.5	49.8	22.9
5	✓	✓	✓	27.2	51.0	25.3

4.5 Visualization Results

To visually showcase the performance of our proposed method, we present a selection of object detection results on novel classes in Fig. 6. The left column displays the support images, while the right column exhibits the query images alongside the ground truth and predicted results. It is worth noting that even if the shape of the query sample differs significantly from that of the support images, our model can accurately identify objects in query images that belong to the same category as the support images.

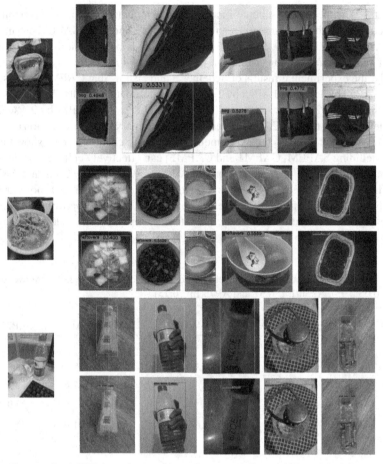

Fig. 6. The one-shot MSW detection results on three novel classes of data. The leftmost column represents the support images. For each category, the first row represents the query image and its ground truth, and the second row represents the prediction results and its confidence score.

5   Conclusion

To tackle the challenge of MSW detection with few labeled samples, we introduced a one-shot MSW detection model based on the Faster R-CNN framework. In addition, a spatial attention-based feature enhancement module is designed to enhance the object-relevant features of query and support feature maps. Moreover, a channel-attention fusion module is proposed to enhance and integrate the category-level features. To assess the effectiveness of our proposed method, we conducted comprehensive comparison and ablation experiments on the MSW dataset. The results demonstrate the superior performance of our approach in detecting novel MSW objects. Furthermore, we have provided visualization results of our experiments, which serve as compelling evidence to validate the effectiveness of our method.

Acknowledgments. This work was supported by the National Key Research and Development Project under Grants 2022YFB3305800–5, and 2019YFC1906002, National Science Foundation of China under Grants 61305026, 62125301, 62203022, 61890930–5, 61903010, and 62021003, Beijing Outstanding Young Scientist Program under Grant BJJWZYJH01201910005020, Beijing Natural Science Foundation under Grant KZ202110005009, CAAI-Huawei MindSpore Open Fund under Grant CAAIXSJLJJ-2021-017A, and Beijing Youth Scholar under Grant No.037.

References

1. Zhang, Q., et al.: A multi-label waste detection model based on transfer learning. Resour. Conserv. Recycl. **181**, 106235 (2022)
2. Zhou, L., et al.: Swdet: anchor-based object detector for solid waste detection in aerial images. IEEE J. Sel. Top. Appl. Earth Observations Remote Sens. **16**, 306–320 (2022)
3. Lin, K., et al.: Toward smarter management and recovery of municipal solid waste: a critical review on deep learning approaches. J. Clean. Prod. **346**, 130943 (2022)
4. Kasina, M., Kajdas, B., Michalik, M.: The leaching potential of sewage sludge and municipal waste incineration ashes in terms of landfill safety and potential reuse. Sci. Total. Environ. **791**, 148313 (2021)
5. Lin, W.: Yolo-green: a real-time classification and object detection model optimized for waste management. In: 2021 IEEE International Conference on Big Data (Big Data), pp. 51–57. IEEE (2021)
6. Panwar, H., Gupta, P., Siddiqui, M.K., Morales-Menendez, R., Bhardwaj, P., Sharma, S.: Aquavision: automating the detection of waste in water bodies using deep transfer learning. Case Stud. Chem. Environ. Eng. **2**, 100026 (2020)
7. Ma, W., Wang, X., Yu, J.: A lightweight feature fusion single shot multibox detector for garbage detection. IEEE Access **8**, 188577–188586 (2020)
8. Huang, Q., Zhang, H., Xue, M., Song, J., Song, M.: A survey of deep learning for low-shot object detection. arXiv preprint arXiv:2112.02814 (2021)
9. Michaelis, C., Ustyuzhaninov, I., Bethge, M., Ecker, A.S.: One-shot instance segmentation. arXiv preprint arXiv:1811.11507 (2018)
10. Fu, K., Zhang, T., Zhang, Y., Sun, X.: OSCD: a one-shot conditional object detection framework. Neurocomputing **425**, 243–255 (2021)
11. Yang, H., Lin, Y., Zhang, H., Zhang, Y., Xu, B.: Towards improving classification power for one-shot object detection. Neurocomputing **455**, 390–400 (2021)
12. Shao, Q., Qi, J., Ma, J., Fang, Y., Wang, W., Hu, J.: Object detection based one-shot imitation learning with an RGB-D camera. Appl. Sci. **10**(3), 803 (2020)
13. Hsieh, T.-I., Lo, Y.-C., Chen, H.-T., Liu, T.-L.: One-shot object detection with co-attention and co-excitation. In: Advances in Neural Information Processing Systems, vol. 32 (2019)
14. Niu, Z., Zhong, G., Yu, H.: A review on the attention mechanism of deep learning. Neurocomputing **452**, 48–62 (2021)
15. Hu, J., Shen, L., Sun, G.: Squeeze-and-excitation networks. In: Proceedings of the IEEE Conference on Computer Vision and Pattern Recognition, pp. 7132–7141 (2018)
16. Wang, Q., Wu, B., Zhu, P., Li, P., Zuo, W., Hu, Q.: ECA-Net: efficient channel attention for deep convolutional neural networks. In: Proceedings of the IEEE/CVF Conference on Computer Vision and Pattern Recognition, pp. 11534–11542 (2020)
17. Vaswani, A., et al.: Attention is all you need. In: Advances in Neural Information Processing Systems, vol. 30 (2017)
18. Bai, T., et al.: An optimized faster R-CNN method based on DRNet and Roi align for building detection in remote sensing images. Remote Sensing **12**(5), 762 (2020)
19. Targ, S., Almeida, D., Lyman, K.: Resnet in resnet: generalizing residual architectures. arXiv preprint arXiv:1603.08029 (2016)

Flue-Cured Tobacco Grading Method Based on a Convolutional Neural Network

Chunjie Zhang[1,2] (ID), Lijun Yun[1,2(✉)] (ID), and Zaiqing Chen[1] (ID)

[1] Yunnan Normal University, Kunming 650000, China
yunlijun@ynnu.edu.cn
[2] Yunnan Key Laboratory of Optoelectronic Information Technology, Kunming 650000, China

Abstract. Artificial flue-cured tobacco grading often has problems such as unstable grading results and low qualification rates, which lead to waste of tobacco resources and conflicts between tobacco farmers and collection stations. To rapidly and accurately recognize tobacco grades, a tobacco grading network called Tacc-Net was proposed. First, the convolution layer, pooling layer, batchnorm layer and SENet are used to build the Tacc-Block. Second, three Tacc-Blocks are connected to extract features, followed by the full connection layer to compose Tacc-Net for classification. Finally, the training was carried out in the tobacco leaf image dataset with 10 grades and more than 4000 images to realize the grade of tobacco leaf images. Compared with the classical neural network, this method has higher accuracy and can classify tobacco images of different grades more accurately.

Keywords: Tobacco Grade · Image Classification · SENet · Convolutional Neural Network

1 Introduction

China is a large flue-cured tobacco producer and consumer country, and in 2021, the total output of flue-cured tobacco reached 202.1 million kg [1]. Flue-cured tobacco leaves are an important raw material for the tobacco industry. In the purchase process, different qualities of tobacco leaves will affect the price of tobacco leaf purchases and the quality of subsequent cigarette production. The quality of tabacco leaves is determined by their grade [2]. According to the national standard of Chinese flue-cure tobacco GB2635–1998, the grade of the tobacco leaf can be determined by its growth position, appearance factor and color. For example, C3F represents the orange grade 3 tobacco leaf in the middle part. The standard divides tobacco into 42 grades, but it is difficult to accurately grade tobacco in practical applications.

The current tobacco grading method is mainly determined by the grading staff [3]. The grading staff rely on their senses and experience to determine the grade of tobacco leaves, which has strong subjectivity and randomness and easily leads to an inaccurate grade of tobacco leaves, which will have a negative impact on cigarette production. At the same time, this is a lengthy and time-consuming task. In the tobacco grading season, a large number of human resources are needed to distinguish tobacco grades, resulting in a waste of resources. However, almost all of the grading features of tobacco can be seen from the tobacco image [4]. It is very useful to use intelligent technology to extract tobacco leaf features and classify their grade, which can help the grading staff grade tobacco leaves quickly and accurately.

In recent years, some computer recognition methods have been proposed by researchers. Traditional algorithms usually extract color, texture, and shape features of tobacco leaves and then use them for classification learning. [5] used PCA to reduce the dimension of tobacco leaf features and then put the features into SVM. GA is used to optimize the selection of SVM parameters, and the recognition rate can reach 96.59%. [6] used blob detection, image thresholding and blob analysis to classify tobacco leaves, and the accuracy was 91.67%. [7] based on the fuzzy pattern recognition algorithm, extracted the appearance characteristics of tobacco leaves and then classified the tobacco sample; the accuracy of the prediction sets was 80.23%. However, this recognition method requires researchers to have a good understanding of the characteristics of tobacco leaves and select the most appropriate algorithm for these characteristics.

Deep learning methods use an end-to-end solution to extract features and then build a classifier [8]. For a certain model, you only need to input sample data, and the prediction result tag will be output automatically. Deep learning does not require manual design and feature extraction and is widely used in the image field. In the field of image classification, Yann LeCun initially deployed LeNet to recognize handwritten characters [9]. Since 2012, representative deep network structures such as AlexNet [10], GoogLeNet [11], VGGNet [12], and ResNet [13] have emerged, which have achieved good results in image processing, such as image recognition [14, 15], object detection [16, 17], image compression [18, 19], and image segmentation [20, 21]. Some researchers have also applied deep learning models to the tobacco industry. [22] Based on a multimodal convolution neural network and near-infrared spectroscopy, a tobacco origin recognition method was proposed. [23] proposed a tobacco plant detection method, and a convolution neural network was used as a feature extractor to extract features in R-CNN. [24] proposed a 1D-CNN based on a one-dimensional convolution depth neural network, and Yazhao Li et al. proposed the CNN-MY model to classify moldy and normal tobacco leaves [25]. However, there are very few deep learning models for tobacco leaf grading. Shixin Wang et al. applied Inception v3 to tobacco leaf images to classify 12 grades of tobacco leaves, with an accuracy of 95% [26]. Mengyao Lu et al. proposed an A-ResNet network and trained eight different levels of tobacco leaf images with an accuracy of 91.3% [27], but it is necessary to collect front and back images of tobacco leaves and build front and back models, the model is slightly complex.

In this research, we propose a flue-cured tobacco leaf grading method based on a convolution neural network. We use the convolution layer, pooling layer, batchnorm layer and SENet to compose the Tacc-Block. Then, three Tacc-Blocks and the full connection layer are connected to compose Tacc-Net. Experiments are carried out on the collected dataset to prove the effectiveness of this method.

2 Model

Although convolutional neural networks are increasingly widely used, their composition is very similar [28, 29]. They are mainly composed of convolutional layers, pooling layers, and fully connected layers. Our model continues to use these architectures and integrates attention mechanisms [30, 31].

2.1 Tacc-Block

As shown in Fig. 1, Tacc-block consists of two parallel paths. Convolution kernels of different sizes are used to extract information from different spaces, such as 3 * 3 and 5 * 5. The BatchNorm layer is behind the convolution layer to accelerate the training of the model. The ReLU activation function is behind the BatchNorm layer to introduce nonlinear characteristics. The features extracted from the two branches are added together, and then the dimensions and computation are reduced through the maxpooling layer. SENet follows the max pooling layer and pays attention to key features.

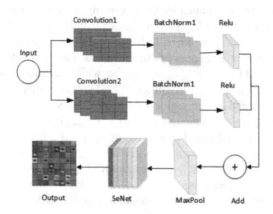

Fig. 1. Tacc-block structure.

The convolution layer is used to obtain the corresponding feature map of the image [32]. As shown in Fig. 2, the convolution kernel slides along the input to perform the convolution operation. In Tacc_Block, we use two different convolution kernels to calculate the original input image to obtain different feature maps.

Batchnorm is a means of normalization [33]; it standardizes the input, which helps to stabilize the network during training.

For each feature map, after convolution, it is necessary to introduce nonlinear characteristics through an activation function [34]. The ReLU activation function is used in this paper, and the corresponding formula is shown in Eq. 1:

$$\mathrm{ReLu}(x_i) = \begin{cases} x_i & x_i > 0 \\ 0 & \text{otherwise} \end{cases} \tag{1}$$

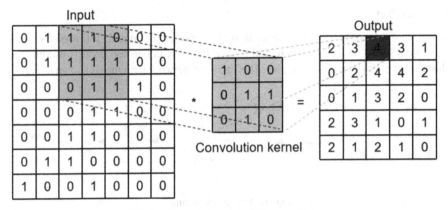

Fig. 2. Convolution calculation process.

The first two paths are added in the add layer, which requires that the output shapes of the two paths are the same.

The max pooling layer can retain the most important feature information and reduce the number of model parameters. The downsampling process for calculating the maximum value can be expressed as Formula (2).

$$x_i = \max\{a_1, ..., a_n\} \tag{2}$$

where n is the area size.

Squeeze and Extinction Network (SENet) is a classic attention mechanism that is widely used by industry experts [35]. The function of the SE attention mechanism is to enhance important features and suppress general features. The SE module includes two parts: squeeze and exception. The module structure is shown in Fig. 3. First, squeeze the input feature graph to obtain the $1 \times 1 \times C$ feature vector with global information. Then, the Exception operation is performed to obtain the importance of each channel. Finally, the vector value and the feature map are weighted to give each channel a different weight.

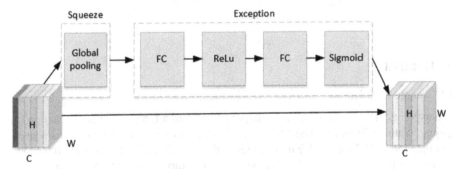

Fig. 3. SE module structure.

2.2 Tacc-Net

In this study, tobacco samples are used as the input of the model, followed by three Tacc-blocks for feature extraction, and finally, the fully connected layer is used as the classifier to classify tobacco samples. The Tacc-Net network structure is shown in Fig. 4.

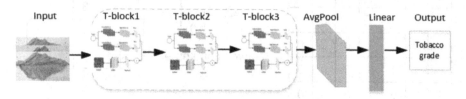

Fig. 4. Tacc-Net structure.

When performing grading tasks, map a preprocessed RGB image of tobacco leaves to $3 \times 256 \times 256$ vectors are sent into the network model, and the global features are extracted by T-block1-T-block3 to generate a $256 \times 4 \times 4$ eigenvector, then send the feature vector to the classification part for classification and recognition, and finally generate a feature vector with 10×1 is taken as the classification result, corresponding to 10 grades of tobacco leaves, and the network structure is shown in Table 1. 32 in Table 1 is the batch size.

Table 1. The network structure

Layer	Input size	Output size
Input	(32, 3, 256, 256)	–
T-block1	(32, 3, 256, 256)	(32, 64, 64, 64)
T-block2	(32, 64, 64, 64)	(32, 128, 16, 16)
T-block3	(32, 128, 16, 16)	(32, 256, 4, 4)
AvgPool	(32, 256, 4, 4)	(32, 256, 1, 1)
Linear	(32, 256)	32 * 10

3 DataSet

3.1 Image Acquisition

The experimental sample data in this paper come from a tobacco collection station in Qujing, Yunnan Province. The FUJIFILM X-43 is used to collect images, its sensor specification is 23.5 mm * 15.7 mm, the resolution of collected pictures is 6000 * 4000, the images have RGB channels, and the output file format is JPEG. When collecting data, the image quality was strictly controlled: the light was uniform when shooting, and the tobacco leaves were free of other impurities. This study collected 10 grades of tobacco samples, including B1F, B2K, B2F, B3F, C2F, C3F, C4F, X2F, X3F and X4F.

3.2 Image Preprocessing

For subsequent experiments, the image samples are processed as follows:

The image is large, and the memory is insufficient. The original tobacco leaf image was resized to 256 * 256 * 3 as the input of the network. Then, normalize the images to the $[-1, 1]$ range.

The processed sample data need to be divided. The training set is the data sample set of model fitting used to train the model, and the test set is used to evaluate the generalization ability of the model. We randomly select 80% of the number of images at different grades to constitute the training set, and the remaining 20% constitute the test set.

Considering that the quantity imbalance of different grades may lead to overfitting when training the model, the data in the training set are expanded. Because the color difference of different grades of tobacco leaves is small, if the color parameters of the image are changed, the classification accuracy will be affected. Therefore, this experiment uses the flipping method to expand the images of the training set. The images in the test set were not enhanced.

Figure 5 shows some tobacco leaf sample images in the dataset.

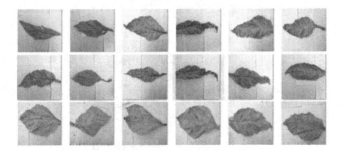

Fig. 5. Tobacco sample images.

The quantity of the dataset is shown in Table 2:

4 Experiment and the Results

4.1 Experimental Process

All tobacco samples were randomly divided, and there was no cross between the training and test sets. In the experimental process, first, at the training stage, the augmented training set samples and label data were input into the Tacc-Net network. The model obtains the classification results through forward propagation, compares with the labels to obtain attenuation, and back-propagates through loss backpropagation to continuously optimize the network parameters. In this process, an optimal model will be obtained for the classification of the test set. The experimental process is shown in Fig. 6.

Table 2. Number of samples of training and testing for the dataset used.

Grade	Samples of training	Samples of testing
B1F	480	60
B1K	480	60
B2F	480	60
B3F	480	60
C2F	480	60
C3F	480	60
C4F	432	53
X2F	480	60
X3F	480	60
X4F	480	60
Total	4752	593

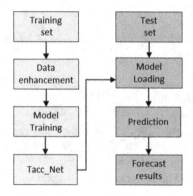

Fig. 6. Experimental Flow Chart.

4.2 Experimental Setup

The experiments use the PyTorch framework, the programming language is Python 3.7, the Linux operating system is used, the GPU uses Nvidia GV100, and the operating system uses Linux 3.10.0 to achieve all the experiments in this article. The environment used in the experiment is shown in Table 3.

In this study, cross-entropy was selected as the loss function, and SGD was selected as the optimization algorithm. The parameters were set as shown in Table 4. During the training process, monitor the accuracy of the test set and save the best weight value.

4.3 Experimental Results

Figure 7 (a) shows the results of testing the loss function of our model on the training set. When the model iterates for approximately 30 epochs, the model starts to converge

Table 3. Experimental environment.

Environment	Parameter/Version
GPU	Nvidia GV100
CUDA	11.6
Pytorch	1.12.1
Pycharm	2020.3
Operating System	Linux 3.10.0

Table 4. Experimental environment.

Parameter	Value
Learning rage	0.001
moment	0.9
Batch size	32
Epochs	100

gradually, and the loss finally stabilizes at approximately 0.02. Figure 7 (b) shows the accuracy curve of our model on the training set. The accuracy of the training set is rising. After approximately 30 epochs, the curve changes less and less, and the model converges, eventually reaching 99% accuracy.

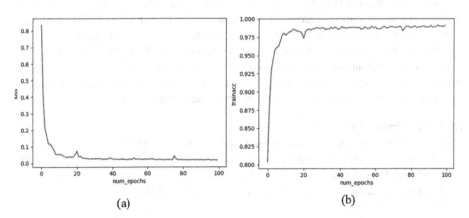

(a)   (b)

Fig. 7. Curve of loss of training set and accuracy of training set.

To display the grading results of each grade in detail, Fig. 8 shows the confusion matrix of the model in the test set. It can be seen that the accuracy of the model in B1F, B1K, B2F, C4F can reach 100%, in B3F, X3F, X4F can reach 98.3%, in X2F can reach 91.7%, in C3F and C2F the accuracy is relatively low, 88.3 and 86.7%, respectively.

The accuracy of the model in the whole test set reached 96.12%. Experiments show that the model designed in this paper is reasonable and feasible and can achieve good classification results.

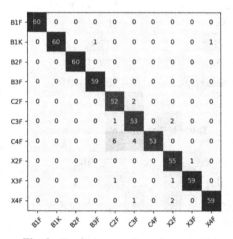

Fig. 8. Confusion matrix on the test set.

4.4 Comparative Analysis

Transfer Learning

Training convolutional neural networks from scratch requires considerable computing power, and transfer learning can use the pretrained model to ensure recognition accuracy while reducing training time [36]. This research studied the deep structure involving AlexNet, VGG, ResNet and DenseNet and compared it with the model proposed in this paper. When using other models for training, we use transfer learning to speed up training. We use the pretrained model on ImageNet, apply it to the tobacco dataset in this paper, retain all other layers, and modify the output layer category to 10.

Evaluating Indicator

To assess the performance of this method, some commonly used metrics are applied. After training, load the weight of the best model for this training to evaluate the precision, recall, F1 and Ti of the model on the test set.

Precision is used to evaluate the correct proportion of the true value in the data predicted to be correct.

$$\text{Precision} = \frac{\text{TP}}{(\text{TP} + \text{FP})} \tag{3}$$

Recall is used to evaluate the correct proportion of all the data with correct true values.

$$\text{Recall} = \frac{\text{TP}}{(\text{TP} + \text{FN})} \tag{4}$$

where TP is true positive, FP is false positive, and FN is false negative.

F1 is the harmonic average of accuracy and recall.

$$F1 = \frac{2PR}{(P+R)} \tag{5}$$

where P is the precision and R is the recall.

T is the processing time of a single picture.

$$T = \frac{\sum_{i=1}^{N} t_i}{N} \tag{6}$$

where N is the total number of images, ti represents the processing time of the ith image, and T represents the average time consumption of a single image.

Comparisons with Classical Models

During the experiment, all the classical models were trained with the method of transfer learning. First, load the pretrained model trained on the ImageNet dataset, fine-tune it, modify the output layer to ten categories, and then train it on the tobacco dataset.

Figure 9 shows the accuracy of this method and other classic models in the test set. From the figure, we can see that the accuracy of AlexNet in the test set is only 91.6%, the accuracy of VGG11 is 93.9%, the accuracy of VGG16 is 94.27%, the accuracy of ResNet18 is 93.75%, the accuracy of ResNet50 is 92.5%, and the accuracy of DenseNet121 is 93.5%. Our method has the highest accuracy, reaching 96.12%, 1.85% higher than the highest VGG16.

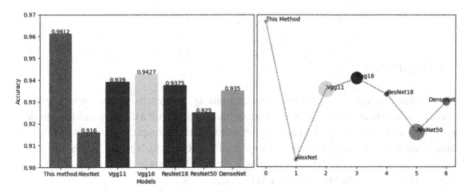

Fig. 9. Accuracies of different models.

Table 5 shows the comparison of the precision, recall and F1 scores between the model in this paper and the classic depth convolution neural network models AlexNet, VGG11, VGG16, ResNet18, ResNet50 and DenseNet121. T in Table 4 represents transfer learning.

Table 6 shows the image processing speed and the size of the models. It can be seen from the table that although AlexNet processes images at a fast speed, only 0.067 s per image, its model is large, reaching 228 MB. By comprehensive comparison, the processing speed and size of the model proposed in this paper are optimal.

Table 5. Comparison results of each model on the test set.

Model	Precision	Recall	F1
T-AlexNet	0.918	0.9194	0.9181
T-vgg11	0.9394	0.9408	0.9395
T-vgg16	0.9425	0.9423	0.9421
T-ResNet18	0.9382	0.9391	0.9378
T-ResNet50	0.9265	0.9267	0.9257
T-DenseNet121	0.9361	0.9367	0.9361
This method	0.9617	0.9619	0.9626

Table 6. Comparison of image processing speed and model size

Model	Speed(s)	Size(MB)
T-AlexNet	0.067	228.2
T-vgg11	0.155	515.2
T-vgg16	0.241	537.2
T-ResNet18	0.221	44.8
T-ResNet50	0.423	94.5
T-DenseNet121	1.444	28.5
This method	0.072	5.7

5   Conclusions

To solve the problems in artificial tobacco grading, in this paper, we integrated the convolution neural network and attention mechanism and built a tobacco grading model: Tacc_Net. First, we collected tobacco samples to build a dataset. Second, Tacc_block is constructed using convolution, batchnorm, pooling, ReLu, SENet, etc. Then, the Tacc-Net model is built using the T-block, pooling layer and fully connected layer. Experiments on the dataset show that this method has high accuracy.

However, the dataset used in this paper is still small. In the future, richer datasets can be used to verify the recognition effect. At the same time, the tobacco leaf image used is static, but in actual industrial production, it is dynamic, and the image quality may be unstable. In the future, we will further study the practicability of this classification method in industrial equipment.

Acknowledgements. This article was supported by the postgraduate program of the Scientific Research Foundation of Education Department of Yunnan Province (Grant No. 2022Y90) and the Science and Technology Plan Project of Yunnan Provice Company of China Tobacco Corporation (Grant No. 2021530000242043).

References

1. China Statistical Yearbook 2022. http://www.stats.gov.cn/sj/ndsj/2022/indexch.htm. Accessed 28 Jul 2023
2. Liu, J., Shen, J.Y., Shen, Z., Liu, R.: Grading tobacco leaves based on image processing and generalized regression neural network. In: ICADE, pp. 89–93. IEEE 345 E 47TH ST, New York, NY 10017 USA (2012)
3. Li, S., et al.: Comparison of tobacco grading methods based on hyperspectral information. Tobacco Sci. Technol. **54**(10), 82–91 (2021)
4. Zhang, F., Zhang, X.: Classification and quality evaluation of tobacco leaves based on image processing and fuzzy comprehensive evaluation. Sensors **11**(3), 2369–2384 (2011)
5. Yao, X., He, F., Ping, A., Luo, H., Guan, Q.: Leaf tobacco grading method based on PCA-GA-SVM. Tobacco Sci. Technol. **51**(12), 98–105 (2018)
6. Harjoko, A., Prahara, A., Supardi, T., Candradewi, I., Pulungan, R., Hartati, S.: Image processing approach for grading tobacco leaf based on color and quality. Int. J. Smart Sens. Intell. Syst. **1**(12), 1–10 (2019)
7. He, Y., et al.: Method for grade identification of Tabacco based on machine vision. Trans. ASABE **61**(5), 1487–1495 (2018)
8. Arora, R., Rai, P., Raman, B.: Deep feature–based automatic classification of mammograms. Med. Biol. Eng. Compu. **58**(4), 1199–1211 (2020)
9. Lecun, Y., Bottou, L., Bengio, Y., Haffner, P.: Gradient-based learning applied to document recognition. Proc. IEEE **86**(11), 2278–2324 (1998)
10. Krizhevsky, A., Sutskever, I., Hinton, G.: ImageNet classification with deep convolutional neural networks. Commun. ACM **60**(6), 84–90 (2017)
11. Szegedy, C., et al.: Going deeper with convolutions. In: CVPR, pp. 1–9. IEEE 345 E 47TH ST, New York, NY 10017 USA (2015)
12. Simonyan, K., Zisserman, A.: Very deep convolutional networks for large-scale image recognition. In: International Conference of Learning Representation, pp. 1409–1556 (2014)
13. He, K., Zhang, X., Ren, S., Sun, J.: Deep Residual Learning for Image Recognition. In: CVPR, pp.770–778. IEEE345 E 47TH ST, New York, NY 10017 USA (2016)
14. Yang, Y., Yun, L., Li, R., Cheng, F., Wang, K.: Multi-view gait recognition based on a Siamese vision transformer. Appl. Sci.-Basel **13**(4), 2273 (2023)
15. Cheng, Y., Wang, H.: A modified contrastive loss method for face recognition. Pattern. Recogn. Lett. **125**, 785–790 (2019)
16. Pan, T., Huang, H., Lee, J., Chen, C.: Multi-scale ResNet for real-time underwater object detection. Signal Image Video Process. **15**(5), 941–949 (2020)
17. Fahad, L., Tahir, S., Rasheed, U., Sqqib, H., Hassan, M., Alquhayz, H.: Fruits and vegetables freshness categorization using deep learning. CMC-Comput. Mat. & Continua **71**(3), 5083–5098 (2022)
18. Krishnaraj, N., Elhoseny, M., Thenmozhi, M., Selim, M., Shankar, K.: Deep learning model for real-time image compression in Internet of Underwater Things (IoUT). J. Real-Time Image Proc. **17**(6), 2097–2111 (2020)
19. Zhang, Q., Zhang, M., Chen, T., Sun, Z., Ma, Y., Yu, B.: Recent advances in convolutional neural network acceleration. Neurocomputing **323**(5), 37–51 (2019)
20. Lin, B., Qu, Y., Xie, J., Li, C.: Deeptongue: tongue segmentation via Resnet. In: ICASSP, pp.1035–1039. IEEE345 E 47TH ST, New York, NY 10017 USA (2018)
21. Khouloud, S., Ahlem, M., Fadel, T., Amel, S.: W-net and inception residual network for skin lesion segmentation and classification. Appl. Intell. **52**(4), 3976–3994 (2021)
22. Zhang, L., Ding, X., Hou, R.: Classification modeling method for near-infrared spectroscopy of tobacco based on multimodal convolution neural networks. J. Anal. Methods Chem. 2020 (2020)

23. Sun, X.P., Peng, J.Y., Shen, Y., Kang, H.W.: Tobacco plant detection in RGB aerial images. Agriculture **10**(3), 57 (2020)

24. Zhai, N., Yun, L., Ye, Z., Wang, Y., Li, Y.: A tobacco storage moldy prediction method based on one-dimensional convolutional neural network. Comput. Eng. Sci. **43**(10), 1833–1837 (2021)

25. Li, Y., Yun, L., Ye, Z., Wang, K., Zhai, N.: Image recognition of moldy tobacco leaves based on convolutional neural network. Comput. Eng. Sci. **43**(03), 473–479 (2021)

26. Wang, S., Yun, L., Ye, Z., Wang, Y.: A tobacco leaf grading processing algorithm based on convolutional neural network. J. Yunnan Minzu Univ. **29**(01), 65–69 (2020)

27. Lu, M.Y., Jiang, S.W., Wang, C., Chen, D., Chen, T.E.: Tobacco leaf grading based on deep convolutional neural networks and machine vision. J. Asabe **65**(01), 11–22 (2022)

28. Dulari, B., et al.: CNN variants for computer vision: history, architecture, application. Chall. Fut. Scope. Electorn. **10**(20), 2470 (2021)

29. Li, Z.W., Liu, F., Yang, W.J., Peng, S.H., Zhou, J.: A survey of convolutional neural networks: analysis, applications, and prospects. IEEE Trans. Neural Networks Learn. Syst. **33**(12), 6999–7019 (2022)

30. Niu, Z.Y., Zhong, G.Q., Yu, H.: A review on the attention mechanism of deep learning. Neurocomputing **452**(10), 48–62 (2022)

31. Li, R., Zheng, S., Duan, C., Yang, Y., Wang, X.: Classification of hyperspectral image based on double-branch dual-attention mechanism network. Remote Sensing **12**(3), 582 (2020)

32. Mei, S., Ji, J., Hou, J., Li, X., Du, Q.: Learning sensor-specific spatial-spectral features of hyperspectral images via convolutional neural networks. IEEE Trans. Geosci. Remote Sens. **55**(8), 4520–4533 (2017)

33. Santurkar, S., Tsipras, D., Ilyas, A., Madry, A.: How does batch normalization help optimization? In: NIPS, 31 Neural Information Processing Systems (NIPS), 10010 North Torrey Pines Rd, La Jolla, California 92037 USA (2018)

34. Dubey, S., Chakraborty, S.: Average biased ReLU based CNN descriptor for improved face retrieval. Multimedia Tools Appl. **80**(15), 23181–23206 (2021)

35. Guo, M., et al.: Attention mechanisms in computer vision: a survey. Comput. Visal Media **8**(3), 331–368 (2022)

36. Zhuang, F., et al.: A comprehensive survey on transfer learning. Proc. IEEE **109**(1), 43–76 (2021)

Uyghur Text Recognition Based on the SVTR Network

Wenhua Yu, Mayire Ibrayim[✉], and Askar Hamdulla

School of Information Science and Engineering, Xinjiang University, Xinjiang Key Laboratory of Signal Detection and Processing, Urumqi, Xinjiang, China
mayire401@xju.edu.cn

Abstract. To address the lack of image datasets for Uyghur text recognition, text image synthesis techniques were used to construct the Uyghur text image datasets; data enhancement techniques such as adding noise, blurring, and brightness changes were used to enhance some of the image in the dataset to varying degrees to further enhance the natural scene features in the constructed dataset; finally, 99.9% text recognition accuracy was obtained on the constructed dataset using the SVTR network with the addition of the Uyghur text dictionary, with a 21.9% increase in accuracy compared to the transformed Latin CRNN network for the same dataset. Compared with other Uyghur text recognition methods under previous machine learning frameworks, the method in this paper can batch process data, automatically extract features to improve efficiency, and have different degrees of improvement in recognition results from a few points to twenty points. The experimental results show that the recognition method using synthetic images and data enhancement techniques under this paper's deep learning network framework can better achieve the recognition task of Uyghur text and achieve better experimental results.

Keywords: Deep Learning · SVTR Network · Uyghur Text · Text Recognition

1 Introduction

At this stage, text recognition has succeeded for mainstream texts such as Chinese and English and is widely used in commercial fields. For example, licence plate recognition, translation, and electronic document recognition, but the recognition of nonmainstream minority texts is still in its infancy. In addition to the original influencing factors of scene text recognition, the challenges of Uyghur text recognition mainly come from the special characteristics of the Uyghur text itself. First, the Uyghur text's structure can be understood intuitively from Fig. 1. The number 0 indicates that Uyghur text is written from right to left; 1 represents the baseline domain of writing, which will be written along a straight line called the baseline, and the baseline has a certain thickness; the forms of words constituting Uyghur text are diversified, with 2, 3, 4, and 5 representing the initial, intermediate, final, and independent forms, respectively; 6 represents a hyphenated segment consisting of four characters, and 9 represents a word consisting of a solitary

M. Zhang et al. (Eds.): CCF NCCA 2023, CCIS 1960, pp. 67–84, 2024.
https://doi.org/10.1007/978-981-99-8761-0_7

letter and two hyphenated segments without a certain regularity [1]; 7 and 8 represent the subsidiary and main strokes, respectively, and usually, there is no connection between the two parts; there are many similar characters that are difficult to distinguish; and there is no single standard for the width and height of characters [1].

Fig. 1. Structural features of the Uyghur text.

This paper uses deep learning methods for Uyghur text recognition, and the main contributions of this paper are as follows: first, to solve the problem of insufficient Uyghur text recognition datasets, synthetic techniques are used to construct Uyghur text datasets; next, data enhancement techniques such as adding noise, blurring and luminance changes are used to extend the data scale and enhance the natural scene features of the datasets; finally, an Uyghur text dictionary is added using a scenario-based text recognition network for mainstream texts (Chinese and English) to obtain 99.9% accuracy of Uyghur text recognition.

2 Related Work

At present, research on the recognition of ethnic minority scripts needs to rely on the relevant language and script environment, so it is usually related to the geographical environment and ethnic gathering. The study of ethnic minority languages and texts has received increasing attention, and an increasing number of scholars and universities have joined the study of ethnic minority scripts. In the same way as the study of text recognition in mainstream languages, recognition can be divided into printed text recognition and handwritten text recognition according to the different fonts of Uyghur texts. The research in this paper is focused on printed Uyghur text recognition. Text recognition in images can be divided into segmentation-based and no-segmentation approaches according to whether segmentation is needed. The segmentation-based approach requires locating the location of each character in the input text image, recognizing each character by a single-character recognizer, and then combining the recognized characters into a string sequence to obtain the final recognition result [2]; the no-segmentation approach takes the whole text line as a whole and directly maps the input text image into the output string sequence [2]. Some scholars mainly use segmentation-based methods in their research on printed Uyghur text recognition. Li used segmentation for connected Uyghur texts [3], followed by subsequent feature extraction and classification recognition. Jia [4] used features such as the number of holes, tail points, intersections, and directional codes to train and recognize Uyghur text models. Hao [5] used CNN to extract features for printed Uyghur text character recognition. After preprocessing by Yu [6], letter segmentation was performed, followed by matching recognition using HOG feature extraction and MLP classifier. Wang [7] used a character segmentation recognition method based on morphology and integral projection for Uyghur text recognition. When recognizing Uyghur text characters obtained from segmentation, the Zernike moment features of Uyghur text characters were extracted, and a Euclidean distance classifier was used for classification and recognition. Wan [8] used the pixel integral projection method to perform line segmentation and word segmentation on text images, innovatively proposed the baseline area white projection segmentation method to perform oversegmentation on connected segments, and then combined threshold judgment rules to eliminate oversegmentation. Based on the traditional projection-based Uyghur character segmentation algorithm, Lang [9] proposed a segmentation algorithm that combines connected domain labelling with vertical projection.

The above Uyghur text recognition methods focus on cutting the Uyghur text to obtain the features before recognition. However, Uyghur text is mainly a phonetic script evolved based on Arabic and Persian scripts, and its character form is very similar to Arabic characters, which belongs to the Turkic language family of the Altaic language family, while in terms of grammatical structure, it belongs to the type of adhesive language [1]. It needs to ensure an accurate cut to achieve text recognition, and because the cut difficulty of characters is greater than the cut difficulty of hyphenation is greater than the cut difficulty of words. The similarity of characters is greater than the similarity of hyphenation, which is greater than the similarity of words [3]. Considering the cut difficulty and similarity, it is difficult to cut Uyghur text and more difficult to ensure an accurate cut. This paper uses mainstream text (Chinese and English) scene text recognition with a single visual model (the model is referred to as SVTR [10]) for Uyghur text recognition in images, which introduces global and local mixing blocks to extract stroke features and intercharacter correlation, respectively, combined with a multiscale backbone network to form a multigrain feature description [10] to extend the application of the model from the mainstream text recognition domain to the nonmainstream text recognition domain.

3   Method

3.1   Overall Architecture of SVTR

The SVTR [10] recognition model uses a single visual model for natural scene text recognition and is different from conventional text recognition models that require visual feature extraction models and sequence models, and the single visual model reduces model complexity and has promising applications. The SVTR [10] network first decomposes image text into small 2D patches called character components because each patch may contain only part characters. Thus, patch-based image tokenization and self-attention capture recognition cues between character components [10]. The entire network consists of three downsamplings, and the three stages of refinement can be seen in Fig. 2 of the overall architecture, which again includes mixing, merging, and combining operations. Local and global mixing blocks and merge or combine operations are designed and iteratively used in each phase to capture local features and elemental dependencies. Throughout the process, the role of each module is inseparable, and the model is highlighted below in modules.

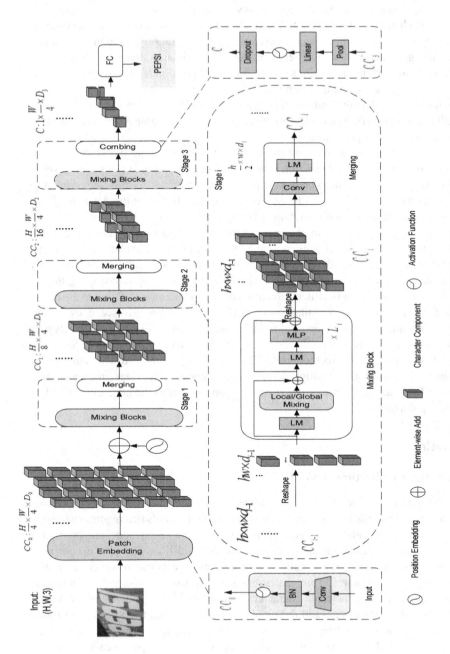

Fig. 2. Overall architecture of SVTR [10].

3.2 Sampling Module

As seen from Fig. 2 of the overall SVTR architecture, the SVTR recognition process is divided into three stages, with three downsampling stages, each time reducing the resolution of the input feature map and expanding the perceptual field layer by layer and the size of the downsampling module, as shown in Fig. 3.

As seen from the size change in the downsampling phase of Fig. 3, patch embedding with overlap is performed using a 3×3 convolution with step size $(2, 1)$, which combines nonlinear and overlap characteristics to increase the receptive field. The downsampling size change is mainly performed on the height, indicating that the width-level text information is richer than the height-level text information. The overall process can be seen from the size change in Fig. 3 [10] as follows: ① the input size is $H \times W$ a three-channel text image, and after the patch embedding module, the size is transformed into the patch of $\frac{H}{4} \times \frac{W}{4}$; ② the three downsampling stages after patch embedding are mainly used to extract features. Combined with the overall architecture of Fig. 2, each stage has a series of mixing blocks and merges. In the final stage, there is also combing; local and global mixing blocks are used to extract the local features and dependencies of the strokes. After the third stage, the feature size becomes $1 \times \frac{W}{4}$, represented by the symbol C; ③ finally, after the FC layer to obtain the character sequence, the output result is PEPSI.

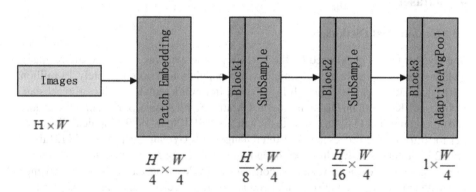

Fig. 3. Downsampling module size variation.

3.3 Mixing Block

Because different text characters have differences and need to rely on character-level features in the recognition process, sequence features are widely used to represent text in images. Considering that sequence features for slicing regions introduce noise, the SVTR network does not use sequence features but uses two mixing blocks to extract features. As shown in Fig. 2 and Fig. 4, two mixing blocks are global mixing blocks and local mixing blocks. As shown in Fig. 4(a), the global mixing block serves to sense character component dependency and extract global features, stroke features, local character morphological features and individual correlations of strokes in characters and weakens the influence of nontext regions. As shown in Fig. 4(b), local mixing block sensing extracts local features and encodes correlations between different features, correlations between multiple characters and correlations between text and nontext regions.

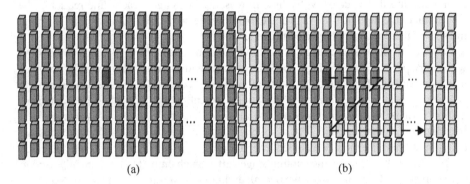

(a)   (b)

Fig. 4. Mixing blocks: (a) global mixing and (b) local mixing.

4   Dataset

4.1   Uyghur Text Dictionary

The Uyghur text is a text used by the Uyghur people, who are mainly in the Xinjiang Uyghur Autonomous Region of China, with a population of approximately 13 million (2015 population within China). It is also used in foreign regions, such as Kazakhstan, Uzbekistan, Kyrgyzstan, Pakistan, Russia, Ukraine, Saudi Arabia, Syria, Turkey, Canada, and other countries [11]. According to the national "GB12050–1989 Graphical Character Set for Information Processing and Interchange with Uyghur Script Code," [12] there are 32 basic letters in Uyghur text, including 8 vowel letters and 24 consonant letters. The Uyghur text dictionary can be constructed by learning the alphabet of Uyghur text with common punctuation marks and referring to the correspondence of common English dictionaries in the English recognition network. The English recognition and dictionary correspondence process is because English contains 26 letters (in case of case-insensitive), and a dictionary needs to be provided during the model training and testing to map all occurrences to the index of the dictionary, so the dictionary needs to contain all characters that are expected to be correctly recognized. For example, the process of constructing a dictionary based on a widely used English text that is stored in the notepad file en.txt according to the letters of the English alphabet, one character per line, and left justified. For example, the dictionary construction based on the widely used English text, which is stored in the notepad file en.txt according to the letters of the English alphabet as a single character per line and left justified.

Assuming that the en.txt dictionary is stored in alphabetical order according to Table 1, then characters are mapped together with numerical indexes, and the numerical indexes are marked in increasing order from 0. Therefore, the English word "bad" is mapped into numerical indexes [1 0 3], and the network in this paper needs to add corresponding dictionaries for different text characters. By comparing the format and content of the English dictionary with the Uyghur alphabet and some common punctuation marks, we can obtain a Uyghur text dictionary containing 114 symbols (the table contains four rows and three columns of space symbols, and the third to eighth columns of the fifteen rows are to be filled with subsequent symbols) (Table 2).

Table 1. 26 English Alphabets (case insensitive).

English dictionary							
a	b	c	d	e	f	g	h
i	j	k	l	m	n	o	p
q	r	s	t	u	v	w	x
y	z						

Table 2. Uyghur text dictionary

English dictionary							
u	g	_	i	m	/	1	I
L	S	V	R	C	2	0	v
a	1	8	5	3	6	9	.
j	p		ق	ا	پ	ل	4
7	ئ	ى	ش	ت	ي	ك	د
ف	ر	و	ن	ب	ه	خ	ى
ج	ۇ	ز	س	م	ژ	گ	ڭ
ژ	ۋ	ح	غ	ھ	ۆ	s	c
e	n	w	P	E	D	U	d
r	b	y	B	o	O	Y	N
T	k	t	h	A	H	F	z
W	K	G	M	f	Z	X	Q
J	x	q	-	!	%	#	?
:	$	,	&	'	É	@	é
(	+						

4.2 Uyghur Text Dataset

In the field of deep learning, datasets play a crucial role in the research process and are an essential part of the experiment. The demand for data volume in text recognition is much greater than that in text detection, rising from a few thousand images for text detection to tens of thousands, hundreds of thousands, or even millions of images for text recognition. Therefore, the training dataset images for text recognition cannot be too small. Suppose the training and test datasets only take up a small part. In that case, it is difficult to ensure that the data features and distribution of the training dataset and the test dataset are similar, resulting in the model fully learning the features of the training dataset and overfitting, leading to insufficient generalization ability of the model. The training results lose conviction, or the trained model does not have generalization. Therefore, in the absence of current open-source natural scene Uyghur text image datasets, this paper uses self-built datasets from the team of the Key Laboratory of Signal Detection and Processing and the Key Laboratory of Multilingual Information Technology in the School of Information Science and Engineering of Xinjiang University for experiments. The synthetic dataset can be generated using existing background images for Uyghur text recognition data using the method provided in [13], or the dataset can be assembled using the method in [14].

The laboratory establishes a dataset containing words and phrases commonly used in Uyghur texts, a test dataset of arbitrary-length word images for text recognition, which is composed of synthetic word images of arbitrary length with a fixed image height of 32 pixels and five backgrounds from light to dark chosen for the image data background. The total number of datasets is 174816, including 158928 word images in the training dataset and 15888 word images of any width in the test dataset; the feature distributions of the training dataset and the test dataset are the same, and the dataset images are named according to the numerical order growth direction starting from the number 0, the rule is ****.jpg. An example of the dataset part is shown in Fig. 5 and Fig. 6 below.

Fig. 5. Example of partial data samples from the training dataset (left) and partial labelling (right)

Fig. 6. Example of partial data samples from the test dataset (left) and partial labelling (right).

5 Experiment

5.1 Image Text Recognition Evaluation Criteria

During experiments, the algorithms usually have a basic assumption that the data distribution is uniform. For category-balanced data, accuracy is generally used as an evaluation metric; for data with unbalanced data categories, a portion of the data from more categories can be discarded to make it comparable to the data from fewer categories; or the data from fewer categories can be synthesized to make it comparable to the data from more categories, and the processing mainly involves data enhancement of the image data to obtain more data. Therefore, category-balanced data directly use accuracy as an evaluation metric, and category-unbalanced data, after the category-balancing process, can also use accuracy as an evaluation metric.

To verify the effectiveness of the text recognition algorithm, recognition accuracy is used as the evaluation criterion. Recognition accuracy is divided into character recognition accuracy and word recognition accuracy, which can be referred to as recognition accuracy. Both recognition rates are the ratio operation between the predicted value and the real value. The difference is that the character recognition rate is compared in terms of characters, and the ratio of the number of recognized characters to the total number of actual characters is counted; the word recognition rate is compared in terms of words, and the ratio of the number of recognized words to the total number of actual words in the image is counted. Because the word recognition rate is in words, each character in a word must be recognized correctly. The word recognition rate requirement is more stringent because errors in individual characters can be tolerated in character recognition. The above two evaluation criteria are commonly used in English datasets. This paper takes the word recognition accuracy as the evaluation index of the text recognition algorithm, which can be expressed as

$$\text{Accuracy} = \frac{N}{M} \times 100\% \tag{1}$$

where M represents the number of all recognized characters, and N represents the number of samples that are fully recognized correctly.

5.2   Experimental Results and Analysis

Experimental Basic Environment: Based on the PaddlePaddle Framework, Intel(R) Xeon(R) Gold 6271C CPU @ 2.60 GHz, NVIDIA-SMI 460.32.03, driver version 460.32.03, CUDA version 11.2, GPU Tesla V100-SXM2. Video Mem 16GB, CPU 2 Cores, RAM 16GB, Disk 100GB, Programming language version Python 3.7 and PaddlePaddle 2.2.0.

To ensure the reliability of the experimental results in this paper, the SVTR network model is first experimentally validated before Uyghur text recognition, and the validation results are compared with the paper's experimental results to determine the reliability of the experimental results and the network model. Because the flying paddle platform has arithmetic power consumption and running time limitations for each day of the week, the validation uses only the synthetic dataset ST as the training set, and the test set is the same as the six datasets in the paper experiments. Because a single card is used, the batch parameters batch_size_per_card: from $512 \rightarrow 256$ and num_workers: from $4 \rightarrow 2$ are adjusted during the training process; the batch parameters batch_size_per_card: from $256 \rightarrow 128$ and num_workers: from $2 \rightarrow 1$ are adjusted during the testing process to ensure that they will not out of memory. The final validation results are compared with the original paper, and the validation comparison table is shown in Table 3. SVTR-T (Tiny) is the experimental result of the original paper, and SVTR-T is the validation result. From Table 3, it can be seen that the validation differs from the original paper by 1.2%, 1.5% and 0.8% on the English regular dataset and by 4.0%, 4.3%, and 1.7% on the English irregular dataset. After comparing the two types of data validation, regular and irregular, the validation gap of the regular dataset is smaller than the validation gap of the irregular dataset. Considering the partial changes in parameters during the training phase dataset, training process, and testing process, the overall network experimental effect is not much different. Therefore, the experimental results of the SVTR network on the PaddlePaddle platform are reliable and can be used for Uyghur text recognition.

Table 3. Validation comparison table.

Method	datasets	IC13	SVT	IIIT5K	IC15	SVTP	CUTE
SVTR-T (Tiny)	MJ+ST	96.3	91.6	94.4	84.1	85.4	88.2
SVTR-T	ST	95.1	90.1	93.6	80.1	81.1	86.5

Because the experimental results of the SVTR network on the PaddlePaddle platform are reliable, the Uyghur character recognition effect can be experimentally verified from the following aspects.

(1) The effect of dataset size change on the recognition effect of the SVTR network.

In this paper, recognition experiments are conducted in the SVTR network and PPOCRv3-SVTR (indicating the PPOCRv3 system using the SVTR recognition algorithm) system by changing the size of the training dataset and test dataset. The recognition models of the SVTR network and PPOCRv3-SVTR system were trained with training data of different sizes. The experiments were verified in the SVTR network and

PPOCRv3-SVTR system with test datasets of different sizes, and the results were compared. The comparison table of the effect of the SVTR network and PPOCRv3-SVTR system is shown in Table 4.

Table 4. Validation comparison table.

Network Types	Training dataset size	Test dataset sizes	Accuracy rate (%)
PPOCRv3-SVTR	5000	3000	75.00
SVTR	5000	3000	80.00
PPOCRv3-SVTR	10000	5000	92.00
SVTR	10000	5000	99.50
PPOCRv3-SVTR	25000	5000	96.10
SVTR	25000	5000	98.50
PPOCRv3-SVTR	158928	15888	97.30
SVTR	158928	15888	99.90

As seen from Table 4, the recognition performance of both the SVTR network and the PPOCRv3-SVTR system improved as the dataset size increased. The improvement is because as more image data are fed into the model, the features of the images are more representative, and the model can learn features that cover more scenes, so the recognition rate of the model is improved. However, unlike the PPOCRv3-SVTR system, the recognition accuracy of the SVTR network decreases when the amount of data is 25,000, which is due to the data enhancement operation performed on the initial 5,000 data. As seen from the experimental data in Table 4, the effect of data enhancement on the SVTR network is more obvious than that of the PPOCRv3-SVTR system. The SVTR system is more obvious in that data augmentation can improve the generalization ability of the model network to meet practical application scenarios.

Commonly used data enhancement methods are translation transformation, flip transformation, random cropping, noise addition, contrast transformation, scaling transformation, and scale transformation. The most direct effect of data enhancement operation is to increase the sample size, which can effectively alleviate the overfitting of the model and eventually enhance the generalization ability of the model. Because the experimental data in this paper are text images, the original labels of the images should be kept unchanged when the data enhancement operation is performed, but if the corresponding labels can be modified after the data enhancement, the network generalization can be better improved, and corresponding to modified labels is a time-consuming and laborious process, so the random cropping processing needs to be disregarded for the time being. The role of panning and flipping transformations in enhancing text features is relatively small and is not considered for the time being. Therefore, for the experimental data and labelling characteristics of this paper, several processing methods, including blurring, increasing noise, and changing brightness are finally selected to enhance the data, and the training set data are changed from 5000 to 25000. Figure 7 shows the same original Uyghur text image, adding noise, reducing brightness, adding blur, and increasing brightness for data enhancement.

Fig. 7. Example of dataset enhancement

(2) Comparison of Uyghur text recognition results with previous methods.

In this paper, the results of previous studies related to the recognition of printed Uyghur texts are compared with the results of this method, and the comparison is shown in Table 5.

The method in this paper is a deep learning method. The network automatically performs the extraction process of image features without manual feature extraction, which can save time and improve the effectiveness of feature extraction. Table 5 shows that the data scale of this paper is larger than the data scale of several thousand images used by previous scholars and because the training and test sets have similar data features and data distributions, which are all commonly used words and phrases. The model fully learns the features of the training set, and the experimental recognition accuracy grows to 99%. The recognition result of this paper's method is 0.47% higher than the highest recognition result (convolutional model [5]) in the past. Because the Uyghur text datasets used in the above methods are self-built datasets, the comparison of different methods' experimental results shows that the model in this paper works better than other experimental methods in the case of self-built datasets. Additionally, because CRNN [15], the converted Latin CRNN [16], the PPOCRv3-SVTR system, and the SVTR (our) network use the same dataset, the accuracy of the converted Latin CRNN [16] increases by 5.2% compared with the CRNN [15] network under the same dataset; the accuracy of using the PPOCRv3-SVTR system increases by 5.2% compared with CRNN [15] and increases by 24.5% and 19.3% over the conversion Latin CRNN network; using the SVTR network increased by 27.1% over the CRNN network, 21.9% over the conversion Latin CRNN, and 2.6% over the PPOCRv3-SVTR system, with significant changes in network accuracy. Comparing the PPOCRv3-SVTR system with the SVTR network, we found that the accuracy difference is 2.6% because PPOCRv3-SVTR is a system that incorporates many modules, so the overall running time is longer, and the ratio of the experimental time of the PPOCRv3-SVTR system to the SVTR network is 5:1. The running time of PPOCRv3-SVTR is too long, and the overall consideration SVTR network works best.

(3) Effect of iteration rounds on recognition results

The neural network in the training process uses the iterative calculation to obtain the relevant weight parameters. After many iterations, it can obtain the ideal parameters to ensure that the experimental process does not introduce other variables, so in the identification of the experimental comparison process, all experimental rounds are used 500 rounds (epoch) of iterative operations, where the best_epoch is 313.

SVTR network, the whole experiment process 500 epochs, each epoch contains 620 global_step, where print_batch_step is set to 10, then every 10 global_step will print

Table 5. Table captions should be placed above the tables.

Methods	Target text	Dataset size	Accuracy rate (%)
Dripping\moving window method+main attachment separation+MQDF classifier [1]	Uyghur	18175	95.06
Position relation merge connected domain+convolution [3]	Uyghur	89600	99.00
Convolution Model [5]	Uyghur	489214	99.43
HOG features+MLP classifier [6]	Uyghur	1762	96.15
Morphology and integral projection+Zernike moment characteristics+Euclidean distance [7]	Uyghur	5000	70.98
Connected domain+vertical projection+Euclidean distance [9]	Uyghur	1408	91.26
PCAM attention mechanism [13]	Uyghur	10015000	96.80
CRNN [15]	Uyghur	174816	72.80
Convert LatinCRNN [16]	Uyghur	174816	78.00
CNN_Succ-2&Conv-4 [17]	Uyghur	10575	96.77
ResNet+BiLSTM+Attention [18]	Uyghur	109379	99.40
GRCNN+ATT [19]	Uyghur	109089	93.59
PPOCRv3-SVTR	Uyghur	174816	97.30
SVTR Model(our)	Uyghur	174816	99.90

out acc, norm_edit_dis, loss, and other parameters. From the beginning of training, the training iteration rounds are from global_step 10 to global_step 550 of the first epoch, the recognition accuracy of the model is almost 0, the model's learning effect is very poor, and the accuracy rate starts to change from around global_step 560. From global_step 690 in the second epoch, the accuracy changes significantly, and the model learns the features in the image better. After 313 iterations, the recognition accuracy on the Uyghur text dataset finally converges to 99.9%. From the analysis of the number of iterations and accuracy, we can see that if the number of iterations is not enough and stops early, the model does not reach stable convergence at this time and the training results; if there are too many iterations, the training time is too long, and resources are wasted.

5.3 Analysis of SVTR Network Limitations

The SVTR network has limitations because SVTR uses absolute encoding; therefore, it does not support variable length and recognizes up to 25 characters of text. The overall structure of SVTR is a backbone+ctchead structure and uses absolute position encoding during training. Absolute positional encoding is a sequence of positional encoding based on a fixed input size, and the positional encoding information is updated with training. However, suppose the inference uses an input size that is inconsistent with the training. In that case, the position encoding obtained from the training cannot participate in the inference, and the runtime will report an error and show the size problem. At this stage, the most common solution for the case of an uncertain number of characters, or a number of image characters greater than 25, is to use the PP-OCRv3 network that introduces the SVTR recognition algorithm. The PP-OCRv3 structure is backbone(lcnet)+neck(svtr)+ctchead, and the backbone uses a lightweight full convolutional network lcnet. There is no absolute position coding, and for an input of size (W variable), lcnet extracts size the obtained feature F. Neck takes a two-layer SVTR global block, no absolute position coding is used, and the feature F goes through SVTR to extract global features and is finally sent to ctchead to decode the result.

Because it is known from the Uyghur text recognition comparison experiment that the time ratio between the PPOCRv3-SVTR system and SVTR network experiment is 5:1 because PPOCRv3-SVTR is an integrated detection and recognition system, the system contains several modules, and the whole operation processing time is long, so the solution to the problem can be used in addition to the PPOCRv3-SVTR network, modification and deletion of the absolute code section can also be considered. Because the data length of the commonly used text recognition dataset does not vary much, the character length is relatively short, and the number of text characters does not exceed 25, the PaddlePaddle learning competition dataset with a large variation in data length is selected. The PaddlePaddle learning competition dataset is the Chinese scene text recognition competition dataset [20], which includes a total of 60,000 images, of which 50,000 are the training dataset and 10,000 are the test dataset. The dataset is collected from Chinese street scenes and formed by intercepting text line areas (e.g., store signs, landmarks, etc.) from the street scene images. All images are subjected to some preprocessing, such as blurring, variable shooting angle, shadow brightness variation, and size variation, and finally, the text area is mapped isometrically to a 48-pixel high image using an affine variation, samples of which are shown in Fig. 8 and Fig. 9.

From the sample examples in Fig. 8 and Fig. 9, it can be seen that the pictures are blurred. The length varies greatly, and because the training dataset has annotation files and the test dataset does not, it is time-consuming and laborious to relabel the test dataset. The data are overly blurred and easily mislabelled, so the training dataset is reclassified into training and test datasets. Because of the problems of mislabelling, unlabelled, and incomplete labelling, the training dataset was filtered by reading the labelled files using gb2312 encoding. The final training dataset was 43,520 images, and the validation dataset was 2,290 images. Experiments were conducted using the redivided dataset, as seen in Table 6; the difference in accuracy before and after the improvement of the same network structure is not very large, but in the inference process after the training test before the improvement of the SVTR-T network, it cannot participate in the normal inference process, and inference shows errors. After the improvement to remove the absolute position encoding can carry out the inference process, inference shows success to facilitate the subsequent inference deployment work. The combination of SVTR with other networks before improvement can also be a good solution to the problem of inference reporting errors [21].

Considering the perspective of experimental data, to better obtain the text features of the dataset, data enhancement was performed on the experimental competition dataset,

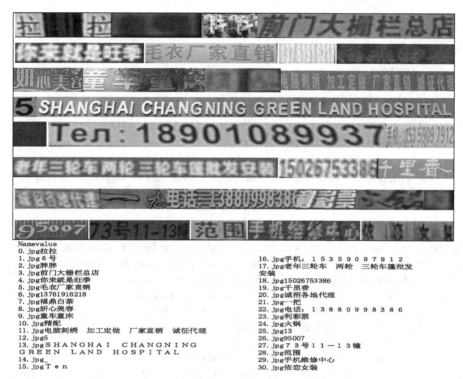

Namevalue
0. jpg拉拉
1. jpg6 号
2. jpg胖胖
3. jpg前门大栅栏总店
4. jpg你来就是旺季
5. jpg毛衣厂家直销
6. jpg13761916218
7. jpg福鼎白茶
8. jpg妍心美容
9. jpg童车童床
10. jpg精配
11. jpg电脑刺绣　加工定做　厂家直销　诚征代理
12. jpg5
13. jpgSHANGHAI　CHANGNING
GREEN　LAND　HOSPITAL
14. jpg
15. jpgT e n

16. jpg手机：１５３５９０９７９１２
17. jpg老年三轮车　两轮　三轮车蓬批发
安装
18. jpg15026753386
19. jpg千里香
20. jpg诚招各地代理
21. jpg一把
22. jpg电话：１３８８０９９８３８６
23. jpg利彩票
24. jpg火锅
25. jpg13
26. jpg95007
27. jpg7３号１１－１３幢
28. jpg范围
29. jpg手机维修中心
30. jpg依恋女装

Fig. 8. Example of partial data samples from the training dataset

Fig. 9. Example of partial data samples from the test dataset

and the text images were borrowed from the idea of Uyghur text dataset enhancement. First, five data enhancement methods were selected: adding salt noise, Gaussian noise, reducing luminance, increasing noise, and adding some blur. From the data enhancement effect in Fig. 10, it can be seen that the effect of adding salt and pepper noise and adding Gaussian noise is similar compared with the original image because the dataset comes from a street scene with different shooting angles, so the difference between the effect of reducing luminance and the original image is small, and the effect of adding blur and increasing luminance is more obvious. Therefore, three data enhancement methods can

Table 6. Comparison table before and after improving absolute coding

Stages	Backbone	Neck	Head	Loss	Acc (%)	infer_rec
Before	SVTR-T	seEncoder (reshape)	CTCHead	CTCLoss	61.021	Error
	ppocrv3(0.5)	SVTR	MultiHead	MultiLoss	45.744	success
	ppocrv3(1)	SVTR	MultiHead	MultiLoss	51.768	success
After	SVTR-T	SeEncoder (reshape)	CTCHead	CTCLoss	59.319	success
	ppocrv3(0.5)	SVTR	MultiHead	MultiLoss	48.669	success
	ppocrv3(1)	SVTR	MultiHead	MultiLoss	52.990	success

be chosen: adding Gaussian noise, increasing brightness, and adding some blur. Because the coding of gb2312 is used to read the annotation file, the codec cannot decode the illegal multibyte sequences after data enhancement. Two solutions are adopted: first, the range of the Chinese character set is expanded because the range from gb2312 to gbk to gb18030 is expanded in turn, and the error is still reported after changing the range of character coding; then, illegal multiobbyte sequences were chosen to ignore these undecoder characters, and ignore ('gb2312', 'ignore') was added after gb2312 encoding. It was found that there were still error reporting problems, so the follow-up work of the SVTR network limitation experiment can be carried out from solving the data enhancement encoding to read the annotation file first and then improving the insufficient points of the network, and the insufficient points of SVTR network improvement are still an important task for experimental research.

Fig. 10. Data enhancement effect

6 Summary and Future Work

In this paper, we use the scene text recognition SVTR network for Uyghur text recognition work and use the image synthesis technique to construct the Uyghur text image dataset. We use data enhancement techniques such as adding noise, blurring, and brightness variation to some images of the dataset. Finally, with the addition of the Uyghur text dictionary, we use the SVTR network in constructing the Uyghur text dataset to obtain 99.9% recognition accuracy.

Although certain results have been achieved in Uyghur text recognition, the literature on Uyghur text recognition is mainly provided by domestic scholars and has not been seen in the international text recognition field. In addition to the common difficulties in the field of text recognition, the recognition of Uyghur text also faces the following problems unique to Uyghur text:

(1) Researchers and scholars use self-built datasets with variable data sizes and a lack of publicly available datasets;
(2) Interference of the writing characteristics of text characters, Uyghur text characters belong to the type of adherent language; there is no uniform size, there is no obvious cut-off point, the characters are difficult to slice, and there is the interference of recognition;
(3) There are characters with similar character structures and various writing forms, which make accurate recognition more difficult;
(4) How to select the scene text recognition network for Uyghur text recognition to make the best effect; Uyghur text recognition technology research is still immature, in the stage of relatively little reference materials and literature.

These problems need to be solved in Uyghur text recognition research. As recognition research advances, it will face various problems, and what we need to do is to determine the problems, solve them, and consider summarizing the experience to apply to other language text recognition, which is of great importance both from the scientific research point of view and the practical application point of view.

Acknowledgement. This work has been supported by the Natural Science Foundation of China (62166043, U2003207).

References

1. Zhu, L.: Study the factors and countermeasures affecting the recognition rate of printed Uyghur language. Xinjiang University (2015)
2. Liu, C.-Y., Chen, X.-X., Luo, C.-J., et al.: A deep learning approach for natural scene text detection and recognition (2021)
3. Nan, L.: Research on printed Uyghur text recognition technology based on Siamese segments. Xi'an University of Electronic Science and Technology (2020). https://doi.org/10.27389/d.cnki.gxadu.2020.002311
4. Jia, Y., Zhang, P., Jia, Y., Shao, X., Liu, M.: Feature extraction of printed Uyghur text based on concatenated segments. Intell. Comput. Appl. **10**(05), 206–209+212 (2020)
5. Hao, H.: CNN-based recognition of printed Uyghur characters. Xinjiang University (2018)
6. Yu-Li, Y.-E.: A method for recognizing printed Uyghur text based on HOG features and MLP classifier. Microcomput. Appl. **33**(06), 30–33 (2017)
7. Wang, X.: Research and application of key technologies for recognizing printed Uyghur text. Xi'an University of Electronic Science and Technology (2017)
8. Jin'e, W.: Research and Implementation of Key Technologies for Printed Uyghur Character Recognition System. Xinjiang University (2013)
9. Xiao, L.: Printed Uyghur word recognition based on syncopation. Xi'an University of Electronic Science and Technology (2015)
10. Du, Y., Chen, Z., Jia, C., et al.: SVTR: scene text recognition with a single visual model. arXiv preprint arXiv:2205.00159 (2022)
11. Baidu Baike – Uighur (2015). 4, 8 http://baike.baidu.com/view/106638.htm

12. Xinjiang University. GB12050–1989, Uyghur coded graphic character set for information processing information exchange. State Administration of Quality Supervision, Inspection, and Quarantine (SBTS), Beijing (1989)

13. Fu, Z.: Research the recognition technology of Vedic characters in scene images. University of Science and Technology of China (2021). https://doi.org/10.27517/d.cnki.gzkju.2021.001139

14. Text recognition data generation. https://textrecognitiondatagenerator.readthedocs.io/en/lat est/tutorial.html#text-distorsions

15. Shi, B., Bai, X., Yao, C.: An end-to-end trainable neural network for image-based sequence recognition and its application to scene text recognition. IEEE Trans. Pattern Anal. Mach. Intell. **39**(11), 2298–2304 (2016)

16. Ibrayim, M., Mattohti, A., Hamdulla, A.: An effective method for detection and recognition of Uyghur texts in images with backgrounds. Information **13**(7), 332 (2022)

17. Palhati, S., Kadir, A., Yasen, A.: Multifont typography wi-ha-cowen keyword image recognition. Comput. Sci. **49**(S2), 615–620 (2022)

18. Tang, J., Gushul, S., Xu, M., Xiong, L., Wang, M.: Scanned body recognition in Uyghur based on deep learning. J. Northeast Normal Univ. (Nat. Sci. Ed.) **53**(01), 71–76 (2021). https://doi.org/10.16163/j.cnki.22-1123/n.2021.01.012

19. Xiong, L.: Research and application of Uyghur language detection and recognition methods. Xinjiang University (2021). https://doi.org/10.27429/d.cnki.gxjdu.2021.000431

20. PaddlePaddle Learning Race: Chinese Scene Text Recognition Dataset. https://aistudio.baidu.com/aistudio/datasetdetail/173448

21. Decimal to Binary: Text Recognition Model Based on Variable-Length SVTR and ONNX Deployment. https://aistudio.baidu.com/aistudio/projectdetail/4436515?channe lType=0&channel=0

Research on Traffic Flow Forecasting Based on Deep Learning

Hong Zhang[1], Tianxin Zhao[1], Jie Cao[1,2,3(✉)], and Sunan Kan[1]

[1] College of Computer and Communication, Lanzhou University of Technology,
Lanzhou 730050, China
17361561705@163.com
[2] Lanzhou City University, Lanzhou 730070, China
[3] Lanzhou University of Technology, Lanzhou 730050, China

Abstract. Traffic flow forecasting (TFF) is the key technology of intelligent transportation systems, plays a vital role in intelligent transportation and has attracted the attention of researchers worldwide. Forecast methods and models based on deep learning (DL) are the current research hotspots in this field. On the basis of the main methods and models of TFF, this paper mainly reviews the related research on TFF based on DL. First, from the perspective of scientometrics, the researchers, countries, and institutions of TFF based on DL are counted, and the cocitation network of keywords, journals, and authors is analysed. Then, TFF methods based on DL are reviewed from three aspects: time series, space-time, and spatiotemporal graphs. This paper focuses on research on forecast methods based on spatiotemporal graphs, clarifies the research trends in this field from the aspects of graph spatiotemporal networks, graph autoencoders, and graph attention networks, and summarizes the structure and characteristics of different forecast models. Finally, from the aspects of applied research and model research, the follow-up research issues, challenges, and future research directions in this field are discussed.

Keywords: Traffic flow forecasting · deep learning · graph neural networks · scientific measurement · ITS

1 Research Background

As economic conditions continue to improve, an increasing number of people are flocking to cities. Government departments continue to expand the urban area, and the number of vehicles on the road increases rapidly. Road congestion and traffic accidents are becoming increasingly serious and have become travel problems faced by residents. Therefore, government departments are eager to develop ITSs (intelligent traffic systems), and TFF is the cornerstone of ITS development. Accurate and real-time forecast results can help relevant departments plan traffic routes more rationally. It can complete vehicle scheduling and diversion and congestion risk assessment and provide the optimal route for residents to travel.

TFF methods can be roughly divided into two categories: methods based on mathematical statistics and methods based on machine learning. Methods based on mathematical statistics include Kalman filtering, nonparametric regression, HA, and ARIMA. Forecast methods based on mathematical statistics are widely used in the field of TFF because of their high computational efficiency and suitability for various scenarios. However, such methods can only describe the linear relationship existing in traffic data and cannot extract the deeper nonlinear relationship, so the forecast accuracy cannot be further improved.

The methods based on machine learning mainly include support vector machine, neural networks, and DL. Neural networks have powerful learning capabilities for traffic data and can capture nonlinear spatiotemporal relationships. However, shallow neural network methods require considerable feature engineering. The DL method uses a multilayer neural network architecture to gradually mine the hidden spatiotemporal features in the data from the lowest level to the highest level under the condition of sufficient historical data. Its fitting ability is particularly powerful, and it can describe more complex nonlinear space-time relationships.

As DL methods have shown strong performance in forecasting tasks, methods based on convolutional neural networks (CNNs) [1] and recurrent neural networks (RNNs) [2] are widely used in TFF. Liu et al. [3] applied the scientometrics method to the research field of TFF for the first time. At the same time, the author lists popular forecast techniques, provides benchmarks for peer research and comparison, and quantifies research progress. Since traffic data are graph-structured data, the method based on the graph convolutional network (GCN) [4] in DL shows a strong ability to process graph-structured data. This method is introduced into the TFF task. A more accurate forecast is achieved. Therefore, this paper organizes and analyses the research on TFF based on DL, mainly including visual analysis of researchers, institutions, keywords, journals, and author cocitations, comparative analysis of the main research methods, and follow-up research directions.

2   Visual Analysis

This paper conducts a scientometric analysis [3, 5] in the field of TFF based on DL.

In this paper, literature records in this research field were retrieved from the WoS (Web of Science) database. At the time of the search work, the WoS database for the search records was limited to the "Web of Science Core Collection". The search box input is' (TS = (traffic AND forecast *) OR TS = (traffic AND predict *) AND (TI = forecast * OR TI = predict * OR TI = estimate *) AND (AK = deep learning *) '. The citation index selects the Science Citation Index Extended Edition (SCI-EXPANDED). A total of 510 literature records were retrieved.

2.1   Author Network Analysis

This paper constructs a collaborative network of authors in this research area, as shown in Fig. 1.

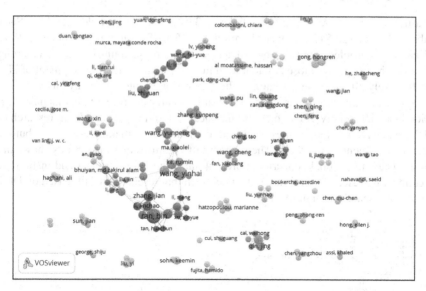

Fig. 1. The coauthorship network

Bin Ran is a Distinguished Professor from Southeast University and the most prolific author in this field. He has published 8 articles on TFF based on DL. Professor Bin Ran has been researching static and dynamic traffic network models for a long time and has achieved much major research. In recent years, he has been mainly engaged in research on ITSs and intelligent networked transportation systems and has made great contributions to dynamic transportation network modelling. Yinhai Wang has published 7 articles in this field. Professor Yinhai Wang is engaged in research work in the field of intelligent transportation, especially the computer processing of traffic data, and has achieved many significant research results, specializing in intelligent transportation information processing. Jian Zhang, Li Li, and Yunpeng Wang each published five articles. Furthermore, given the collaborative relationship, there are several research teams in the collaborative network, and prolific authors are usually at the center of the team to which they belong. The first team includes Yinhai Wang, Zhiyong Cui, and others, and there is a cooperative relationship between them. On the second research team, Bin Ran is the author of the center, and Jian Zhang, Linchao Li, Wenqi Lu, Xu Qu, Yonggang Wang, Huachun Tan, and others have cooperative relationships. In the field of TFF based on DL, you can follow the research trends and journal articles of these highly productive authors to obtain the latest research in this field.

2.2 Author's Country and Institution Analysis

This paper constructs a network distribution map composed of the author's country and organization, as shown in Fig. 2. The figure shows the author's country, and 13 countries/regions have published more than ten articles. They are China (280 articles, 54.90%), United States (113 articles, 22.15%), South Korea (23 articles, 4.50%), Spain (20 articles, 3.92%), England (19 articles, 3.72%), Canada (18 articles, 3.52%), Germany

(18 articles, 3.52%), Australia (17 articles, 3.33%), Italy (14 articles, 2.74%), Saudi Arabia (13 articles, 2.54%), France (12 articles, 2.35%), Singapore (10 articles, 1.96%), and Japan (10 articles, 1.96%). The linkages between these countries are quite strong, indicating that they have close collaboration in TFF research. The development of ITSs can effectively alleviate the common traffic congestion problem in many cities.

At the same time, a large number of institutions carry out research in this field, such as Southeast University. It can be seen that these institutions are all doing research on TFF based on DL and have achieved fruitful research results, making great contributions to the development of this field. The diversity of countries and institutions shows that TFF has become a global concern. At present, many countries/regions and institutions are conducting research in this area. It can be seen that research on TFF based on DL is the current research hotspot of TFF.

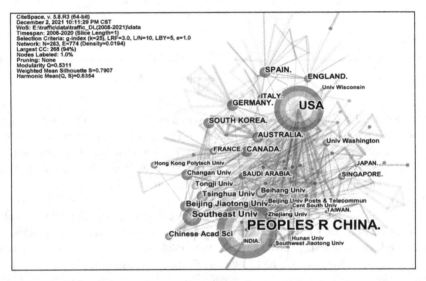

Fig. 2. The network of author institutions and nations

2.3   Keyword Network Analysis

In this section, author keywords are analysed by constructing a keyword network to analyse the hotspots and emerging trends in the research field of TFF.

In all selected articles, a total of 2156 keywords were obtained. Here, the threshold is set to 4, that is, a keyword appears at least 4 times, and 115 keywords are obtained. Figure 3 is a keyword network. The largest node in Fig. 3 belongs to "DL", the frequency of occurrence is 149, and the frequency of occurrence exceeding 25 is "Machine learning" (133); "Predictive models" (53); "TFF" (44); "Learning (artificial intelligence)" (29); "Traffic engineering computing" (28); "Road traffic" (25) and "neural networks" (25). In addition, "Learning (artificial intelligence)", "Predictive models", "DL", "Machine learning" and other nodes are all very close in distance, which means that the connection between DL, machine learning, and artificial intelligence is very close. This shows that the research methods of TFF are diversified, and they are all related to each other.

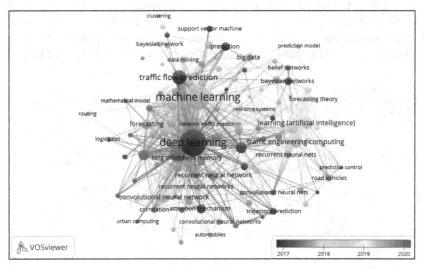

Fig. 3. The network of keywords

Figure 3 constructs an overlay visualization of keywords to show the evolution of research topics over time to analyse emerging research hotspots. Years of publication are differentiated by overlaying visualizations with different colors, with warm colors (e.g., red) indicating that keywords appear primarily in recent articles and cool colors (e.g., blue) indicating keywords appearing in earlier articles. Figure 3 shows some red themes appearing in articles published in recent years, including "graph convolutional network", "spatiotemporal correlation", "multitask learning", and "convolutional neural network". This shows that they are an emerging trend in the research field of TFF, and it can be seen that TFF based on graph convolution has been a research hotspot in the past two years. Blue nodes, such as "Bayesian network" and "support vector machine", which were research hotspots in the first five years, are slowly disappearing.

At the same time, the characteristics of the main keywords and their relationships can be visually displayed through the time zone map. Figure 4 shows the time zone map from 2008 to 2020. The largest node is "DL", followed by keywords such as "neural network", "model", and "machine learning". The technologies involved in this research include neural networks, Bayesian networks, Kalman filtering, support vector machines, big data, attention mechanisms, etc., indicating that the research methods are diverse. Combining the time zone view and the current research status, the technological development in this field can be divided into two periods. In the first period (2008–2015), the most common keywords in this period are "neural network", "machine learning" and "support vector machine". They lay the foundation for applying DL to the field. Due to the increasing amount of traffic data, big data technology and machine learning are applied to this research field, and the use of data mining to predict traffic flow is welcomed by the majority of researchers. In the second period (2016–2020), research in this field increased rapidly, and the most published articles were published in this period. DL is able to process nonlinear data and introduce it into TFFing, with many excellent results. With the deepening of research, DL methods are further refined. CNN, RNN, and GCN are the mainstream forecast models. On this basis, feature extraction and spatiotemporal correlation methods have also received more attention. At the same time, attention mechanisms and reinforcement learning are also widely used in TFF.

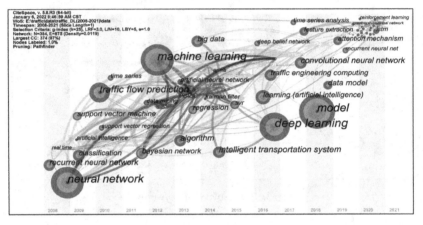

Fig. 4. Timezone map

2.4 Journal Cocitation Network Analysis

The journals that play an important role in this field are analysed by counting the source journals that published these 510 articles.

Figure 5 shows the journal cocitation network. The highly cited journals include Transportation Research Record (frequency = 230), Journal of Transportation Engineering (frequency = 156), and Neural Computer & Applications (frequency = 154). It can be seen that these journals contribute the most to this research field.

2.5 Author Co-Citation Network Analysis

Author cocitation networks were used to analyse relationships between authors. If two authors' articles are cited in the same article and their names appear in the reference, it is called a coauthorship. Figure 6 shows the author's cocitation network. The five most frequently cited authors include Yisheng Lv (frequency = 155, China), Xiaolei Ma (frequency = 130, China), Eleni I. Vlahogianni (frequency = 117, Greece), Sepp Hochreiter (frequency = 116, Germany), and Billy M. Williams (107, USA).

Yisheng Lv is a Ph.D. from the Chinese Academy of Sciences. His research interests are DL, intelligent transportation, etc. Lv et al. [6] published an article on TFF based on DL in 2015.

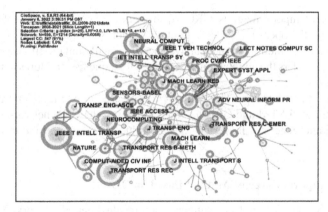

Fig. 5. The journal cocitation network

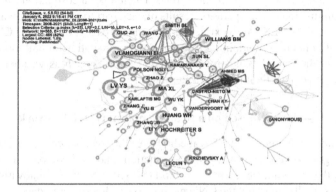

Fig. 6. The author cocitation network

3 Research Methods

The method based on DL has become the mainstream trend in TFF research. The following analysis is based on DL-based time series forecast methods, spatiotemporal forecast methods, and spatiotemporal graph forecast methods. This paper focuses on the study of spatiotemporal graph forecasting methods and analyses the structure and characteristics of different models from three aspects: graph spatiotemporal networks, graph autoencoders, and graph attention networks.

3.1 Time Series Forecast Method Based on DL

The principle of RNN is to process the input information at the previous moment and retain it in the operation of the current information and then extract the time-series correlation between the input data multiple times. Therefore, the neural network has the ability of "memory".

Long short-term memory (LSTM) [7] is a common variant of RNN that utilizes three gating combinations to obtain long-term features, which enhances the RNN's ability to extract temporal features. GRU [8] simplifies the gated structure of the LSTM method, making the operation faster. Although networks such as LSTM and GRU are used in forecast tasks, their internal recursive operations will limit the efficiency of model training, which hinders the application of sequence-to-sequence structures in forecasting tasks.

CNN is used in the task of TFF and can also be used to extract temporal features. Compared with the LSTM and GRU network structures, the CNN network structure is more concise and generates multistep forecast values at the same time to avoid error accumulation [9].

3.2   Spatiotemporal Forecast Method Based on DL

Zhang et al. [10] designed a deep spatiotemporal residual neural network. The method uses the residual convolution module of the same structure for time series modelling from three aspects: adjacency, periodicity, and trend. The temporal correlations are fused by a weighted summation of the operation results of each part to extract temporal features.

Some methods use LSTM to extract temporal features and use the 2D CNN model to extract spatial features, combining the two aspects for spatiotemporal modelling. At the same time, these models incorporate external features such as weather and other information and achieve high forecast accuracy [11–14].

3.3   Forecasting Method Based on a Spatiotemporal Graph Network

The traditional two-dimensional CNN method uses the road network as a regular two-dimensional grid to simulate the spatial association, and each subregion in the road network has the same adjacency relationship [15]. After countless innovative studies, many scholars finally migrated the CNN method to graph-structured data and proposed the graph convolution method, which makes the processing of these data more efficient [16].

Since traffic data are time-series data, extracting spatiotemporal features and fusing them is the current research focus [17]. Graph spatiotemporal networks, graph attention, and graph autoencoders have been used to extract spatiotemporal features and have shown strong advantages.

Graph Spatiotemporal Network
1. Time series feature extraction based on CNN.

Yu et al. [18] designed and proposed spatiotemporal graph convolutional networks (STGCNs), as shown in Fig. 7.

The STGCN method uses gated linear units (GLU) to form a 1-D gated CNN to simulate time-series correlation and extract time series features. A graph convolution method is used to simulate spatial association to extract spatial features. The temporal dimension adopts 1-D causal convolution to extract temporal dependencies. When capturing temporal features with a temporal convolutional layer, the input sequence undergoes 1D causal convolution along the temporal dimension. In addition, the GLU gating mechanism is used for activation to obtain the output. Diao et al. [19] designed and proposed the DGCNN framework.

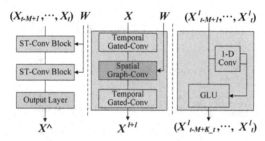

Fig. 7. Spatiotemporal graph convolutional networks

Wu et al. [20] designed a new spatiotemporal graph model Graph WaveNet. The gated TCN layer captures temporal features through dilated causal convolution (see Fig. 8). Increasing the number of dilated causal convolutional layers leads to exponentially larger receptive fields.

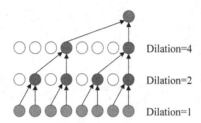

Fig. 8. Dilated casual convolution

2. Time series feature extraction based on RNN.

Zhao et al. [21] designed the temporal graph convolutional network T-GCN. Its network architecture is shown in Fig. 9. The author believes that RNN is the most widely used when dealing with sequence data, especially its variants LSTM network and GRU. GRU is widely used for time series feature extraction due to its few parameters and short learning and training time.

GRU can preserve long-term dependencies. Based on this, Chen et al. [22] used hoplinks to extract periodic temporal dependencies. Since the long-term back-propagation of the deep network will bring about exploding and disappearing gradients, the author adds residuals to the recurrent graph network to overcome this defect. Wang et al. [23] stacked 2 layers of LSTM to predict the traffic time and added two influencing factors of traffic lights and road intersections to the forecast results.

Graph Autoencoder

The autoencoder (AE) takes traffic data with some connections as input and captures spatiotemporal features to achieve the forecast task. AE usually utilizes CNN, RNN, and GCN to extract spatiotemporal features. Li et al. [24]proposed the diffusion convolutional recurrent neural network (DCRNN), and the model framework is shown in Fig. 10.

In the work of Lin et al. [25], the AE-based graph filter is used to learn and train the data of shared bicycles and taxis to complete the task of capturing spatiotemporal

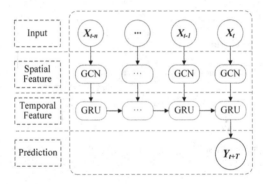

Fig. 9. Temporal graph convolutional networks

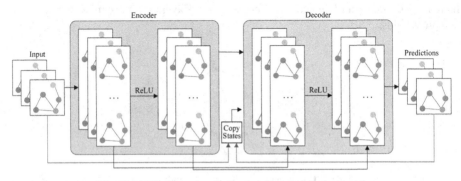

Fig. 10. Diffusion convolutional recurrent neural network

features. Zhao et al. [26] completed the task of spatiotemporal feature extraction through hierarchical recursive AE, and the acquisition of temporal features was achieved through a 3-layer RNN-based AE architecture. Guo et al. [27] designed an encoder-decoder structure to realize TFF. The decoder layer used an autoregressive method to generate output. Bai et al. [28] argue that the decoder architecture based on a recurrent neural network suffers from error accumulation. Therefore, the encoders and decoders that extract long and short time series features are separately learned and trained to improve the existing error accumulation problem and improve the forecast performance.

Graph Attention Network

Graph attention networks (GAT) [29] introduce attention mechanisms in spatiotemporal graph networks. It calculates the weights of neighboring road nodes, and then the central road nodes are represented by their updates.

Guo et al. [30] proposed attention-based spatial-temporal graph convolutional networks (ASTGCNs). Guo et al. [27] believed that the simple application of traditional multihead attention (MHSelfAttention) to traffic signal sequence transformation would lead to a mismatch problem and could not effectively extract local trend information in the traffic network.

Currently, TFF models based on DL have shown superior performance. Compared with classical algorithm models, complex spatiotemporal correlations can be extracted, and higher forecast accuracy can be achieved. However, this type of model is complex to construct and has poor interpretability [31]. Various DL-based TFF models have unique advantages and disadvantages [32]. Multiple models can be combined by connecting them one after the other or side-by-side. For example, the combination of GCN and GRU can improve the forecast performance. To simultaneously extract spatiotemporal features of traffic flow data, combined models are most widely used. The combined forecast model combines the advantages of multiple models, avoids the defects of a single model, and performs better than a single model. However, at the same time, the model becomes more complex. The learning and training time is longer, and improper combination will reduce the forecast accuracy.

Although combined models are complex to model and time-consuming to train, a proper combination of individual models has better predictive performance and higher accuracy. Combined with the spatiotemporal features of the road network, appropriate models are selected in the spatiotemporal dimension to extract spatiotemporal features.

4 Challenges and Research Directions in TFF

Many scholars and researchers have proposed innovative methods, and the accuracy of forecasting has also been significantly improved. However, with the continuous development of DL, the research has gradually deepened, and there is still a broad space for development. Therefore, this paper will discuss future research trends from the two aspects of model research and application research.

5 Model Research

Since traffic data are generally graph-structured data, the spatiotemporal graph network method has shown a strong ability to process graph-structured data, and it is the prevailing trend to use this method to achieve forecasting results. Therefore, there is still a broad research space for the representation and processing of graph-structured data. The following discusses and analyses dynamic graph modelling, deep-level modelling of spatiotemporal graph networks, and spatiotemporal multigraph modelling.

Dynamic Graph Modelling
At present, most road network graph structures processed by spatiotemporal graph network methods are static graphs. These methods [18, 20, 21] use static adjacency matrices to process graph information. As time changes, the relationship between nodes remains unchanged. Only a few methods use dynamic graph structures. The spatiotemporal graph network processing dynamic graph is a difficult point. Defining a road network as a dynamic graph, the vertices and edges are variable and irregular, and it is more difficult to address.

A few scholars did not use a predefined adjacency matrix when using spatiotemporal graph networks to extract hidden correlations and spatiotemporal associations between nodes on a graph. Instead, they address the dynamic graph structure using a dynamic adjacency matrix, which is learned from road network graph data. In the work of Diao et al. [19], more accurate TFF is achieved by exploiting the dynamic graph structure. The dynamic TFF is completed by generating the dynamically changing Laplace matrix. GCN relies on predefined graph structure information. Therefore, Wu et al. [33] did not use well-defined graph structure information but proposed a graph learning layer.

If the spatiotemporal graph network model is extended to the dynamic graph model, it will become a new breakthrough in the field of TFF.

Deep Modelling of Spatiotemporal Graph Networks
Compared with shallow machine learning, DL constructs deep hidden representations with different abstraction levels, which shows stronger advantages in TFF [35]. From the perspective of graph DL, only a few of the currently existing spatiotemporal graph network models build deep structures [20, 34]. Li et al. [36] studied the oversmoothing problem in deep networks. In a spatiotemporal graph network, its central road node is characterized by aggregating the information of neighboring road nodes. When the number of layers of the spatiotemporal graph network increases, the difference between the central road node and the neighboring road nodes will be smaller, and the forecast result will be worse. To achieve more accurate forecasting results, it is essential to establish a deeper spatiotemporal graph network and solve the problem of oversmoothing. Therefore, there is still much research space for deep modelling of spatiotemporal graph networks.

Spatiotemporal Multigraph Modelling
With the deepening of TFF research, researchers have used the information carried by multiple graphs to conduct spatiotemporal multigraph modelling.

In the work of Lv et al. [37], multiple graphs are constructed jointly with the spatial correlation of the road network and the semantic correlation between roads, which enables more refined spatiotemporal modelling. Similarly, Lu [38] et al. considered geographic proximity and contextual spatial information. Song et al. [34] established a spatiotemporal synchronization graph and used GCN to act on the graph to capture the local spatiotemporal dependencies.

Multiple graphs can incorporate more information into the spatiotemporal forecast of traffic flow. However, how to construct multigraphs and extract effective information to realize spatiotemporal multigraph neural network modelling is still a problem worthy of further study.

5.1 Application Research

At present, many existing TFF methods are limited to short-term forecasting, and there are few studies under abnormal conditions [39], while large-scale TFF also needs further research.

TFF Considering External Features
The actual traffic state is affected not only by the time series data of traffic flow but also by external factors such as weather conditions, POI (point-of-interest) and traffic accidents. Currently, only a few scholars consider external features when making forecasts. In

the literature [40–42], the external feature POI is added and preprocessed to achieve more effective forecasting when making traffic forecasts. Meanwhile, the literature [10, 14, 42] added the weather factor as an external feature of the TFF. In the process of constructing the spatiotemporal graph network, if researchers can take these external features into account and fuse the spatiotemporal features with the external features, more useful information can be extracted. This is a future research hotspot.

Large-Scale TFF
As the road network expands, the scale of traffic flow data becomes increasingly larger, and the graph becomes larger. The increasing number of nodes and edges in large graphs brings difficulties to accurate and fast forecasting. The difficulty of processing large graphs using spatiotemporal graph networks increases. Most current TFF models use global public datasets PeMS, METR-LA, LOOP [43], and NYC Taxi. However, the actual observed traffic flow data will continue to grow larger, and these datasets will not meet the forecasting requirements. To determine how to use graph neural networks to process large-scale graph data, some scholars have also conducted related research [44].

6 Summary

In this paper, a scientometric method is used to analyse the research field of TFF based on DL. The analysis results show that the high-yield authors mainly include Ran Bin, Wang Yinhai, and others. Southeast University, Tsinghua University, and Beijing Jiaotong University are the research institutions that publish the most papers. Keyword analysis shows that "graph convolutional network", "spatiotemporal correlation", "multitask learning", and "attention mechanism" are emerging research hot words in this field. It provides valuable information for research in this field through visualization techniques. It describes the global research status of TFF based on DL.

This paper sorts out the methods or models of TFF. It mainly studies and discusses time series forecasting, spatiotemporal forecasting and spatiotemporal graph forecasting based on DL. This paper focuses on the introduction of spatiotemporal graph forecasting methods from three aspects: graph spatiotemporal networks, graph autoencoders and graph attention networks. The representative mainstream forecast models of each part are analysed, and the advantages and disadvantages of each model are discussed. Multiple models can be appropriately combined to improve the accuracy of a single model and improve predictive performance.

Two major issues that need further research in this field are discussed, including issues in application research and model research, and future research directions are clarified. In terms of model research, dynamic graph modelling, deep-level modelling of spatiotemporal graph networks, and spatiotemporal multigraph modelling are key issues that need to be studied in the future. In terms of application research, it mainly focuses on considering external characteristics and large-scale TFF research.

References

1. Ma, X., Dai, Z., He, Z., et al.: Learning traffic as images: a deep convolutional neural network for large-scale transportation network speed forecast. Sensors **17**(4), 818-1–818-16 (2017)

2. Bogaerts, T., Masegosa, A.D., Angarita-Zapata, J.S., et al.: A graph CNN-LSTM neural network for short and long-term traffic forecast based on trajectory data. Transp. Res. Part C-Emerging Technol. **112**, 62–77 (2020)
3. Liu, J., Wu, N., Qiao, Y., et al.: A scientometric review of research on traffic forecast in transportation. IET Intel. Transport Syst. **15**(1), 1–16 (2021)
4. Zhang, H., Chen, L., Cao, J., et al.: A combined TFF model based on graph convolutional network and attention mechanism. Int. J. Modern Phys. C **32**(12), 2150158-1–2150158-21 (2021)
5. Zhao, X.: A scientometric review of global BIM research: analysis and visualization. Autom. Constr. **80**, 37–47 (2017)
6. Lv, Y., Duan, Y., Kang, W., et al.: TFF with big data: a DL approach. IEEE Trans. Intell. Transp. Syst. **16**(2), 865–873 (2015)
7. Chen, P., Fu, X., Wang, X.: A graph convolutional stacked bidirectional unidirectional-LSTM neural network for metro ridership forecast. IEEE Trans. Intell. Transp. Syst. 1–13 (2021)
8. Hussain, B., Afzal, M.K., Ahmad, S., et al.: Intelligent TFF using optimized GRU model. IEEE Access **9**, 100736–100746 (2021)
9. Zhang, J., Zheng, Y., Qi, D., et al.: DNN-Based forecast model for spatiotemporal data. In: Proceedings of the 24th ACM SIGSPATIAL International Conference on Advances in Geographic Information System, pp. 92-1–92-4 (2016)
10. Zhang, J., Zheng, Y., Qi, D., et al.: Deep spatio-temporal residual networks for citywide crowd flows forecast. In: 31st AAAI Conference on Artificial Intelligence, pp. 1655–1661 (2017)
11. Yao, H., Tang, X., Wei, H., et al.: Revisiting spatial-temporal similarity: a DL framework for traffic forecast. In: 33rd AAAI Conference on Artificial Intelligence/31st Innovative Applications of Artificial Intelligence Conference/9th AAAI Symposium on Educational Advances in Artificial Intelligence, pp. 5668–5675 (2019)
12. Xingjian, S., Chen, Z., Wang, H., et al.: Convolutional LSTM network: a machine learning approach for precipitation nowcasting. In: Advances in Neural Information Processing Systems, pp. 802–810 (2015)
13. Lv, Z., Xu, J., Zheng, K., et al.: LC-RNN: a DL model for traffic speed forecast. In: IJCAI International Joint Conference on Artificial Intelligence, pp. 3470–3476 (2018)
14. Yao, H., Wu, F., Ke, J., et al.: Deep multi-view spatial-temporal network for taxi demand forecast. In: 32nd AAAI Conference on Artificial Intelligence/30th Innovative Applications of Artificial Intelligence Conference/8th AAAI Symposium on Educational Advances in Artificial Intelligence, pp. 2588–2595 (2018)
15. Niepert, M., Ahmed, M., Kutzkov, K.: Learning convolutional neural networks for graphs. In: International conference on machine learning, pp. 2014–2023 (2016)
16. Kipf, T.N., Welling, M.: Semisupervised classification with graph convolutional networks. arXiv preprint arXiv:1609.02907 (2016)
17. Defferrard, M., Bresson, X., Vandergheynst, P.: Convolutional neural networks on graphs with fast localized spectral filtering. In: Proceedings of the 30th International Conference on Neural Information Processing Systems, pp. 3844–3852 (2016)
18. Yu, B., Yin, H., Zhu, Z.: Spatiotemporal graph convolutional networks: a DL framework for traffic forecast. arXiv preprint arXiv:1709.04875, 1–7 (2017)
19. Diao, Z., Wang, X., Zhang, D., et al.: Dynamic spatial-temporal graph convolutional neural networks for traffic forecast. In: 33rd AAAI Conference on Artificial Intelligence/31st Innovative Applications of Artificial Intelligence Conference/9th AAAI Symposium on Educational Advances in Artificial Intelligence, pp. 890–897 (2019)
20. Wu, Z., Pan, S., Long, G., et al.: Graph wavenet for deep spatial-temporal graph modelling. arXiv preprint arXiv:1906.00121 (2019)
21. Zhao, L., Song, Y., Zhang, C., et al.: T-GCN: a temporal graph convolutional network for traffic forecast. IEEE Trans. Intell. Transp. Syst. **21**(9), 3848–3858 (2020)

22. Chen, C., Li, K., Teo, S.G., et al.: Gated residual recurrent graph neural networks for traffic forecast. In: 33rd AAAI Conference on Artificial Intelligence/31st Innovative Applications of Artificial Intelligence Conference/9th AAAI Symposium on Educational Advances in Artificial Intelligence, pp. 485–492 (2019)
23. Wang, D., Zhang, J., Cao, W., et al.: When will you arrive? Estimating travel time based on deep neural networks. In: Thirty-Second AAAI Conference on Artificial Intelligence, pp. 2500–2507 (2018)
24. Li, Y., Yu, R., Shahabi, C., et al.: Diffusion convolutional recurrent neural network: data-driven traffic forecast. In: International Conference on Learning Representations (2018)
25. Lin, L., He, Z., Peeta, S.: Predicting station-level hourly demand in a large-scale bike sharing network: a graph convolutional neural network approach. Transp. Res. Part C-Emerg. Technol. **97**, 258–276 (2018)
26. Zhao, J., Zhu, T., Zhao, R., et al.: Layerwise recurrent autoencoder for real-world TFF. In: 9th international conference on intelligence science and big data engineering (IScIDE), pp. 78–88 (2019)
27. Guo, S., Lin, Y., Wan, H., et al.: Learning dynamics and heterogeneity of spatial-temporal graph data for traffic forecast. IEEE Trans. Knowl. Data Eng. 1 (2021)
28. Bai, L., Yao, L., Kanhere, S.S., et al.: STG2seq: spatial-temporal graph to sequence model for multistep passenger demand forecast. In: 28th International Joint Conference on Artificial Intelligence, IJCAI 2019, pp. 1981–1987 (2019)
29. Veličković, P., Cucurull, G., Casanova, A., et al.: Graph attention networks. arXiv preprint arXiv:1710.10903 (2017)
30. Guo, S., Lin, Y., Feng, N., et al.: Attention based spatial-temporal graph convolutional networks for TFF. In: 33rd AAAI Conference on Artificial Intelligence/31st Innovative Applications of Artificial Intelligence Conference/9th AAAI Symposium on Educational Advances in Artificial Intelligence, pp. 922–929 (2019)
31. Bai, J., Zhu, J., Song, Y., et al.: A3T-GCN: attention temporal graph convolutional network for traffic forecast. Isprs Int. J. Geo-Inf. **10**(7) (2021)
32. Wang, X., Ma, Y., Wang, Y., et al.: TFF via spatial temporal graph neural network. In: 29th Worldwide Web Conference (WWW), pp. 1082–1092 (2020)
33. Wu, Z., Pan, S., Long, G., et al.: Connecting the dots: Multivariate time series forecast with graph neural networks. In: Proceedings of the 26th ACM SIGKDD International Conference on Knowledge Discovery & Data Mining, pp. 753–763 (2020)
34. Song, C., Lin, Y., Guo, S., et al.: Spatial-temporal synchronous graph convolutional networks: a new framework for spatial-temporal network data forecast. In: Proceedings of the AAAI Conference on Artificial Intelligence, pp. 914–921 (2020)
35. Nagy, A.M., Simon, V.: Survey on traffic forecast in smart cities. Pervasive Mob. Comput. **50**, 148–163 (2018)
36. Li, Q., Han, Z., Wu, X.-M.: Deeper insights into graph convolutional networks for semisupervised learning. In: Thirty-Second AAAI conference on artificial intelligence, pp. 3538–3545 (2018)
37. Lv, M., Hong, Z., Chen, L., et al.: Temporal multi-graph convolutional network for TFF. IEEE Trans. Intell. Transp. Syst. **22**(6), 3337–3348 (2021)
38. Lu, B., Gan, X., Jin, H., et al.: Spatiotemporal adaptive gated graph convolution network for urban TFF. In: Proceedings of the 29th ACM International Conference on Information & Knowledge Management, pp. 1025–1034 (2020)
39. Wang, Z., Su, X., Ding, Z.: Long-term traffic forecast based on LSTM encoder-decoder architecture. IEEE Trans. Intell. Transp. Syst. **22**(10), 6561–6571 (2021)
40. Geng, X., Li, Y., Wang, L., et al.: Spatiotemporal multi-graph convolution network for ride-hailing demand forecast. In: Proceedings of the AAAI Conference on Artificial Intelligence, vol. 33, pp. 3656–3663 (2019)

41. Lin, Z., Feng, J., Lu, Z., et al.: DeepSTN+: context-aware spatial-temporal neural network for crowd flow forecast in metropolis. In: Proceedings of the AAAI Conference on Artificial Intelligence, vol. 33, pp. 1020–1027 (2019)
42. Liang, Y., Ke, S., Zhang, J., et al.: GeoMAN: multilevel attention networks for geo-sensory time series forecast. In: Proceedings of the 27th International Joint Conference on Artificial Intelligence, pp. 3428–3434 (2018)
43. Cui, Z., Henrickson, K., Ke, R., et al.: Traffic graph convolutional recurrent neural network: a DL framework for network-scale traffic learning and forecast. IEEE Trans. Intell. Transp. Syst. 21(11), 4883–4894 (2019)
44. Lee, J.B., Rossi, R.A., Kong, X., et al.: Higher-order graph convolutional networks. arXiv preprint arXiv:1809.07697 (2018)

Driver Fatigue Monitoring Based on Facial Multifeature Fusion

Jie Wang[1], Weiwei Zhang[1(✉)], Jinlong Zhao[1], and Jun Guo[2]

[1] Xi'an Siyuan University, Shaanxi 710038, China
25971519@qq.com
[2] Northwestern University, Shaanxi 71027, China

Abstract. In response to the problems of low efficiency and inaccuracy of exist-ing fatigue driving recognition and detection algorithms, this paper proposes a machine learning-based driver fatigue detection algorithm. First, an adaptive median filtering algorithm is used to denoise the collected images, and then the Summed-area table is used to calculate its Har Like eigenvalue. Second, the Adaboost face detection and recognition algorithm and the tracking algorithm that predicts the relocation of the target position are used to quickly extract the features of the tracked face, and the improved cascade regression Tree model is used to locate the face feature points. The support vector machine algorithm is used to classify the collected eye feature values, setting a threshold to determine whether the eyes are in a closed state, and fusing the feature values of the mouth and head. Finally, through a fatigue detection algorithm based on multifeature weighted summation, repeated experimental simulations were conducted on the trained dataset to determine the weight values of the eye parameters as 0.55, the mouth parameters as 0.25, and the head parameters as 0.20. Based on the differ-ences in the weight values of the feature values obtained from the simulation exper-iments, the fatigue level was divided into awake, mild fatigue, moderate fatigue, and severe fatigue. Repeated experimental data testing shows that the method has greatly improved the accuracy and recognition speed of sleep-deprived driving recognition and detection. Tests on a dataset of simulated driving have shown that our model has an average accuracy of approximately 95.1%.

Keywords: Machine learning · Feature point localization · Fatigue testing · Cascaded regression tree model · Support vector machine

1 Introduction

Fatigued driving is one of the main causes of traffic accidents. Due to the driver being in a monotonous environment for a long time and driving with high intensity, excessive energy consumption and psychological decline can easily affect their normal driving. At the same time, when drivers are fatigued, their perception and judgment of external things decrease to varying degrees, which can easily lead to traffic accidents. Therefore, studying a recognition and monitoring system based on driver fatigue status is beneficial for reducing the incidence of traffic accidents caused by fatigued driving and is of great significance for ensuring the safety of drivers' lives.

Currently, there are two main methods of driver fatigue detection based on driver physiological parameters and behavioural characteristics. Driver fatigue detection is based on EEG, ECG and EMG parameters. The detection of driver behavioural characteristics uses computer vision to analyse the driver's facial features and extracts the characteristics of the driver's eye movement characteristics, mouth characteristics and head position to determine whether the driver is in a fatigue state. The behavioural feature detection method allows for a lower cost and more reliable acquisition. The literature [1] presents a wearable EEG-based convolutional neural network approach for fatigue driving monitoring and early warning. The data acquisition of wearable EEG and the detection of the drowsy state of vehicle drivers are utilized. If the system detects the driver status as drowsy, the system will issue an alert. The system was experimentally proven to have a classification accuracy of 95.59% and further demonstrates the feasibility of the method. In [2], the authors propose a robust facial landmark localization model for eye localization and state evaluation. The eye aspect ratio (EAR) is calculated by extracting features of the eye to determine its extent, while the model is adapted to different scenarios. The literature [3] proposes a noninvasive deep neural network-based driver drowsiness detection system that uses a combination of convolutional neural network algorithms and recurrent neural network algorithms to classify drivers into three levels of drowsiness and evaluates and tests its system using the collected experimental dataset. The literature [4] proposes a fatigue detection algorithm based on the fusion of multiple features of the driver's face. A modified convolutional neural network of YOLOv3 is used while eliminating the subtle effects in the collected data features, and finally, the driver state is detected by building a driver fatigue state assessment model. The literature [5] presents an auxiliary system for driver fatigue detection systems, which detects the driver's head characteristics and determines whether the driver is in a state of fatigue based on the data collected from the head. The literature [6] proposed an improved Bayesian algorithm through which the number of blinks of the driver's eyes was counted and judged by the prediction interval, and then the number of blinks of the driver was analysed by the grey relational entropy method. Finally, the number of blinks detected was used to judge whether the driver was in a fatigued driving state.

Most of the aforementioned research methods are based on the eye selecting its feature points and establishing relevant algorithmic models [7]. This paper proposes a multifeature fusion weighting algorithm based on the driver's face, which calculates a weighted sum of the taken feature parameters, resulting in a driver-based fatigue recognition and monitoring method. The method contains more feature points than a single feature point monitoring method and is more optimized, more accurate and easier to implement than traditional algorithms. This paper first introduces the Haar-like-based AdaBoost face classifier algorithm for face detection [8]. Considering the driver's head activity during driving, a kernel correlation tracking algorithm incorporating adaptive template update and predictive target position relocation is used on the basis of face recognition detection. Second, a cascade regression algorithm and support vector machine algorithm are used to achieve mouth. Second, based on the cascade regression algorithm and support vector machine algorithm, the state of the mouth, head and eye is identified, and the collected data are classified. Third, the weighted sum is calculated according to the eye parameters, mouth parameters and head parameters, and the driver

state is classified as awake, mild fatigue, moderate fatigue and severe fatigue according to the results of the parameter weighting calculation [9]. Finally, the feasibility and
effectiveness of the proposed algorithm for driver fatigue identification and detection is
verified through extensive experiments [10].

2 Driver Face Detection and Tracking

2.1 Image Preprocessing

Due to various factors that may affect the collection and storage process, the image
may be damaged to varying degrees, resulting in image degradation and uneven light
distribution. Therefore, to ensure the accuracy of subsequent recognition and detection,
this article adopts adaptive median filtering to denoise the image. Adaptive median
filtering can adjust the filtering window according to different noise concentrations in
the image.

2.2 Face Detection Using the Adaboost Algorithm Based on Haar-Like Features

Harr-like features are widely used in facial recognition representations [11]. In this
article, we use an extended feature library of Harr-like features, which are mainly divided
into four categories: linear features, edge features, point features, and diagonal features.
The difference between the sum of the grayscale values of all pixels in the white rectangle
and the sum of the grayscale values of all pixels in the black rectangle is used as the
Harr-like feature value to further intuitively reflect the grayscale changes of the image.

The integration graph can be used to quickly calculate the eigenvalues of the Harr
Like mentioned above. Any point on the integration graph (m,n) represents the sum of
the grayness of all pixels in the current rectangular area from the upper left edge of the
gray image. The calculation formula for the integration graph is:

$$O'(m, n) = \sum_{x=0}^{x \leq m} \sum_{y=0}^{y \leq m} O(m, n) \tag{1}$$

Among them, O(m,n) represents the size of the point (m,n) grayscale value, and the
calculation formula can be further simplified through iterative operation:

$$O'(m, n) = O'(m - 1, n) + O'(m, n - 1) + O(m, n) - O'(m - 1, n - 1) \tag{2}$$

By using the calculation method of the integration graph mentioned above, the Harr-
like eigenvalues can be calculated. First, a classifier is selected based on the training
dataset. Second, a strong classifier is constructed by weighting the weak classifier.
Finally, the constructed multiple strong classifiers are concatenated according to the
AdaBoost algorithm principle to form a stacked classifier, which further improves the
detection speed and accuracy through the stacked classifier [12]. In the AdaBoost algorithm, each weak classifier is a decision stump, i.e., the simplest decision tree. Each
decision stump predicts the class of the sample based on the weight distribution of the
current sample. In each iteration, the AdaBoost algorithm updates the weights of the

samples based on the classification of the current sample, so that the weights of the mis-classified samples increase and the weights of the correctly classified samples decrease. In this way, each weak classifier pays more attention to the previously misclassified samples, thus gradually improving the performance of the classifier.

Cascading classifier is an enhanced form of AdaBoost algorithm based. It forms a more complex classifier by stringing multiple weak classifiers together. The output of each weak classifier is used as an input to the next layer of classifiers, thus creating a nested structure. The principle of cascading classifiers is to strengthen the performance of the classifiers layer by layer, so that each layer is able to deal with noise and anomalies that cannot be handled by the previous layers. In this way, cascading classifiers can handle complex datasets more robustly, with higher classification accuracy and better generalisation ability.The principle of building a stacked classifier is as follows:

Define the dataset and labels, go through Z cycles to obtain a weak classifier, and cascade them to obtain a strong classifier:

$$Z = \{(x_i, y_i)\} \, i = 1, 2, 3 \ldots, N \tag{3}$$

where x_i is the coordinate value of the image, y_i is the classification label of the dataset, and y_i is taken as -1 and 1 to facilitate subsequent calculations. $y_i = 1$ indicates that face images are included in the captured data, $y_i = -1$ indicates that the face image is not included in the captured data. The specific algorithm procedure is as follows:

① Initialise weights: for each sample in the training set, initialise a weight, usually of equal value. The weights indicate the importance of the samples in the current training phase.

② Weak Classifier Training: Select a weak classifier as the base classifier and obtain a classifier by training it using the current sample weights.

③ Classifier weight calculation: calculates the error rate of the current classifier on the training set. Classifiers with lower error rates will be given higher weights to focus more on these misclassified samples in subsequent training.

④ Sample weight update: Based on the error rate of the classifiers, the weights of the samples are updated. Misclassified samples are given higher weights to make the next weak classifier pay more attention to these difficult to classify samples.

⑤ Combining weak classifiers: the weak classifiers obtained from the current training are added to the cascading classifiers and their weights are calculated based on their error rates on the training set.

The AdaBoost face recognition and detection algorithm based on Harr-like features exists in the open-source library of OpenCV [13]. This article uses OpenCV for face detection. The experimental results show that the AdaBoost facial recognition and detection algorithm based on Harr-like features can eliminate interference caused by skin color, resulting in higher recognition accuracy and fast, effective and accurate extraction of facial features [14]. Figure 1 shows the results of openCV experimental testing.

2.3 Facial Target Tracking Algorithm

Due to changes in the range of facial recognition positions caused by facial movements during driving, the accuracy of facial recognition can be affected to a certain extent.

Fig. 1. OpenCV experimental results.

Therefore, it is necessary to better locate the accurate position of the face and improve the efficiency and robustness of detection [15]. This article adopts a kernel correlation tracking algorithm that integrates adaptive template update and predicted target position relocation to track and recognize the driver's face.

The kernel correlation tracking algorithm that integrates adaptive template updates and predicted target position repositioning is a further improvement on the multifeature scale adaptive kernel correlation filter (SAMF). This algorithm can better solve the problem of inaccurate recognition and detection caused by changes in the range of facial recognition position changes caused by facial activity during driving, further improving the robustness of detection. During the detection process, subtle changes in identifying targets can lead to changes in feature values, so it is necessary to continuously update the filter model. Considering the linear relationship between the previous image frames and the detection target, to ensure tracking accuracy, the speed and feature changes of the detection target are selected as the filter update mechanism. The updated filter framework structure is shown in Fig. 2.

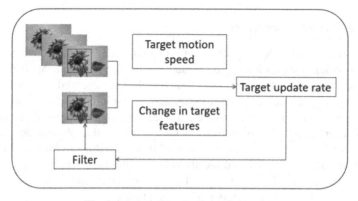

Fig. 2. Update filter framework diagram

To better reflect the changes in speed, the relationship between the target update rate (u) and target motion speed (v) was proposed: Simulate using MATLAB, as shown in Fig. 3:

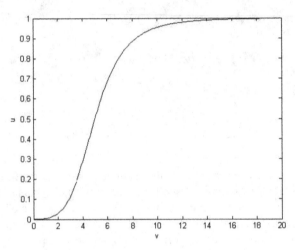

Fig. 3. Function image

According to the function image in Fig. 3, when the target motion speed is $v > 4$, it is detected that the target is in rapid motion. When the target motion speed is within the range of [4, 5.1], the slope of each point is greater than 0.2. Therefore, the maximum slope will be reached when the target motion speed is approximately 5, and it is also better suited for the movement changes of facial target recognition caused by facial activity during the driver's driving process, improving detection accuracy.

3 Driver's Eye and Mouth State Recognition

3.1 Facial Feature Localization

To further improve the accuracy of target recognition and the influence of external factors, this article uses an improved cascaded regression tree to locate facial feature points before recognizing the driver's eyes and mouth. The improved cascade regression tree model uses affine transformation parameters to initialize the face shape, making the processed face features closer to the real face, further improving the convergence speed and accuracy, and finally realizing feature point location. A universal algorithm framework for human faces is first proposed [16], followed by an improved cascaded regression tree algorithm for facial localization. Finally, the position of facial feature points is estimated through pixel strength. The algorithm is divided into three processes: establishing a model, training a model, and model fitting.

The specific steps for facial feature point localization are as follows:

Step 1. Image pre-processing: pre-process the input face image, while calculating the input face picture and shape, extracting the directional gradient histogram features of the picture and direction, and establishing the mapping relationship between the face picture and the face shape, in order to carry out the subsequent face detection and feature point localisation.

Step 2. Face detection: x pixels are randomly selected near the feature points of the face, and the x pixels produce x^2 pixels of difference features, using the trained face detection model to detect the face in the preprocessed image until the face region in the image is found.

Step 3. Face feature point localisation: constructing a random feature difference set from the difference features obtained in step 2, and performing feature point localisation on the detected face. Simultaneous face feature point localisation:

a. Preliminary feature point localisation using the cascade regression tree model.
b. Fine-tuning the results of the preliminary localisation using the already trained face feature model.
c. Repeat steps a and b until a satisfactory result is achieved or a preset number of iterations is reached.

Step 4. Fine positioning of facial feature points: for inaccurate positioning of feature points, the already trained face feature model and the improved cascade regression tree model can be used:

a. Preliminary feature point localisation using the cascade regression tree model.
b. Use the already trained face feature model to fine tune the results of the preliminary localisation.
c. Repeat steps a and b until a satisfactory result is achieved or a preset number of iterations is reached.

Step 5. Face feature point tracking: Use the trained face feature model and the improved cascade regression tree model to track the face feature points:

a. Use the trained face feature model and the improved cascade regression tree model to locate the feature points of the face in the current frame.
b. Calculate the transformation matrix of the face from the localised feature points.
c. using the transformation matrix, transform the face of the next frame and locate the feature points.
d. Repeat steps a to c until a preset number of iterations is reached.

The face features are positioned as shown in Fig. 4.

3.2 Eye Feature Recognition

On the basis of facial feature point localization in 3.1, a support vector machine-based eye recognition method is proposed by using the position of feature points to further accurately locate the human eye. Research has shown that the aspect ratio of the human eye is the most reflective feature. In response to this article, it is necessary to extract parameters such as the proportion of frames for eye closure, the maximum duration of continuous eye closure, and the blink frequency for the driver's eyes.

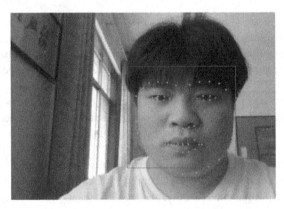

Fig. 4. Face feature experiment

First, the Euclidean distance formula is used to calculate the aspect ratio (EAR) of the eyes, and six key points of the eyes in both open and closed states are selected, as shown in Fig. 5.

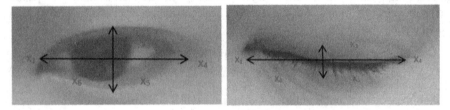

Fig. 5. Key Points in Open and Closed Eyes

Formula for calculating the aspect ratio of the eyes:

$$EAR = \frac{||x_2 - x_6|| + ||x_3 - x_5||}{||x_1 - x_4|| + ||x_1 - x_4||} \tag{4}$$

Euclidean distance formula:

$$L(a, b) = \sqrt{(x_a \cdot x - x_b \cdot x)^2 + (x_a \cdot y - x_b \cdot y)^2} \tag{5}$$

The Euclidean distance between the horizontal and vertical states can be expressed as:

$$e_1 = L(x_1, x_4) \tag{6}$$

$$e_2 = \frac{L(x_2, x_6) + L(x_3, x_5)}{2} \tag{7}$$

The eye aspect ratio was calculated by substituting the Euclidean distances of the horizontal and vertical states into the formula EAR:

$$EAR = \frac{e_1}{e_2} \tag{8}$$

Second, a support vector machine is used to classify the EAR calculation results mentioned above [17]. The essence of the support vector machine is to find the maximum interval between two types of datasets in two-dimensional space and the maximum hyperplane l between multiple datasets in multidimensional space. It is essentially an optimization problem, as shown in Fig. 6.

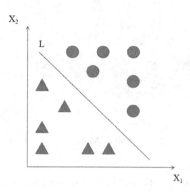

Fig. 6. Support vector machine binary classification problem

The steps to adopt the support vector machine algorithm are as follows:

① Training dataset: Use (x_1, y_1), $(x_2, y_2)...(x_n, y_n)$ to represent the dataset;

② The x_n in the dataset represents the vector, which is the coordinate position of the nth data in the N-dimensional space, and y_n is used to represent the label of the dataset. Here, $+1$ and -1 represent the data label, $+1$ represents the positive sample, and -1 represents the negative sample;

③ The hyperplane expression can be derived from the linear equation: $w^T x + b = 0$ (where w^T represents the w transposition matrix, and w in the expression is a constant);

④ A conclusion can be derived from the linear separability of the dataset: $y_i[w^T x_i + b] \geq 1$;

⑤ According to the distance formula from a point to a straight line, the distance formula from a point to a hyperplane can be obtained: $d = \frac{|w^T x + b|}{||w||}$, where $||w||$ represents the module of w, $||w|| = \sqrt{w_1^2 + w_2^2 + w_3^2 + ... + w_m^2}$;

⑥ According to the conclusion derived from ⑤, it can be simplified as $d = \frac{1}{||w||}$. To achieve the maximum value of d, it is necessary to minimize $||w||$ and finally transform the minimization problem $||w||$ into a convex optimization problem for the solution.

Support vector machine classification results are used to determine whether the eyes in the image are in a closed eye state.

3.3 Mouth Feature Recognition

Due to the driver's involuntary yawning during fatigued driving, the mouth movement characteristics of the driver are more obvious and have a significant degree of closure.

In the algorithm for extracting mouth features, the Euclidean distance formula, which is the same as the eye recognition method, is still used to calculate the mouth aspect ratio (MAR). At the same time, six key points of the mouth in the open and closed states are selected, as shown in Fig. 7.

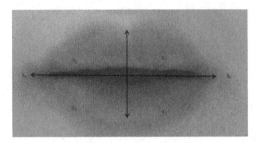

Fig. 7. Extraction of Mouth Feature Points

The camera collects images of the driver's face and mouth area, extracts the driver's facial features, including the features of the mouth area, through face recognition technology, uses machine learning algorithms to train and classify the features of the mouth area to achieve recognition of mouth movements, including yawning, etc. Finally, the monitoring of mouth movements is combined with other fatigue driving detection indicators, such as head tilt, to achieve early warning and monitoring of driver fatigue driving. The mouth area is identified as shown in Fig. 8.

Fig. 8. Recognition of the mouth area

Through the analysis and comparison of several sets of test data, the method of mouth monitoring and recognition based on facial multifeature fusion for the driver fatigue driving monitoring system proposed in this research has achieved better results in both mouth movement recognition and fatigue driving detection and has high feasibility and practical value in practical applications. The results of the experiments on mouth characteristics are shown in Table 1.

Table 1. Mouth test data

Testers	Mouth status (open mouth/closed mouth)
Tester 1	open mouth
Tester 2	open mouth
Tester 3	closed mouth
Tester 4	open mouth
Tester 5	closed mouth
Tester 5	open mouth

4 Driver's Head Feature Recognition

The most prominent feature of driver fatigue is the continuous nodding of the head. We can collect the frequency of the driver's head nodding to determine whether the driver is in a fatigued driving state and use the nodding frequency as an important parameter for subsequent calculation of the weighted sum [18]. This article stipulates that if the frequency of driver nodding during a certain cycle exceeds a certain threshold, it is determined as fatigued driving. Therefore, a method for analysing the frequency of head nodding is proposed, which calculates the nodding frequency over a period of time and uses MATLAB to simulate and draw its relationship diagram, as shown in Fig. 9.

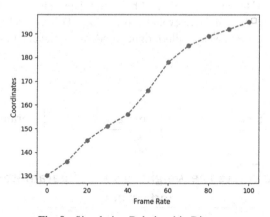

Fig. 9. Simulation Relationship Diagram

Image capture of the driver's head area by means of a camera. Extraction of the driver's facial features, including those of the head region, by face recognition technology. Machine learning algorithms are used to train and classify the features in the head region to achieve recognition of head posture, including head state, number of nods, number of yawns, etc. This is combined with other fatigue detection indicators to monitor driver fatigue. Some of the head monitoring data are shown in Table 2.

Table 2. Experimental data on the head state

Testers	Head condition	Number of nods	Number of yawns
Tester 1	positive	5	2
Tester 2	slanting	7	3
Tester 3	positive	3	5
Tester 4	positive	4	4
Tester 5	slanting	5	3
Tester 6	positive	6	4
Tester 7	slanting	2	2
Tester 8	slanting	3	5
Tester 9	positive	5	3
Tester 10	positive	2	2

5   Based on Multiple Feature Weighting and Fatigue Recognition

Evaluating the fatigue status of drivers based on the aforementioned single eigenvalue has certain limitations, while the accuracy is not particularly high. Therefore, this article proposes a multifeature weighted and fatigue detection algorithm that takes weight values for the parameters of the eyes, mouth, and head and then judges the degree of fatigue based on the weight values of the relevant feature values. This method divides the degree of fatigue into four types: awake, mild fatigue, moderate fatigue, and severe fatigue, as shown in Fig. 10.

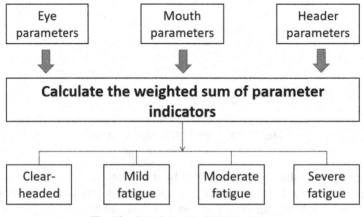

Fig. 10. Calculating the Weighted Sum

The specific steps are as follows:

① Based on the characteristic value parameters of the eyes x_1, mouth x_2, and head x_3 mentioned above, the weight values for the accuracy of driver fatigue judgment are selected, and the calculation formula is as follows:

$$Y = \alpha \cdot x_1 + \beta \cdot x_2 + \gamma \cdot x_3 \tag{9}$$

The feature parameters of the eyes, mouth, and head are multiplied by their corresponding weights and then added and summed to obtain the fatigue value Y of the driver's weighted sum.

② By conducting repeated experimental simulations on the training set data, the weight values of the three feature values of the eyes, mouth, and head were determined. The corresponding weight values are shown in Table 3. The weight values of the experimental simulation feature parameters indicate that eye features are the most important for driver fatigue judgment, followed by eye and head parameters.

Table 3. Characteristic Value Parameter Weight Values

characteristic parameter	Eye parameters	Mouth parameters	Header parameters
Feature parameter weight value	0.55	0.25	0.20

③ According to the differences in the weight values of the characteristic value parameters obtained from simulation experiments, the state is divided into four levels: awake, mild fatigue, moderate fatigue, and severe fatigue. The comprehensive parameter values correspond to the weight value and fatigue level to determine the driver's fatigue level. The corresponding relationship between fatigue level and parameter values is shown in Table 4.

Table 4. Relationship between Fatigue Degree and Parameter Values

Fatigue level	clear-headed	fatigue		
		Clear and mild fatigue	Moderate fatigue	Severe fatigue
Weighted fatigue value of characteristic parameters Y	$Y < 0.35$	$0.35 \leq Y < 0.55$	$0.55 \leq Y < 0.80$	$0.80 \leq Y < 1.0$

6 System Testing

System testing environment: Processor: Intel (R) Core (TM) i5-10200H CPU @ 2.40 GHz 2.40 GHz; Belt RAM: 16.0 GB. Video capture device: HUAWEI Kirin ISP 5.0 image processing technology, which can capture facial image data from the camera.

To demonstrate the reliability of the series of algorithms proposed in this article, real-time videos of drivers driving vehicles were recorded on safe closed roads. The speed of the test vehicle was controlled at 15 km/h. During the recording of the driving process, the drivers were asked to simulate driving vehicles in different states, with the visual frequency controlled for approximately 5 min. Finally, based on the recorded video data, a series of algorithms proposed in this article were integrated for calculation and analysis. The experimental results are shown in Table 5. The test data show that the algorithm proposed in this article is feasible and reliable.

Table 5. Tes. The results

Testers	Video length/s	Number of consecutive eye closures/time
Tester 1	282	8
Tester 2	290	9
Tester 3	286	10
Tester 4	291	9
Tester 5	288	7
Tester 6	290	11
Tester 7	281	8
Tester 8	285	9
Tester 9	291	10
Tester 10	293	9
Tester 11	295	11
Tester 12	280	8
Tester 13	283	12
Tester 14	284	11
Tester 15	286	12
Tester 16	287	10

7   Conclusion

Aiming at the main cause of most traffic accidents from fatigued driving, this paper proposes a multifeature-based weighted summation algorithm to identify and detect the degree of driver fatigue, combined with Adaboost face recognition and detection and support vector machine and other related algorithms to monitor the features of the driver's eyes, mouth and head, which is conducive to improving the disadvantages of the traditional detection system of monolithic features, the face proposed in this paper The multifeature fusion driver fatigue algorithm in this paper achieves significant improvements in the efficiency of fatigue driving monitoring and other aspects and improves the accuracy of fatigue driving detection.

References

1. Zhu, M., Chen, J., Li, H., Liang, F., Han, L., Zhang, Z.: Vehicle driver drowsiness detection method using wearable EEG based on convolution neural network. Neural Comput. Appl. 33(20), 13965–13980 (2021)
2. Ling, Y., Luo, R., Dong, X., Weng, X.: Driver eye location and state estimation based on a robust model and data augmentation. IEEE Access 9, 67219–67231 (2021)
3. Arefnezhad, S., Samiee, S., Eichberger, A., Frühwirth, M., Kaufmann, C., Klotz, E.: Applying deep neural networks for multi-level classification of driver drowsiness using vehicle-based measures. Expert Syst. Appl. 162, 113778 (2020)
4. Li, K., Gong, Y., Ren, Z.: A fatigue driving detection algorithm based on facial multi-feature fusion. IEEE Access 8, 101244–101259 (2020)
5. Pilataxi, J., Vinan, W., Chavez, D.: Design and implementation of a driving assistance system in a car-like robot when fatigue in the user is detected. IEEE Latin Am. Trans. 14(2), 457–462 (2016)
6. Sun, W., Zhang, X., Wang, J., He, J., Peeta, S.: Blink number forecasting based on improved Bayesian fusion algorithm for fatigue driving detection. Math. Probl. Eng. (2015)
7. Ji, Y., Wang, S., Lu, Y., Wei, J., Zhao, Y.: Eye and mouth state detection algorithm based on contour feature extraction. J. Electron. Imaging 27(5), 1 (2018)
8. Baohu, Y., Li, L.A.N., Yong, D.: Face detection based on skin color segmentation and AdaBoost algorithm. Sci. Technol. Eng. 13(11), 3119–3125 (2013)
9. Jo, S.P., Park, J.H., Lee, I., Kim, S.H., Kim, M.U., Kim, J.T.: Driver Fatigue Evaluation Methods for Commercial Vehicles (2013)
10. Pan, T., Wang, H., Si, H., Li, Y., Shang, L.: Identification of pilots' fatigue status based on electrocardiogram signals. Sensors 21(9), 3003 (2021)
11. Kim, J., Kim, S., Han, Y., et al.: Night vehicle detection using variable haar-like feature. J. Measur. Sci. Instrum. 2(04), 337–340 (2011)
12. Segundo, M.P.P., Silva, L., Bellon, O.R.P., Queirolo, C.C.: Automatic face segmentation and facial landmark detection in range images. IEEE Trans. Syst. Man Cybern. Part B (Cybern.) 40(5), 1319–1330 (2010)
13. Vishnu, R., Vishvaragul, S., Srihari, P., Nithiavathy, R.: Driver drowsiness detection system with opencv and keras. J. Phys. Conf. Ser. (2021)
14. Zhang, J.Y., Qiu, W.W., Fu, H.J., Zhang, M.T., Ma, Q.G.: Review of techniques for driver fatigue detection. Appl. Mech. Mater. 433, 928–931 (2013)
15. Reddy, B., Kim, Y.H., Yun, S., Seo, C., Jang, J.: Real-time driver drowsiness detection for embedded system using model compression of deep neural networks. In: Proceedings of the Computer Vision and Pattern Recognition Workshops, Honolulu, HI, USA, 21–26 July 2017, pp. 438–445 (2017)
16. Lyu, J., Yuan, Z., Chen, D.: Long-term multigranularity deep framework for driver drowsiness detection. arXiv 2018, arXiv:1801.02325 (2018)
17. Chen, C., Seo, H., Jun, C.H., Zhao, Y.: Pavement crack detection and classification based on fusion feature of LBP and PCA with SVM. Int. J. Pavement Eng. 23(9), 3274–3283 (2022)
18. Wei, W., Weidong, M., Mengdan, F., Han, Q.: Real-timeface recognition based on selective detection and multiscale matching. Comput. Eng. Des. (2018)
19. Dua, M., Shakshi, Singla, R., Raj, S., Jangra, A.: Deep CNN models-based ensemble approach to driver drowsiness detection. Neural Comput. Appl. 33, 3155–3168 (2021)

20. Doudou, M., Bouabdallah, A., Berge-Cherfaoui, V.: Driver drowsiness measurement technologies: current research, market solutions, and challenges. Int. J. Intell. Transp. Syst. Res. **18**, 297–319 (2020)
21. Shen, H.M., Xu, M.H.: Design and implementation of embedded driver fatigue monitor system. Science and Engineering Research Center. Proceedings of 2015 International Conference on Artificial Intelligence and Industrial Engineering (AIIE 2015) (2015)
22. Zhou, C., Li, J.: A real-time driver fatigue monitoring system based on lightweight convolutional neural network (2021)
23. Chen, S., Sun, Y., Zhang, H., Liu, Q., Lv, X., Mei, X.: Speech fatigue detection based on deep learning. J. Phys. Conf. Ser. (2022)
24. Mollicone, D., et al.: Predicting performance and safety based on driver fatigue. Accid. Anal. Prev. **126**, 142–145 (2019)
25. Ning, Z., et al.: When deep reinforcement learning meets 5G-enabled vehicular networks: a distributed offloading framework for traffic big data. IEEE Trans. Ind. Informat. **16**(2), 1352–1361 (2019)
26. Amin, H.U., Yusoff, M.Z., Ahmad, R.F.: A novel approach based on wavelet analysis and arithmetic coding for automated detection and diagnosis of epileptic seizure in EEG signals using machine learning techniques. Biomed. Signal Process. Control **56**, 101707 (2020)
27. Tsipouras, M.G.: Spectral information of EEG signals with respect to epilepsy classification. EURASIP J. Adv. Signal Process. **2019**(1), 1–17 (2019). https://doi.org/10.1186/s13634-019-0606-8
28. Tuncer, T., Dogan, S., Páawiak, P., Acharya, U.R.: Automated arrhythmia detection using novel hexadecimal local pattern and multilevel wavelet transform with ECG signals. Knowl.-Based Syst. **186**, 104923 (2019)
29. Celona, L., Mammana, L., Bianco, S., Schettini, R.: A multi-task CNN framework for driver face monitoring. In: Proceedings of the 2018 IEEE 8th International Conference on Consumer Electronics-Berlin (ICCE-Berlin), Berlin, Germany, 2–5 September 2018, pp. 1–4 (2018)
30. Zuojin, L., Shengbo, L., Renjie, L., Bo, C., Jinliang, S.: Online detection of driver fatigue using steering wheel anglesfor real driving conditions. Sensors **17**(3), 495 (2017)
31. Jiang, Y., Guo, S., Deng, S.: Denoising and chaotic feature extraction of electrocardial signals for driver fatigue detection by Kolmogorov entropy. J. Dyn. Syst. Meas. Contr. **141**(2), 245–258 (2018)
32. Knapik, M., Cyganek, B.: Driver's fatigue recognition based on yawn detection in thermal images. Neurocomputing **338**(2019), 274–292 (2019)
33. Qin, X., Yiwei, S., Xuefeng, Z.: Progress of driving fatigue monitoring methods based on PERCLOS. Autom. Technol. Appl. **27**(6), 43–46 (2008)
34. Buendia, R., Forcolin, F., Karlsson, J., Arne Sjöqvist, B., Anund, A., Candefjord, S.: Deriving heart rate variability indices from cardiac monitoring—an indicator of driver sleepiness. J. Crash Prev. Injury Control **20**(3), 249–254 (2019)
35. Sun, Y., Tang, Z.: Traffic accident analysis and control countermeasures of fatigue driving on expressway. J. Phys. Conf. Ser. (2021)
36. Chen, L., Zhi, X., Wang, H., Wang, G., Zhou, Z., Yazdani, A., Zheng, X.: Driver fatigue detection via differential evolution extreme learning machine technique. Electronics **9**(11), 1850 (2020)
37. Tang, X., Guo, F., Shen, J., Du, T.: Facial landmark detection by semi-supervised deep learning. Neurocomputing **297**, 22–32 (2018)
38. Patacchiola, M., Cangelosi, A.: Head pose estimation in the wild using convolutional neural networks and adaptive gradient methods. Pattern Recognit. **71**, 132–143 (2017)
39. Zhao, Z., Zhou, N., Zhang, L., Yan, H., Xu, Y., Zhang, Z.: Driver fatigue detection based on convolutional neural networks using EM-CNN. Comput. Intell. Neurosci. (2020)

Analysis of SME Investment Relationships with the Help of Multiple Topology Layouts

Yipan Liu⬤, Song Wang$^{(\boxtimes)}$ ⬤, and Shijie Chen⬤

School of Computer Science and Technology, Southwest University of Science and Technology,
Mianyang 621010, Sichuan, China
wangsong@swust.edu.cn

Abstract. By analysing enterprise relationship networks across various dimensions, including enterprise investment relationships, industry affiliations, and risk diffusion, governments and investors can identify correlations between enterprises and mitigate risks in a timely manner. This approach enables government entities and investors to identify the level of interconnectedness between enterprises and proactively mitigate risks. During their development, enterprises require financing to grow, leading to investment relationships that can be both collaborative and antagonistic in nature. Currently, the analysis of enterprises primarily focuses on their economic characteristics, with a lack of multidimensional analysis of enterprise relationships. To address the aforementioned issues, we propose analysing enterprises in a specific region by integrating various dimensions. We use the force-directed and community partition algorithms in 3 dimensions to create clustered views of enterprise communities. In the 2.5 dimension, enterprises are classified into different levels based on their characteristics using spatial location transformations to achieve feature correlation analysis. Finally, a risk diffusion model is implemented based on the mortgage relationships and operational characteristics of enterprises, using a risk diffusion algorithm within a 2 dimensional detailed network. Building upon the aforementioned ideas, we developed a small and medium-sized enterprise investment relationship system using multiple network topology layouts to analyse investment relationships between enterprises. We then verified the effectiveness of our design. The experimental data are mainly from Shanghai, China.

Keywords: Multidimensional · Enterprise relationship · Feature association · Risk diffusion

1 Introduction

Over the past 40 years, small and medium-sized enterprises (SMEs) in China have evolved from small and weak entities to strong and resilient businesses. They have continuously grown and expanded, becoming a main driving force behind economic development. SMEs in China have played a critical role in the country's economy, contributing over 50% of tax revenue, more than 60% of GDP, over 70% of technological innovation, and more than 80% of urban employment. As such, they have become an

© The Author(s), under exclusive license to Springer Nature Singapore Pte Ltd. 2024
M. Zhang et al. (Eds.): CCF NCCA 2023, CCIS 1960, pp. 117–134, 2024.
https://doi.org/10.1007/978-981-99-8761-0_10

indispensable and important sector. The European Union defines SMEs as companies with fewer than 250 employees and an annual turnover of less than €50 million. These enterprises account for 99% of all enterprises in the EU and have a significant impact on the EU economy [1]. Compared to large enterprises, SMEs face challenges when competing in complex markets and have relatively weaker market resistance capabilities. SMEs often lack sufficient resilience in the face of unstable factors such as natural disasters. SMEs seek financing for rapid development, which can be advantageous but also entails certain risks due to the cooperative and competitive nature of the relationship between investors and investees. The invested party hopes to receive long-term financial assistance from the investor to support sustainable development, but this often conflicts with the investor's desire for short-term profit. The investment relationships between enterprises connect them to each other, forming a network of interconnected enterprise relation-ships. Well-developed enterprises contribute to the stability of the network of interfirm relationships. However, businesses may face difficulties during their development, such as financial or environmental issues, which could lead to their decline, ultimately affecting the network of interfirm relation-ships. In some cases, this can even cause large-scale diffusion of enterprise risks, such as financial crises.

Investment relations connect different enterprises to form a vast network of enterprise relation-ships. Network analysis is widely applied in physical, biological, social, and information systems. Graphs can be used to model many types of relationships and processes. In computer science, graphs are used to represent communication networks, and data structures, such as links between web pages. The network topology of a graph can represent the functional connections between brain regions, which interact to produce various cognitive processes. In this representation, vertices correspond to different brain regions and edges represent the connections between them. The investment relationships between enterprises can be viewed as a network relationship. In graph theory, different enterprises can be regarded as nodes, and the investment relationships between enterprises can be regarded as edges. Therefore, we can transform the relationships between enterprises into a network for further analysis and processing.

Traditional enterprise analysis often focuses solely on the internal operational characteristics of the enterprise, while network analysis, when utilized, often only superficially presents the relationships between enterprises, lacking in-depth information extraction. In multidimensional network topologies, analysis can be conducted from different perspectives. In large-scale relationship networks, utilizing three-dimensional network topology to display the relationships can help avoid cluttered structures and achieve effective exploration. In the 2.5-dimensional approach, nodes can be classified based on their characteristics, and the level of association between nodes at different levels can be observed. To examine local network details and analyse the diffusion of node risk, 2D visualization can be utilized.

Based on the issues and analysis methods mentioned above, we propose using network topology structures of various dimensions to analyse the relationships between enterprises. First, in response to the complex network of relationships formed by investments, we utilize community partitioning and 3D network visualization to enable effective exploration and analysis by observers. Simultaneously, we can utilize the 2.5-dimensional approach to conduct feature correlation analysis of enterprises. For instance, we can classify enterprises into different hierarchies based on their business scope. Considering the weak risk-resistance ability of small and medium-sized enterprises, the intercorrelation among these enterprises can be analysed by combining their investment relationships with their own characteristics. This analysis can be used to determine the degree of interrelation among the enterprises. Ultimately, a risk diffusion model is generated by combining the investment relationships and the characteristics of the enterprises. The model simulates the resilience of the enterprise network and enables early warning of potential impacts.

2 Related Work

The analysis of enterprise relationships in different dimensions can be mainly divided into two aspects: the analysis of small and medium-sized enterprises, and the analysis and application of a complex network. The analysis of SMEs mainly focuses on their business operations and abnormal information; The analysis of complex networks mainly focuses on network innovation and network application.

2.1 Analysis of SMEs

SMEs are an important part of the world economy. Zhibing [2] has developed a new financial metric, the contagion effect, to quantify the contagion consequences of guarantee chains in such networks. He has also developed a visual analysis tool [3] designed to monitor and mitigate systemic risk in conglomerate network secured loans. Guido [4] used the mechanism of distributing guarantees to assess the impact of guarantees on SMEs' access to credit. Stjepan [5] examined the impact of business development grant programs and found that grant programs had a positive impact, particularly for smaller companies. Dvorský [6] studies the credit risk factors for SMEs and their assessment methods, and finds that the entrepreneur's age, gender and education level all have an impact on the results. Through an online questionnaire survey of SMEs in the Czech Republic and Slovakia, Anna [7] found that personnel risk is one of the most important business risks for SMEs. Nenad [8] presented a conceptual framework for investigating the factors influencing the failure of SMEs and their levels of recovery. By deriving a structural equation model, researchers have found that both individual and nonindividual characteristics significantly influence the success of SMEs. Among these factors, external nonpersonal factors appear to have the greatest impact. Bolek [9] conducted a survey aimed at identifying and assessing the internal and external factors affecting the existence of information security risks in Slovak smes and agribusinesses. Siti [10] established a credit risk model for SMEs in Malaysia to predict the loan defaults of SMEs, and emphasized the importance of establishing a robust credit risk model for the low-cost and low nonperforming loan management of private banks. Bojing [11] proposes a novel model for enterprise credit ratings through a graph neural network. A heterogeneous-attention-network-based model (HAT) [12] is proposed to facilitate SME bankruptcy prediction using publicly-accessible data and has two major components: a heterogeneous neighborhood encoding layer and a triple attention output layer. This review provides a methodological overview of network techniques and discusses how network analysis can be used in public health, such as the spread of disease.

2.2 Analysis of Complex Network

In physical, biological, social, and information systems, network analysis can be used to model many types of relationships and processes. This book [13] introduces the basic concepts, mathematical representation, structure and location attributes of social network analysis and provides readers with a theoretical basis for social network analysis. Johannes [14] describes three areas of structural approaches to network analysis: location analysis and generalized block modelling, network evolution and dominant path analysis, and multilevel network analysis. This review [15] provides a methodological overview of network techniques and discusses how network analysis can be used in public health, such as the spread of disease. Aiming at the problem that the existing visualization of multilayer networks cannot clearly show the community structure, the author [16] proposes a visualization layout of multi-layer network topology based on Louvain community detection.

Edge binding can reduce confusion in the same unified area for a diagram with a high edge density [17]. Christoph [18] introduces an uncertain network visualization technique based on node link graphs that overcomes the limitations of force-oriented layouts by providing insight into the probability distribution of the entire network through probability graph lay-outs and Monte Carlo processes. In terms of 3D networks, Enns et al. proved that 3D objects with depth cues can accelerate visual search compared with 2D objects [19]. Network analysis is also applied to enterprise relationship research. Cheng [20] proposed a new method to evaluate the risk of contagion chains in the banking industry using deep neural networks to reduce or prevent potential systemic financial risks, enable loan managers to monitor risks from a broader perspective and avoid financial institutions suffering significant financial losses. Based on the k-shell decomposition method, Xiangfeng [21] proposes a new risk assessment strategy, NetRating, to evaluate the risk level of each firm participating in the secured loan, and extends it to deal with the direct guarantee network. Yang [22] proposes an innovative financial risk analysis framework for supply chain mining based on graphs. By mining the interactive relationship between small and medium-sized enterprises, it captures the topo-logical structure and time change information related to the credit of small and medium-sized enterprises and improves the performance of financial risk analysis.

The main focus of enterprise analysis is to study the nature of the enterprise itself, without considering the factors that may affect it. The existing research on the relationships between enterprises has not considered the characteristics of the enterprises themselves. Therefore, by combining their own characteristics, enterprises can be analysed from a multidimensional network perspective.

3 Multidimensional Enterprise Relationship Network

Small and medium-sized enterprises (SMEs) are a crucial component of the national economy. To keep pace with the rapidly developing society, SMEs need to develop rapidly themselves. However, most of the time, they have to secure funding from outside sources, which results in the formation of a complex enterprise relationship network.

Unfortunately, SMEs have low resilience in emergency situations, and this intricate network can become quite fragile during critical moments. Investors and government officials aim to stay informed about the development status of SMEs and various industries and conduct timely assessments of enterprise risks to prevent unnecessary risk diffusion.

Considering the aforementioned phenomenon, to gain a better understanding of the status of local enterprises, we propose a multidimensional topo-logical network analysis that allows for a comprehensive examination of enterprises from multiple perspectives. By utilizing network and graph theory, we analyse the degree of correlation between enterprises, particularly those formed by investment, and consider the unique characteristics of each enterprise. Through this approach, we can analyse the relationships between enterprises from various dimensions and perspectives. Finally, we conduct a detailed analysis of the risk diffusion of enterprises (Fig. 1).

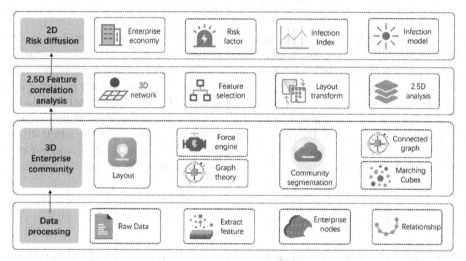

Fig. 1. Enterprise multidimensional analysis process

3.1 Enterprise Investment Relationship Network in 3D

In large-scale relational networks, 3D networks can alleviate the visual confusion caused by overlap and crossover. In this section, we propose the construction of enterprise networks and the division of enterprise communities from a three-dimensional perspective. The three-dimensional construction and division of enterprise relationships enables better observation of the correlations between enterprises.

The division of enterprise communities under three dimensions enables observation of both the internal situation of the community and differentiation between enterprise communities. It mainly involves two key problems: first, the spatial position relationship between enterprises, and second, the boundaries of the enterprise communities.

In this paper, we present a process for generating a 3D enterprise community network topology diagram using enterprise node relational data (Fig. 2).

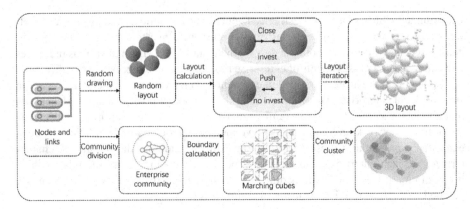

Fig. 2. Enterprise community display

In terms of the layout of enterprise nodes (Fig. 2A), we use the 3D force engine in the D3 force to process the data nodes and enterprise connection relationships to obtain location information for each node. Here, we introduce the force balance model in three dimensions (Formula 1). In formula one, $F(i)$ represents the resultant force of node i. k_{ij} is the corresponding entry in the spring constant matrix, l_{ij} is the distance between node i and node j, and l_o is the original distance between these two nodes. d_{ij} is the unit vector from node i to node j, q_{ij} is the corresponding entry in the damping coefficient matrix, v_j and v_i are the velocity vectors of node j and node i. f_i is the external force acting on node i. When $F(i)$ is less than a certain threshold value, node i is regarded as reaching the equilibrium state.

$$F(i) = \sum \left(\frac{k_{ij} * \left(l_{ij} - l_o\right)}{l_o} + q_{ij} * \left(v_j - v_i\right) * d_{ij} \right) + \sum f_i \tag{1}$$

In a complex enterprise relationship network, each maximum connected subgraph is referred to as an enterprise community. The enterprise relationship network can be represented as a graph, and Formula 2 (shown in FIG. 2.B) can be used to obtain each maximum connected subgraph, or enterprise community. Let us start with one side: f_n represents a collection of nodes in a network, and f_e denotes the edge involved in the node set. The loop is repeated until there is no intersection between the existing node set $f_n(E_i)$ and the remaining node set $f_n(E_n)$. Finally, every maximum connected graph in the network is found.

$$G_c = set \left(\sum_{i=1}^{m} \sum_{\substack{E_i=e_i \\ E_n=E-E_i}}^{f_n(E_n) \cap f_n(E_i)=\emptyset} E_i = f_e(f_n(E_n) \cap f_n(E_i)) \right) \tag{2}$$

To demarcate the boundaries of the enterprise community, we use the following algorithm: for each enterprise community, we obtain the position of each node after 3D-force engine calculation, and after bringing the enterprise nodes into Marching Cubes, we obtain the grid model of the enterprise community (Fig. 3C).

Finally, three.js is used to present the enterprise community relationship network under the three-dimensional network (Fig. 3D).

3.2 Industry Association Analysis in a 2.5D Network

Investment relationships are not the only characteristic of an enterprise. Traditional features, such as parameter comparison, can be easily understood by observers when the size of the enterprise object is small. However, when there are too many comparison objects, it can be difficult to start. Therefore, we introduce 2.5 dimensional feature association analysis.

Under the condition of maintaining the original enterprise community investment relationship network, to better observe the distribution of enterprise characteristics, the universality level is set up to realize the custom analysis.

Enterprises have many characteristics. For example, at the level of enterprise type, different enterprises can be classified into different industries according to their business scope, which helps to understand the development of regional industries. The enterprise management level can understand the development status of the enterprise community. Additionally, the enterprise risk level provides insight into the health of the enterprise community.

For example, at the level of enterprise type, industry correlation analysis can help investors and government organizations understand the development situation of regional enterprises. Industries can be classified into ten categories based on the International Standard Industry Classification, including (Table 1):

Table 1. Industry type.

number	Industry type
1	Agriculture, hunting, forestry and fishing
2	Mining and quarrying
3	Manufacturing industry
4	Electricity, gas and water supply
5	Construction industry
6	Wholesale and retail, restaurants and tourism
7	Transportation, warehousing and postal services
8	Finance, real estate, insurance and commercial services
9	Community, social and personal services
10	Other activities that cannot be classified

To gain a better understanding of the development situation of regional enterprises, we designed a 2.5-dimensional model to analyse the correlation between enterprise characteristics (as shown in Fig. 3). For instance, we used industry classification to categorize enterprises into different groups based on the International Standard Industry

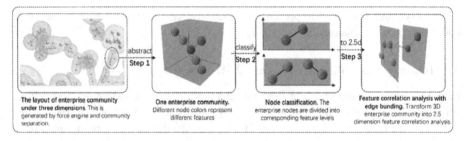

The layout of enterprise community under three dimensions. This is generated by force engine and community separation.

One enterprise community. Different node colors represent different features

Node classification. The enterprise nodes are divided into corresponding feature levels

Feature correlation analysis with edge bunding. Transform 3D enterprise community into 2.5 dimension feature correlation analysis.

Fig. 3. 2.5 Dimension transformation

Classification. Figure 3 illustrates the process of converting a three-dimensional enterprise community into a 2.5-dimensional model. Each enterprise community is extracted and labelled according to its characteristics, and then divided into corresponding feature levels. By applying the edge-binding algorithm, we can observe the correlation between different levels and track the development of the enterprise at each level.

$$
\begin{pmatrix} x'_e \\ y'_e \\ l \end{pmatrix} = \begin{pmatrix} s_x & 0 & 0 \\ 0 & s_y & 0 \\ 0 & 0 & s_z \end{pmatrix} \begin{pmatrix} \cos\theta & -\sin\theta & 0 \\ \sin\theta & \cos\theta & 0 \\ 0 & 0 & 1 \end{pmatrix} \begin{pmatrix} x_e \\ y_e \\ z_e \end{pmatrix} + \begin{pmatrix} t_x \\ t_y \\ t_z \end{pmatrix} \tag{3}
$$

We define a spatial transformation to transform enterprise nodes in three-dimensional space into 2.5-dimensional space according to their own enterprise node characteristics. In Formula 3, l represents the 2.5 dimension level to which the characteristics of enterprise nodes are mapped. x'_e and y'_e represent the spatial coordinates of enterprise nodes after transformation. s_x, s_y, s_z represent the scale. θ represents the angle of rotation. t_x, t_y, t_z represent the translation vector.

$$
F = F(s) + F(r_1) + F(a) + F(r_2) \tag{4}
$$

$$
F(s) = -k_1 * (l - d) * n \tag{5}
$$

$$
F(r_1) = -c_1 * (v\_rel * n) * n \tag{6}
$$

$$
F(a) = k_2 * e^{\left(\frac{d_{ij}}{sigma}\right)} * n_{ij} \tag{7}
$$

$$
F(r_2) = \frac{k_3}{(d_{ij} - epsilon)^2} * n_{ij} \tag{8}
$$

To achieve a better observation effect, the edges between the 2.5 dimensional levels are visually gathered together in space, which is realized by edge bundling (Fig. 4). The red lines show the original edge and the green lines show the changed effect. Formulas 4–8 show the principle of edges involved in FDEB edge binding algorithm. F represents the net force on the edges. $F(s)$, $F(r_1)$, $F(a)$, $F(r_2)$ represent the spring force, friction force, gravity, and repulsive force, respectively. k represents the corresponding constant,

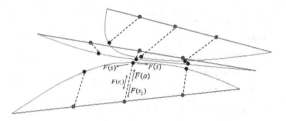

Fig. 4. 2.5 Edge bund in 3D

v_rel represents the relative velocity, n is the direction vector of the side point, d_{ij} is the distance between the edge nodes, *sigma* and *epsilon* represent the range of force action.

Based on the classification of enterprises using the 2.5-dimensional model, we incorporated investment relationships and regional data into our analysis objectives. Our objectives mainly include the following:

1) We analyse the correlation between different industries.
2) We analyse the distribution of enterprises in different industries.
3) We analyse the geographical distribution of different industries.

3.3   Enterprise Risk Diffusion in a 2D Network

Investment relationships connect enterprises and form a network of relationships. Small and medium-sized enterprises (SMEs) are often vulnerable to risks, and external factors can potentially lead to the collapse of these enterprises. In this network of corporate relationships, a failing business may cause risks to spread across the network like a virus (see Fig. 5).

Fig. 5. Risk diffusion

Algorithm: Risk transmission model

Input:

target network $G(V,E)$, venture business V_r,

maximum number of iterations M, threshold value $tValue$

Output: Risk communication network $G_r(V_r, E_r)$

1:    Initialize parameters $G_r(V_r, E_r) = v_r$

2:    **for**(i = 0; i < count(E); i++) **do**

3:        a = E_i.source, b = E_j.target

4:        a.neighbors.push(b), b.neighbors.push(a)

5:    **for**(i=0; i < M; i++) **do**

6:        V_r.foreach(function(risk_item){

7:            risk_item.neighbors.foreach(function(neighbor_item){

8:            if(neighbor not in V_r){

9:            $R(i) = \sum_{j=1, i\neq j}^{n} A_{ij} * w_{ij} * (X_i - X_j) + MInflu(i)$

10:            if ($R(i) < tValue$){V_r.push(neighbor_item)}}}}))

11:    **return** $G_r(V_r, E_r)$

Based on the existing investment relationships and enterprise characteristics, we propose an enterprise risk communication model. When an enterprise suffers losses due to certain factors, it can seek help from relevant enterprises. If an enterprise provides assistance to another venture, we will consider whether the venture can bear the risk

$$R(i) = \sum_{j=1, i\neq j}^{n} A_{ij} * w_{ij} * (X_i - X_j) + MInflu(i) \tag{9}$$

In this paper, a propagation index $R(i)$ (Formula 4) is proposed to represent the possibility of propagation from venture enterprise node i to the neighboring node. The enterprise relation network in this paper mainly involves the investment relation and the management information of the enterprise. A_{ij} represents the investment relationship between enterprise i and enterprise j (weight of edge), w_{ij} is a weight coefficient used to measure the influence of enterprise i on enterprise j, X_i and X_j represent an indicator of the business condition of an enterprise. We add $MInflu(i)$ to indicate human influence and whether the enterprise supports the venture. When $R(i)$ is below a certain threshold, the risk is about to spread.

In the above algorithm, in the enterprise relationship network $G(V, E)$, V represents the enterprise node, and E represents the investment relationship between enterprises. A risk contagion radius is set up to simulate different degrees of diffusion for emerging venture enterprises. At the same time, a threshold $tValue$ is set for enterprises in the infection chain to control the influence of infection. When an enterprise encounters a risk, the first step is to query the neighbors between enterprises. For these neighbors, we need to determine whether they appear in the existing risk diagram $G_r(V_r, E_r)$. $G_r(V_r, E_r)$ represents the relationship network formed by existing venture enterprises. The communication index is calculated for $G_r(V_r, E_r)$ medium - risk enterprise neighbors. If the

Diffuse value is lower than a certain transmission threshold, the risk is transmitted to neighbors. The cycle is repeated until the radius of infection reaches M. Finally, the new communication risk network $G_r(V_r, E_r)$ is obtained.

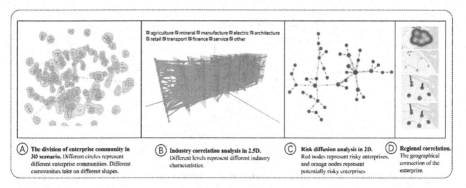

Fig. 6. Analysis process

4   Case Study

4.1   Introduction

Building upon the content in Sect. 3, we have conducted enterprise analysis across various dimensions, as shown in Fig. 6. Figure 6A displays the division of enterprise communities in three dimensions, with each enclosing circle representing a distinct enterprise community network. Figure 6B showcases the arrangement of enterprises across different industries in 2.5 dimensions, with each plane denoting an industry, red nodes representing enterprises, and line segments between plane levels indicating investment relationships between enterprises. Finally, Fig. 6C presents a risk diffusion network of an enterprise in 2-dimensional space, with red nodes representing risk enterprises and yellow nodes signifying risk diffusion enterprises. Figure 6D depicts a regional correlation analysis of enterprises, utilizing a thermal map to represent the distribution of enterprises, a network diagram to represent the relationship between enterprises, and a bar chart to indicate the asset size of enterprises.

4.2   Enterprise Community Division in 3D

The enterprise community division in this paper is mainly based on the investment relationships between enterprises. Although a 3D perspective is conducive to displaying a larger scale enterprise relationship network, it is necessary to address the arrangement of the enterprise relationship network, the extraction of enterprise communities, and the generation of enterprise community surrounding clusters from a three-dimensional perspective.

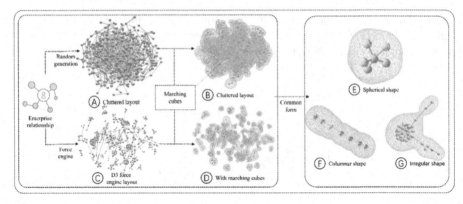

Fig. 7. Three-dimensional layout

A good network relationship arrangement is conducive to better analysis of enterprise relationships. Figure 7 shows the enterprise relationship network in three dimensions. Figure 7C depicts the randomly generated layout of enterprise nodes, where blue nodes represent enterprises and green line segments represent investment relationships between enterprises. Without any spatial arrangement rules (Fig. 7A), the enterprise relationship network appears chaotic and it is difficult to distinguish the relationships between nodes. However, after importing the force engine, the distribution of the relationship network is displayed in Fig. 7C. Figures 7B and 7D show the network relationships that can be rotated and scaled in three dimensions. Although some neighborhoods can be identified in Fig. 7A, there is an overall lack of clear visual effects. To address this issue, we introduce the concept of enterprise community clusters, which surround different enterprise communities to achieve boundary division. Figure 7B and 7C show the enterprise community network relationships after the introduction of the Marching Cubes algorithm. However, Fig. 7B is generated based on a random layout and there is overlap between communities. In contrast, Fig. 7D shows the surrounding clusters formed after the force engine, which are clearly divided. By comparing Fig. 7B and Fig. 7D, it can be observed that adding the community surrounding the cluster helps to divide the relationship network in 3D into different areas, achieving a better effect of community scope differentiation.

The inclusion of the force engine and Marching Cubes algorithm enables the partial research on the display characteristics of individual enterprise communities. For example, we extracted several enterprise community network diagrams (FIG. 7E, FIG. 7F, FIG. 7G) that appear more frequently in FIG. 7D. In FIG. 7E, the distribution of enterprise communities is concentrated and spherical, while in FIG. 7F, the distribution is more divergent and shows a columnar shape. In FIG. 7G, some regions are concentrated, while others are divergent, which has the common characteristics of the first two types. It is evident that the enterprise community cluster is another way of presenting enterprise community relations. By observing the enterprise relationship network, the nodes in the spherical area are relatively close, while the nodes in other areas are more dispersed. Therefore, the generation of enterprise community clusters in three dimensions helps observers better understand the correlation between enterprises.

4.3   Feature Analysis in 2.5D

Enterprises possess various characteristics, including asset size, establishment time, risk information, and more. Based on the available feature information, the enterprises are divided into different levels in 2.5 dimensions. This allows for a customized observation of the correlation between different features.

Enterprises exhibit varying characteristics, and in this analysis, industry types are selected for examination in 2.5 dimensions. The type of local enterprise can serve as a reflection of the local development situation. Following the international Standard Industry Classification in Sect. 3.2, enterprises are divided into ten types. We utilize a 2.5 dimensional network to conduct an industry analysis of local enterprises.

Figure 8 presents the analysis of local enterprises in dimension 2.5. Figure 8A displays the association of enterprises in different industries, with each plane dimension representing an industry. Figure 8B demonstrates the selection of different industries, allowing for the correlation between them to be shown. Figure 8C depicts the development of enterprises in each industry.

Observing the industrial development status shown in Fig. 8C, the red node represents the enterprise, and the line segment represents the investment relationship between enterprises. There are numerous enterprises in the electronics industry, wholesale and retail industry, transportation industry, financial industry, and service industry in this region, and they are closely connected. This indicates that the development of enterprises in this region is inclined towards emerging industries, which reflects the local characteristics of metropolis enterprise development. When examining the development status of the construction industry in this region, the horizontal axis represents the event of enterprise establishment, and the vertical axis represents the size of enterprise assets. From the observation of Fig. 8C, it can be concluded that most construction enterprises are in the upper half, indicating that the assets of construction enterprises in this region are large. This also reflects the high value of the real estate market in this region.

Several relatively developed industries are analysed, as shown in Fig. 8B. The edges between planes were optimized using edge binding calculations to reduce visual clutter (Fig. 8B). The lines between planes represent the investment relation-ships between enterprises. Figure 8B1 shows the connection between finance and electronics, Fig. 8B2 shows the connection between finance and re-tail and wholesale, Fig. 8B3 shows the connection between finance and transportation, and Fig. 8B4 shows the connection between finance and services. Based on the observations and analysis, it can be concluded that among these popular industries, the financial industry is closely related to the transportation and service industries, followed by the eletronic industry and the retail and wholesale industry. Similarly, pairwise analysis could be conducted for each pair of industries, but due to space constraints, only the above correlations are presented.

At the same time, regional analysis is added to show the geographical distribution of enterprises. Figure 8D shows the distribution of enterprises in some electronic information industries. It can be seen that enterprises of this type are mainly distributed in the central and eastern regions.

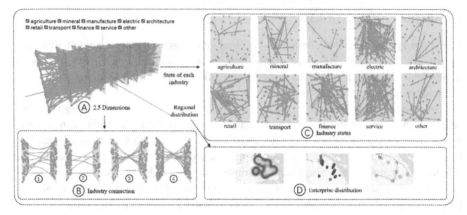

Fig. 8. 2.5-dimensional industry analysis

4.4 Risk Diffusion in 2D

The introduction of the 2D planar network topology diagram can help to see the details of the network. We introduce the risk propagation model to observe the local relationship network in 2D.

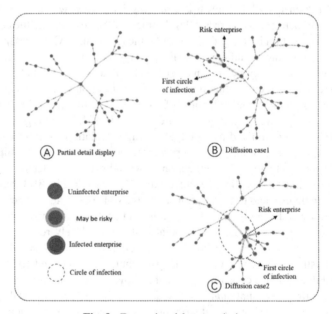

Fig. 9. Enterprise risk transmission

Figure 9 illustrates the communication effect diagram of the enterprise risk communication model in two dimensions. This figure aims to demonstrate the communication effect of enterprise risk in specific scenarios based on the study of the enterprise risk diffusion model in Sect. 3.3. In Fig. 9A, a partially detailed enterprise relationship network topology is presented, where blue nodes represent risk-free enterprises. Figures 9B and 9C show the communication effects of risks generated by different enterprises. The red nodes represent risky enterprises, the yellow nodes represent potentially risky enterprises, and the red dotted line indicates the result of the first round of communication. To set the scope of risk transmission, we used a risk radius of 2, which means two rounds at most. In the transmission process, a subjective factor is added, and the enterprise can choose whether to support the infected enterprise or not. Therefore, we can observe that in the first round of encirclement, some enterprises did not change. Furthermore, some enterprises chose to support the original risk-infected enterprises in the first round of risk transmission, which may lead to the enterprises becoming risky enterprises in the future. Analogously, enterprises that support risky enterprises in the first round have a certain probability of risk. Based on the first round, neighboring enterprises will choose whether to provide support or not, resulting in the second round of risk diffusion.

5 Evaluation

To verify the effectiveness of the multidimensional network analysis on regional enterprises, we designed a user evaluation questionnaire. We invited 20 participants, including business leaders, finance students, and professionals in the visualization field, to evaluate the analysis effects of enterprises using multiple dimensions. Specifically, we evaluated the division of the enterprise community in three dimensions, the industry association analysis in two and a half dimensions, and the risk diffusion model in two dimensions. The evaluation method used a 5-point system, where the lowest score represented "very dissatisfied" (1), and the highest score represented "very satisfied" (5), with the intermediate scores representing different degrees of satisfaction (Table 2).

Table 2. Questionnaire

Question	Industry type
Q1	whether it can effectively divide the position of enterprise nodes in three dimensions
Q2	Whether the community cluster can effectively surround the enterprise community
Q3	Whether the effect of industry correlation analysis is obvious under the 2.5 dimension
Q4	Whether enterprise risk diffusion is effective in two dimensions
Q5	Whether it can effectively understand the overall situation of regional enterprises

The user evaluation results are presented in Fig. 10. Based on the results, our paper can effectively position enterprise nodes in three dimensions (Q1). The community cluster can also properly surround the enterprise community (Q2). Our community analysis, industry association analysis, and enterprise risk diffusion of regional enterprises can effectively and quickly comprehend local enterprises (Q5). However, in the industry association analysis in 2.5 dimensions, due to the large number of nodes and levels, it is necessary to switch between different levels to observe the degree of association between different industries (Q3). For enterprise risk diffusion, we may need to incorporate additional characteristics to evaluate the risk diffusion of enterprises (Q4).

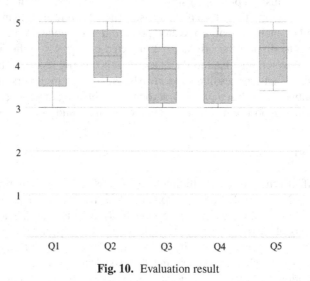

Fig. 10. Evaluation result

6 Conclusion

This paper aims to observe the complex network formed by the investment relationships between enterprises from three dimensions: 3D, 2.5D and 2D. The enterprise community is divided into three dimensions, utilizing a cluster to achieve better encirclement. In the 2.5 dimension, enterprises are categorized into different industry planes for observing and analysing the correlation between industries. The diffusion of local enterprise risk is analysed in two dimensions. Starting from the overall large-scale enterprise community division, to analyzing the correlation between enterprises and industries, and then examining the spread of local enterprise risk, this approach can effectively analyse the situation of local enterprises from different dimensions, ranging from the macro level to the micro level. However, there are still some deficiencies, such as (1) the 2.5 dimension having too many industry levels, which requires manual screening, and (2) in the two dimensions, more factors can be considered for enterprise risk diffusion, such as the operation characteristics of the enterprise and whether it is a dishonest enterprise.

Acknowledgements. This work was supported by Natural Science Foundation of Sichuan Province (Grant No. 2022NSFSC0961) the Ph.D. Research Foundation of Southwest University of Science and Technology (Grant No. 19zx7144) the Special Research Foundation of

China (Mianyang) Science and Technology City Network Emergency Management Research Center(Grant No. WLYJGL2023ZD04).

References

1. Bak, O., et al.: A systematic literature review of supply chain resilience in small–medium enterprises (SMEs): a call for further research. IEEE Trans. Eng. Manag. (2020)
2. Niu, Z., Li, R., Wu, J., et al.: iConViz: interactive visual exploration of the default contagion risk of networked-guarantee loans. In: 2020 IEEE Conference on Visual Analytics Science and Technology (VAST), pp. 84–94. IEEE (2020)
3. Niu, Z., Cheng, D., Zhang, L., et al.: Visual analytics for net-worked-guarantee loans risk management. In: 2018 IEEE Pacific Visualization Symposium (PacificVis), pp. 160–169. IEEE (2018)
4. De Blasio, G., De Mitri, S., D'Ignazio, A., et al.: Public guarantees to SME borrowing. A RDD evaluation. J. Bank. Financ. **96**, 73–86 (2018)
5. Srhoj, S., Lapinski, M., Walde, J.: Impact evaluation of business development grants on SME performance. Small Bus. Econ. **57**, 1285–1301 (2021)
6. Dvorský, J., Schönfeld, J., Kotásková, A., et al.: Evaluation of important credit risk factors in the SME segment. J. Int. Stud. (2018)
7. Kotaskova, A., Belas, J., Bilan, Y., et al.: Significant aspects of managing personnel risk in the SME sector. Manag. Market. Challenges Knowl. Soc. **15**(2), 203–218 (2020)
8. Nikolić, N., Jovanović, I., Nikolić, Đ., et al.: Investigation of the factors influencing SME failure as a function of its prevention and fast recovery after failure. Entrep. Res. J. **9**(3), 20170030 (2018)
9. Bolek, V., Látečková, A., Romanová, A., et al.: Factors affecting information security focused on SME and agricultural enterprises. Agris Online Papers Econ. Inf. **8**(665–2016–45137), 37–50 (2016)
10. Yahaya, S.N., Mansor, N., Bakar, M.H.: Credit risk model: the conceptual framework of SME financing. Int. J. Res. Rev. Appl. Sci. **26**(2), 113–119 (2016)
11. Feng, B., Xu, H., Xue, W., et al.: Every corporation owns its structure: corporate credit rating via graph neural networks. In: Yu, S., et al. (eds.) Pattern Recognition and Computer Vision: 5th Chinese Conference, PRCV 2022, Part I. LNCS, vol. 13534, pp. 688–699. Springer, Cham (2022). https://doi.org/10.1007/978-3-031-18907-4_53
12. Zheng, Y., Lee, V.C.S., Wu, Z., et al.: Heterogeneous graph attention network for small and medium-sized enterprises bankruptcy prediction. In: Karlapalem, K., et al. (eds.) PAKDD 2021, Proceedings, Part I. LNCS, vol. 12712, pp. 140–151. Springer, Cham (2021). https://doi.org/10.1007/978-3-030-75762-5_12
13. Wasserman, S., Faust, K.: Social network analysis: methods and applications (1994)
14. Glückler, J., Doreian, P.: Social network analysis and economic geography—positional, evolutionary and multilevel approaches. J. Econ. Geography **16**(6), 1123–1134 (2016)
15. Luke, D.A., Harris, J.K.: Network analysis in public health: history, methods, and applications. Annu. Rev. Public Health **28**, 69–93 (2007)
16. Zhang, X., Wu, L., Yao, Z., et al.: A multilayer network topology visualization layout based on Louvain community detection. In: 2018 IEEE Third International Conference on Data Science in Cyberspace (DSC), pp. 760–763. IEEE (2018)
17. Holten, D., Van Wijk, J.J.: Force-directed edge bundling for graph visualization. Comput. Graph. Forum **28**(3), 983–990 (2009)
18. Schulz, C., Nocaj, A., Goertler, J., et al.: Probabilistic graph layout for uncertain network visualization. IEEE Trans. Visual Comput. Graphics **23**(1), 531–540 (2016)

19. Enns, J.T., Rensink, R.A.: Influence of scene-based properties on visual search. Science **247**(4943), 721–723 (1990)
20. Cheng, D., Niu, Z., Zhang, Y.: Contagious chain risk rating for networked-guarantee loans. In: Proceedings of the 26th ACM SIGKDD International Conference on Knowledge Discovery & Data Mining, pp. 2715–2723 (2020)
21. Meng, X., Tong, Y., Liu, X., et al.: NetRating: credit risk evaluation for loan guarantee chain in China. In: Wang, G., Chau, M., Chen, H. (eds.) Intelligence and Security Informatics. PAISI 2017. LNCS, vol. 10241, pp. 99–108. Springer, Cham (2017). https://doi.org/10.1007/978-3-319-57463-9_7
22. Yang, S., Zhang, Z., Zhou, J., et al.: Financial risk analysis for SMEs with graph-based supply chain mining. In: Proceedings of the Twenty-Ninth International Conference on International Joint Conferences on Artificial Intelligence, pp. 4661–4667 (2021)

An Iterative Selection Matching Algorithm Based on Fast Sample Consistency

Yanwei Wang[1]($\boxtimes$), Huaide Fu[1], Junting Cheng[2], Xianglin Meng[1], and Zeming Xie[1]

[1] School of Mechanical Engineering, Heilongjiang University of Science and Technology, Harbin 150022, China
wangyanwei@usth.edu.cn

[2] School of Mechanical and Electrical Engineering, Chuzhou University, Chouzhou 239099, China

Abstract. The matching algorithm of feature point pairs is a research hotspot in machine vision at present. However, in the current mainstream algorithm, the method to deal with the mismatched point pairs generated in the matching process depends on the distance between descriptors as the constraint condition. Although the mismatching can be eliminated, the number of correctly matched feature points will also decrease. Therefore, an iterative selection algorithm based on fast sample consistency is proposed. First, the Fast Sample Consensus (FSC) is combined with the iterative selection matching algorithm to find the maximum consistent set; Then, the minimum optimal sampling number is determined according to the distance of the matching point pair, and four groups of data are selected to calculate the transformation model; Finally, the transformation model is applied to the image to be registered. Experiments show that the algorithm increases matching accuracy by almost 8% while simultaneously saving roughly 25% of the time cost.

Keywords: Feature matching · fast sample consistency · Iterative selection · minimum and optimal number of samples

1 Introduction

As a basic technology in machine vision, the application of image registration technology in subsequent image processing, such as picture stitching, binocular vision, target identification and tracking, face recognition, etc. [1], is crucial. Generally speaking, there are two sorts of image calibration methods: characteristic matching and neighbourhood intensity matching based on points to be matched [2]. Intensity matching needs to find local matching of a certain area, and at the same time, it also needs to add the constraint of parallax continuity in the neighbourhood to achieve global matching. The method based on feature matching selects the appropriate matching feature unit according to the characteristics of the environment and the application field. The feature component unit can include: boundary feature, linear feature, corner point, etc. This kind of matching method is widely used because it has the characteristics of fast computation speed, good robustness to illumination and high matching accuracy.

M. Zhang et al. (Eds.): CCF NCCA 2023, CCIS 1960, pp. 135–143, 2024.
https://doi.org/10.1007/978-981-99-8761-0_11

Feature-based matching methods mainly include three steps: feature detection, feature matching, transform estimation and resampling [2]. In recent years, many feature point extraction algorithms applied to image registration have been proposed, such as SIFT algorithm with scale invariance [3]. In order to extract the scale invariance of feature points using SIFT algorithm and speed up the calculation, a SURF feature point detection algorithm based on SIFT algorithm was proposed [4]. Classic Harris algorithm [5], etc. The feature points (or corner points) extracted by these algorithms do not change the affine transformation of the picture. However, when aiming for feature point matching, the distance between each descriptor and query descriptor in the descriptor subset is trained, and then all distances are sorted, and an optimal matching descriptor is found for each query descriptor by setting the threshold of distance. This registration method is prone to mismatches. For example, there is a query descriptor in the image to be registered, but noise makes feature points in the image unable to be matched. However, according to the matching constraints, the feature point corresponding to the query descriptor will also find a matched feature point in the image. The characteristic points in this case are called outliers. So there is often the problem of how to eliminate outliers and increase the accuracy of matching.

The existence of outliers has a negative impact on the accuracy of the final result of image registration. In this paper, an iterative selection algorithm based on fast sample consistency is proposed, which aims to increase the number of correct matching point pairs and reduce the time cost through iterative selection.

2 Classical Algorithm

RANSAC stands for "Random Sample Consensus", is a commonly used algorithm to delete mismatches, which was first proposed by Fischler and Bolles in 1981 [6]. This technique calculates the parameters of a mathematical model using a dataset that includes outliers. Assuming that all the data conform to a certain law, the law is obtained through random sampling, and the law that makes more data conform to is found through repeated sampling. In this case, the outliers have no influence on the estimated value. Hence, it can also be referred to as an outlier detection method. The algorithm can be considered as a non-deterministic algorithm, meaning it yields plausible results with a certain probability that increases with each iteration. It is important to note that this holds true only when the number of iterations does not exceed the maximum specified iterations. It is constantly updated rather than a fixed value, and the expression of the number of iterations k is:

$$k = \frac{\log(1-p)}{\log(1-w^m)} \tag{1}$$

where, p is the feasibility that all points selected randomly from the dataset during certain iterations are intra-office points, w is the probability that one intra-office point is selected from the data set each time, and m is the number of selected matching points.

The algorithm is stable when the number of outliers is small, but when the number of outliers is large, not only the stability decreases, but also the complexity of the estimation of the homicity matrix increases, resulting in a long time. This is due to the large number of outliers and the need to identify the maximum consensus set among randomly chosen samples in each iteration in order to compute the final parameters for the transformation model. Moreover, the model of the fitting object in the subsequent image matching is homologous matrix H, which has 8 degrees of freedom and requires at least 4 groups of corresponding point pairs to calculate the matrix model. However, in practical applications, the calculated point pairs usually contain noise and the position deviation of the corresponding pixel points. As a result, in order to obtain more accurate calculation results, the transformation model needs to calculate far more than 4 groups of point pairs, which brings a large amount of calculation to the program. The following is the formula for calculating the Homography matrix:

$$
\begin{pmatrix} x_2 \\ y_2 \\ 1 \end{pmatrix} = \begin{pmatrix} h_1 & h_2 & h_3 \\ h_4 & h_5 & h_6 \\ h_7 & h_8 & 1 \end{pmatrix} \begin{pmatrix} x_1 \\ y_1 \\ 1 \end{pmatrix} \tag{2}
$$

According to this mathematical model, scholars usually randomly select 4 groups of optimal matching point pairs, calculate the homography matrix H, optimize it through the number of inner layers, and define the minimum number of sample sets:

$$
n = \min\{N_0, \max\{n_0, n_0 \log_2 \mu N_0\}\} \tag{3}
$$

where, N_0 is the total matching point pair (≥ 4), and n_0 is the step size. It's μ that a scaling factor.

In addition, in terms of removing outliers, progressive consistent sampling (PROSAC) is an optimization of classic RANSAC sampling by sampling from an ever-increasing set of optimal corresponding points [7]. Xiaofeng Wang et al. proposed an improved RANSAC algorithm combining feature matching confidence with grid clustering in order to improve the matching accuracy of RANSAC algorithm when it is affected by external interference. This algorithm increases the probability of the existence of internal points and avoids the mismatched results caused by external interference [8]. Igor Djurovi [9] put forward the QML_RANSAC estimator, combined the quasi-maximum likelihood and RANSAC, and compared the obtained result with the current estimate by using the maximum likelihood heurist function to improve the efficiency of removing false matches. Gang Du et al. changed the judgment of outliers from Euclidean distance to area and expanded the search scope. In order to obtain highly reliable RANSAC internal points, Mingchun Sun et al. combined RANSAC algorithm with kd_tree algorithm and adopted quadric surface fitting method to improve the operation accuracy of RANSAC. Xianghong Chen et al. combined deep learning to extract global and local features and conduct loop candidate frame verification on RANSAC, thus improving algorithm stability. Guo Jia et al. designed a method to calculate homography matrix by employing a ranking system based on the quality of feature matching, the algorithm successfully addresses the issue of random sampling in RANSAC and significantly reduces the time required for feature matching [10].

3 Fast Sample Consistency Algorithm

3.1 Algorithm Introduction

Fast Sample consistency (FSC algorithm for short) algorithm 12 is that for a given pair of images, assuming that $f_r(x, y)$ is the benchmark graph and $f_s(x, y)$ is the graph to be matched, the relation between them is represented by a global affin-e transformation model which can reflect most deformities. The relationship between the reference image and the image to be matched can be described as a two-dimensional plane:

$$f_s(x, y) = I(f_r(x, y), \theta) \qquad (4)$$

where, θ is the parameter of affine transformation model, and the approximate expression converted to one-dimensional relation is:

$$f_s(x, y) = I(f_{rx}(x, y), f_{ry}(x, y)) \qquad (5)$$

The communication between f_r and f_s is established by formula (4), and the feature point sets of two images are extracted as follows:

$$C_r\{p_1, p_2, p_3, \ldots, p_m\}$$
$$C_s\{p_1, p_2, p_3, \ldots, p_n\} \qquad (6)$$

Assuming that the corresponding point set is:

$$P\{p_1, p_2, p_3, \ldots, p_i\} \qquad (7)$$

The coordinate of p_i is (x_i, y_i), there are several outliers in point set P. In order to reduce outliers and reduce time consumption and increase stability, the FSC algorithm was used for the corresponding point set C_s to extract the subset C_h with high matching accuracy, and the maximum consistent set was found in the subset C_h.

SIFT feature extraction still has strong stability under the disturbance of illumination, noise, perspective, zoom and rotation, so the algorithm is utilized for feature point extraction. SIFT special point detection should first construct a scale space and subsequently detect extreme points within the scale space, then determine the candidate special points and the direction of the special points in the light of the extreme point set, and finally generate feature descriptors for matching.

3.2 SIFT Feature Matching Algorithm

SIFT feature matching utilizes the distance Ratio between the closest and second nearest neighbors to determine the similarity of key points between two images. To register the image, a critical point is selected in the reference image, and the closest as well as the second nearest key points are located in the image. The distance Ratio is used to solve the distance ratio. In this matching process, many mismatches exist in the matching process. The expression of Ratio is:

$$Ratio = \frac{d}{D} \qquad (8)$$

where, d is the nearest neighbour distance, D is the second nearest neighbor distance.

In formula (8), the nearest neighbor of the key point is the correct corresponding point of the point by default, but it is found in the experiment that the correct corresponding point also exists in the next nearest neighbor. Based on this possibility, this paper adopts the iterative selection matching algorithm to judge the adjacent points of each key point iteratively from far to near. In an effort to enhance iteration speed and reduce computational load, Set the number of adjacent points to 20.

4   C-FSC Algorithm We Raised

Lowe, the author of SIFT, recommends the threshold value of Ratio as 0.8, that is, when Ratio > 0.8, it is considered that this group is wrong to match [11]. When Ratio < 0.8, the number of SIFT matching points will be reduced, but the matching result is relatively stable. The smaller the Ratio value, the harsher the conditions for constructing points between matching points, the higher the accuracy of matching results, but the longer the time. To shorten feature matching length and enhance the accuracy of matching point pairs, this paper adopts the FSC algorithm to increase the correct matching point pairs, effectively reducing the time length and improving the accuracy of matching point pairs. The specific method is as follows: before the Ratio is obtained, two ratio parameters d_l and d_h are set. The correspondence relationship in subset C_h is obtained through d_l, and C is represented as the consensus set, in which the correspondence relationship is obtained through d_h. The conversion error signifies the largest consensus set obtained, which is denoting as:

$$e(c_i, \theta) = ||(x_i^{\sim}, y_i^{\sim}) - T(x_i, y_i), \theta|| \tag{9}$$

where, θ is the transform model parameter (depending on the number of samples). The specific process is shown in Fig. 1.

Firstly, SIFT algorithm is used to match the features of two images to find the corresponding set C_h, and the consensus set C is obtained according to the conversion error. In the consensus set C, the matching points are sorted based on the closet neighbor distance. The minimum optimal point is taken as the representative data set, and the minimum sampling number is sorted according to the distance from far to near by Formula (4). Then, four data sets were randomly selected to estimate the model variables of the representative data set C, and the model parameters were applied to all data sets to find the inner serial number of each pattern parameter. Meanwhile, the optimal model parameters were selected according to the number and variance of inlays. Finally, the optimal model parameters were applied to the consensus set to find the corresponding point pair most suitable for the model, and the final model was calculated.

5   Experimental Results and Analysis

The algorithm is based on the environment: Intel (R) Core (TM) i5-6300HQ + 2.30GHz CPU, 8GB memory, Win10 64-bit operating system, programming tool for Visual Studio2019 created cmake environment, the reference pictures used in the experiment and

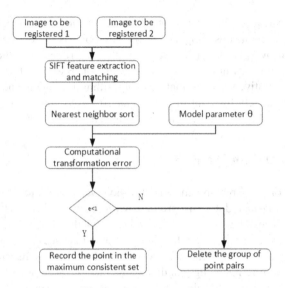

Fig. 1. Image registration

to be registered pictures for the laboratory UAV shooting. In this paper, several groups of experimental results based on SIFT combined with RANSAC, SIFT combined with fast sample consistency were compared, and the results are illustrated in Fig. 2.

In the Fig. 2, figure(a) and figure(b) are the two groups of source images to be registered. In the Fig. 3, figure(a) and figure(b) describe the matching results of feature point pairs obtained by combining SIFT feature extraction algorithm with violence matching. It can be seen from these two images that without mismatched filtering, the registration effect of feature point pairs is poor and adds a lot of work to the later image fusion, which improves the running time of the system. Figure (c) and Figure (d) are the effect maps of matching point pairs after RANSAC algorithm filtering, which greatly reduces the number of matching point pairs, but there are still a few mismatches, which are not completely deleted. According to the above description, in the process of image fusion, the transformation matrix is calculated to randomly sample four groups of matching point pairs, which still have errors in the calculation of transformation matrix. Figure (e) and (f) illustrate that the algorithm we raised is more efficient in filtering mismatches. The results are analyzed in combination with Table 1.

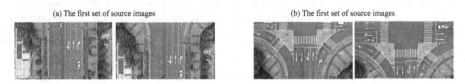

(a) The first set of source images   (b) The first set of source images

Fig. 2. Image to be registered

As can be seen from Table 1, after the combination of FSC and iterative selection, the matching point pairs were purified to a certain extent, achieving a high registration accuracy. Simultaneously, owing to the growth of the amount of iterati-ons, the program duration also increases correspondingly. However, the program running time does not increase under the combination of FSC algorithm. After filtering out the mismatched point pairs and calculating the corresponding transformation matrix, a more ideal image fusion effect can be obtained. Table1 Comparison results between the feature matching method and RANSAC algorithm.

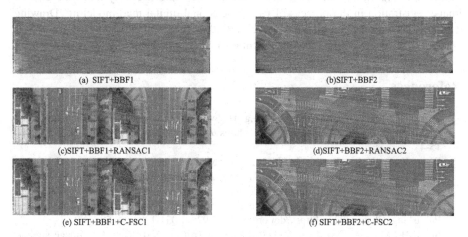

(a) SIFT+BBF1

(b)SIFT+BBF2

(c)SIFT+BBF1+RANSAC1

(d)SIFT+BBF2+RANSAC2

(e) SIFT+BBF1+C-FSC1

(f) SIFT+BBF2+C-FSC2

Fig. 3. Image matching

Table1. The results of feature matching method and RANSAC algorithm are compared

Methods	Time(s)	Logarithm of matching points (pairs)	Match the logarithm of the points correctly (pairs)	Matching accuracy (%)
SIFT + BBF1	16.712563	18869	-	-
SIFT + BBF2	14.165642	14198	-	-
SIFT + BBF1 + RANSAC1	22.653782	445	339	76.18%
SIFT + BBF1 + RANSAC2	25.846725	763	571	74.83%
SIFT + BBF1 + C-FSC1	16.793249	434	366	84.33%
SIFT + BBF2 + C-FSC2	19.100471	741	617	83.26%

6 Summary

According to the characteristics of urban road 2D digital map modeling, the filtering algorithm of mismatching existed in the feature matching point pairs was studied, and the iterative selection based on FSC algorithm was proposed, and the optimal model was determined by the minimum sampling number, so as to compute the maximum consistence set of the entire consistence set. This algorithm can increase the number of matching point pairs rather than blindly remove outliers. According to the experimental results, this algorithm can better deal with the matching accuracy and time cost of image registration in the process of two-dimensional digital map modeling. Drawing comparisons with the common RANSAC algorithm, the running time of the program is decreased by 25%, and the matching accuracy is improved by nearly 8%.

References

1. Zhang, H.: Image registration. In: Zhang, H. (ed.) Advanced Neuro MR Techniques and Applications, pp. 83–94. Elsevier (2021). https://doi.org/10.1016/B978-0-12-822479-3.000 15-4
2. Wang, X., Su, Y., Liu, R., Qu, Q., Liu, H., Yi, G.: Medical image registration method based on simulated CT. In: Huang, D.-S., Jo, K.-H., Jing, J., Premaratne, P., Bevilacqua, V., Hussain, A. (eds.) Intelligent Computing Methodologies: 18th International Conference, ICIC 2022, Xi'an, China, August 7–11, 2022, Proceedings, Part III, pp. 719–728. Springer International Publishing, Cham (2022). https://doi.org/10.1007/978-3-031-13832-4_59
3. Sri, K.H., Manasa, G.T., Reddy, G.G., Bano, S., Trinadh, V.B.: Detecting image similarity using SIFT. In: JeenaJacob, I., Gonzalez-Longatt, F.M., Shanmugam, S.K., Izonin, I. (eds.) Expert Clouds and Applications: Proceedings of ICOECA 2021, pp. 561–575. Springer Singapore, Singapore (2022). https://doi.org/10.1007/978-981-16-2126-0_45
4. Beiyi, W., Xiaohong, Z., Weibing, W.: Feature matching method based on SURF and fast library for approximate nearest neighbor search. Integr. Ferroelect. **218**(1), 147–154 (2021). https://doi.org/10.1080/10584587.2021.1911336
5. Elliott, J., Khandare, S., Butt, A.A., Smallcomb, M., Vidt, M.E., Simon, J.C.: Automated tissue strain calculations using Harris corner detection. Ann. Biomed. Eng. **50**(5), 564–574 (2022). https://doi.org/10.1007/s10439-022-02946-9
6. Riu, C., Nozick, V., Monasse, P.: Automatic RANSAC by likelihood maximization. Image Process. Line **12**, 27–49 (2022). https://doi.org/10.5201/ipol.2022.357
7. Hua, C., Pana, R., Chen, Y.: Binocular ranging method based on improved ORB-RANSAC. Laser Optoelect. Progr. **58**(22), 288–293 (2021)
8. Wang, X., Wang, B., Ding, Z., Zhao, T.: Research on feature matching based on improved RANSAC algorithm. In: Liu, H., Yin, Z., Liu, L., Jiang, L., Gu, G., Wu, X., Ren, W. (eds.) Intelligent Robotics and Applications: 15th International Conference, ICIRA 2022, Harbin, China, August 1–3, 2022, Proceedings, Part III, pp. 477–484. Springer International Publishing, Cham (2022). https://doi.org/10.1007/978-3-031-13835-5_43
9. Djurović, I.: QML-RANSAC: PPS and FM signals estimation in heavy noise environments. Signal Process. **130**, 142–151 (2017). https://doi.org/10.1016/j.sigpro.2016.06.022
10. Guo, J., He, X., Ma, X., Du, S., Wang, J.: Matching of small packages of traditional Chinese medicine based on improved RANSAC algorithm. ITM Web Conf. **45**, 01016 (2022). https://doi.org/10.1051/itmconf/20224501016

11. Liu, Z.: Design of incomplete 3D information recognition system based on SIFT algorithm. In: Huang, C., Chan, Y.-W., Yen, N. (eds.) 2020 International Conference on Data Processing Techniques and Applications for Cyber-Physical Systems: DPTA 2020, pp. 1485–1490. Springer Singapore, Singapore (2021). https://doi.org/10.1007/978-981-16-1726-3_193
12. Ashraf, R., Ahmed, N.: FRANSAC: Fast RANdom sample consensus for 3D plane segmentation. Int. J. Comput. App. **167**(13), 30–36 (2017). https://doi.org/10.5120/ijca20179 14558

Unpaired Image Dehazing for Real Hazy Images

Hongwei Zhao[1,2], Yanting Pei[1,2(✉)], Yi Jin [1,2(✉)], Yaping Huang[2], Shengchun Wang[3], and Yidong Li[1,2]

[1] Key Laboratory of Big Data & Artificial Intelligence in Transportation, Ministry of Education (Beijing Jiaotong University), Beijing, China
{ytpei,yjin}@bjtu.edu.cn
[2] School of Computer and lnformation Technology, Beijing Jiaotong University, Beijing 100044, China
[3] Infrastructure Inspection Research Institute, China Academy of Railway Sciences Corporation Limited, Beijing 100044, China

Abstract. Recently, image dehazing has achieved good performance benefiting from deep learning, but most of them are aimed at synthetic hazy images that have corresponding haze-free images. However, in some practical applications, the acquired images always contain haze in hazy weather, which makes it difficult to obtain pairs of haze-free images. Therefore, image dehazing for real hazy images is very important and challenging because there are no corresponding haze-free images. Therefore, we propose an unpaired image dehazing method to solve the dehazing problem of unpaired real hazy images, which contains the unpaired training module and the supervised training module. For the unpaired training module, we first use a cycle generative adversarial network to generate dehazed images. Then, we use perceptual loss to make the features of dehazed images and unpaired haze-free images more consistent to improve image dehazing performance. Finally, we use instinct properties of clear images to further improve image dehazing performance. For the supervised training module, we design a pseudo labelling scheme to train the model using dehazed images generated from the unpaired training module as pseudo haze-free images, so that we can conduct supervised training to further increase the performance of image dehazing. In addition, we collect a real hazy image dataset from real high-speed railway scenarios, named the HRHI (High-speed Railway Hazy Image) dataset, which contains real hazy images and unpaired haze-free images. To verify the generality of our method, we also collect a real sandstorm image dataset from real high-speed railway scenarios, named the HRSI (High-speed Railway Sandstorm Image) dataset. Expensive experimental results on the HRHI and generic hazy image datasets show the effectiveness of our method, and the experimental results on the HRSI dataset prove the generality of our method.

Keywords: Real hazy image · Unpaired image dehazing

M. Zhang et al. (Eds.): CCF NCCA 2023, CCIS 1960, pp. 144–161, 2024.
https://doi.org/10.1007/978-981-99-8761-0_12

1   Introduction

Haze is very common in our real life, which not only affects the visual effect, but also affects subsequent high-level visual tasks, for example, image object detection. Previous image dehazing methods [1,4,5,9,12,34,35,44] mainly use the atmospheric scattering model [21] shown below to remove haze,

$$I(i) = J(i)t(i) + A(1 - t(i)). \tag{1}$$

In Eq.(1), $I(i)$ denotes the hazy image, $J(i)$ denotes the haze-free image, $t(i)$ denotes the medium transmission, and A denotes the global atmospheric light. Early image haze removal methods mainly use prior knowledge to remove haze, such as the dark channel prior [12].

At present, most image dehazing methods are mainly based on convolutional neural network (CNNs) [5,13,14,17,19,24–26,33,37,42]. Cai et al. [5] presented the first CNN-based image haze removal method. Li et al. [17] presented an image haze removal method by using a reformulated atmospheric scattering model. These methods [5,13,17] are CNN-based image haze removal methods that rely on the atmospheric scattering model. These methods [14,19,24–26,37,42] are end-to-end CNN-based image haze removal methods that can directly recover haze-free images from the input hazy images. Thanks to the application of deep learning, the existing image haze removal methods have achieved very good image dehazing effects. However, they are mainly trained in a supervised manner, which requires many pairs of hazy and haze-free images, as shown in Fig. 1 (a). However, in many practical applications, such as the very important high-speed railway, as shown in Fig. 1 (b), it is unrealistic to acquire many hazy images with paired haze-free images. The pairs of hazy images are usually synthetic hazy images, and most existing image haze removal methods train dehazing models on synthetic hazy images with the paired haze-free images. They achieve good dehazing performance on synthetic hazy images, but their performance is very poor when applied to real hazy images. Therefore, image dehazing is very important and challenging for real hazy images in some practical applications.

To alleviate the problem that real hazy images have no corresponding haze-free images and supervised training cannot be carried out, Li et al. [18] proposed an image dehazing method by using semi-supervised training, Shao et al. [30] presented a domain adaptation image haze removal method, Chen et al. [6] presented a synthetic-to-real image dehazing method guided by physical priors, and Yu et al. [40] presented a multi-scale domain adaptation method to bridge the domain gap between synthetic hazy images and real hazy images. These methods can alleviate the above problem by using synthetic hazy images to help solve the real hazy image removal problem.

Image dehazing methods [8,38] only use hazy images and unpaired haze-free images to solve hazy image dehazing problems. Cycle-Dehaze [8] is an image dehazing method based on CycleGAN [43]. Yang et al. [38] proposed a disentangled image haze removal method that generates haze-free images in an unpaired manner. These image dehazing methods show the great potential of unpaired

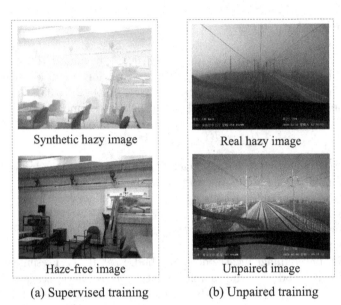

Synthetic hazy image

Real hazy image

Haze-free image

Unpaired image

(a) Supervised training   (b) Unpaired training

Fig. 1. Supervised and unpaired image training. (a) For synthetic hazy images, there are corresponding haze-free images, which can be trained in a supervised manner; (b) For real hazy images, there are no corresponding haze-free images, so we can use unpaired haze-free images for unpaired training.

image dehazing for enhancing the haze removal performance of real hazy images. However, they cannot exploit and take full advantage of the useful information of unpaired haze-free images, and there is still room for improvement in image haze removal on real hazy images.

Most of the above image haze removal methods are all aimed at synthetic hazy images, resulting in poor effects on real hazy images in practical applications. To address the inadequacies of these methods, in this paper, we propose an unpaired image dehazing method, which can solve real hazy image dehazing without paired haze-free images. Our method contains an unpaired training module and a supervised training module. For the unpaired training module, we first use a cycle generative adversarial network to generate the dehazed images. Then, we use perceptual loss to make the features of the dehazed images and unpaired haze-free images more consistent to increase the image dehazing performance. Finally, we use the instinct properties of clear images to further improve the performance of image dehazing. For the supervised training module, we propose a pseudo labelling scheme by treating the dehazed images generated from the unpaired training module as pseudo haze-free images to conduct supervised training to further leverage the image dehazing performance.

The main contributions are shown below:

- We collect a real hazy image dataset and a real sandstorm image dataset from real high-speed railway scenarios, named the HRHI (High-speed Railway Hazy

Image) dataset and HRSI (High-speed Railway Sandstorm Image) dataset, respectively.

- We propose an unpaired image dehazing method to solve the problem of real hazy image dehazing. We first propose unpaired training based on CycleGAN and use perceptual loss and the instinct properties of the clear images to generate clearer dehazed images. Then, we propose to take the dehazed images generated from the unpaired training module as pseudo haze-free images to conduct supervised image dehazing training.
- Many experiments on the HRHI, D-HAZY and HRSI datasets demonstrate the effectiveness and generality of our proposed method.

2   Related Works

2.1   Image Dehazing

Previous image haze removal methods are traditional methods, for example, prior-based methods [4,12,44]. He et al. [12] proposed a dark channel prior for image haze removal. Meng et al. [1] presented a haze removal method based on boundary constraints and the weighted L_1-norm. Zhu et al. [44] presented a color attenuation prior for image haze removal. Berman et al. [4] proposed a non-local prior for image haze removal.

At present, most image dehazing methods are based on deep learning [5, 13,14,17,19,24–26,37,42]. The performance of image dehazing is constantly improved due to the use of deep learning. Cai et al. [5] proposed a CNN-based image haze removal method that first gains medium transmission and then recovers haze-free images by using an atmospheric scattering model. Li et al. [17] directly generated haze-free images according to re-formulated atmospheric scattering model. Li et al. [19] adopted a conditional generative adversarial network for image haze removal. Ren et al. [26] proposed a multi-scale gated fusion network for image dehazing. Qu et al. [25] transformed image haze removal to image-to-image translation and presented a GAN-based image dehazing method. Qin et al. [24] presented a feature fusion attention network for image dehazing. Hong et al. [14] proposed an image dehazing method by using knowledge distillation. Wu et al. [37] presented an image dehazing method by using contrastive learning in which negative and positive samples are hazy images and clear images, respectively. The above image dehazing methods achieve good image dehazing performance, but they mainly aim at synthetic hazy images and training in a supervised manner.

To solve the problem of real hazy image dehazing, Li et al. [18] presented an image dehazing method by using semi-supervised training that contains supervised learning and unsupervised learning branches. Shao et al. [30] presented a image dehazing method by using domain adaptation that contains two image dehazing modules and an image translation module. Chen et al. [6] presented synthetic-to-real dehazing guided by using physical priors, which first trains the dehazing model on synthetic hazy images and then uses unlabelled real hazy images to further fine-tune the model. The above image dehazing methods use not only real hazy images but also synthetic hazy images.

Image dehazing methods [8,38] do not use synthetic hazy images, but only use real hazy images and unpaired haze-free images to address real hazy image removal. Cycle-Dehaze [8] proposed an image dehazing method based on Cycle-GAN [43] by combining perceptual loss and cycle-consistency loss. Yang et al. [38] presented a disentangled image haze removal method that recovers haze-free images in unpaired supervision. However, they do not fully utilize the useful information of unpaired images. Therefore, we present an unpaired image dehazing method for solving the real hazy image dehazing problem in this paper.

2.2   Generative Adversarial Networks

Goodfellow et al. [11] proposed a generative model estimation procedure that trains a generative model and a discriminative model simultaneously. The generative model maximizes the probability of discriminative model error. There are many variants of generative adversarial networks (GANs), such as Cycle-GAN [43], conditional generative adversarial network (CGAN) [22], Dual-GAN [39], Wasserstein GAN [3], bidirectional generative adversarial network (BiGAN) [7] and coupled generative adversarial networks (CoGAN) [20]. In addition, GANs and their variants are extensively used in many computer vision tasks, such as image dehazing [19], image deraining [41] and style transfer [16].

3   Proposed Method

We first introduce the overall framework of our method and then describe the unpaired training module and the supervised training module in this section.

3.1   Method Overview

Supervised training cannot be conducted directly because of the difficulty of collecting the corresponding haze-free images. Therefore, we present an unpaired image haze removal method to address the problem of real hazy image dehazing. Our proposed method includes two modules: one is the unpaired training module, and the other is the supervised training module. The frame diagram is shown in Fig. 2. For the unpaired training module, we propose a CycleGAN-based unpaired training module. In particular, we first use CycleGAN [43] to train the image haze removal network. Then, we use perceptual loss to improve the image dehazing performance. To further improve the image dehazing performance, we constrain the instinct attributes of clear images to train the model, such as the dark channel prior. For the supervised training module, due to the lack of paired haze-free images, we take the dehazed images generated from the unpaired training module as pseudo haze-free images for supervised training. The parameters of the generator and discriminator are shown in Table 1 and Table 2, respectively. Next, we introduce the unpaired training module and the supervised training module in detail.

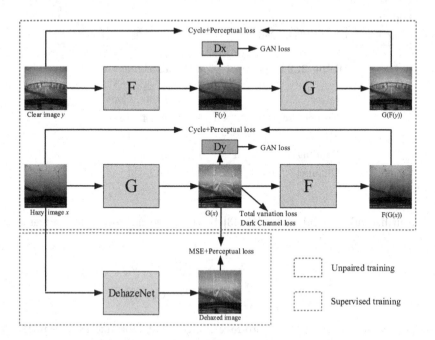

Fig. 2. The overview framework of our method, which contains the unpaired training module and the supervised training module. For the unpaired training module, we used CycleGAN and perceptual loss and some properties of the clear images to generate clearer dehazed images. For the supervised training module, we use the generated dehazed images from the unpaired training module as pseudo haze-free images to conduct supervised image dehazing training.

3.2 The Unpaired Training Module

We assume that the real hazy images belong to the X domain and the unpaired haze-free images belong to the Y domain. The purpose is to transform the X domain into the Y domain to obtain dehazed images. We set hazy image $x \in X$ and unpaired haze-free image $y \in Y$. We first train the dehazing network based on CycleGAN [43]. Our model contains generators G and F, where generator G denotes the mapping from the X domain to the Y domain and generator F denotes the mapping from the Y domain to the X domain. Our model also includes two discriminators, D_Y and D_X, where D_X is used to distinguish between hazy image x and generated hazy image $F(y)$ and D_Y is used to distinguish between haze-free image y and dehazed image $G(x)$.

Table 1. The parameters of the generator.

Layer	Conv	Conv	Conv	ResnetBlock (6)	UConv	UConv	Conv
Kernel size	7×7	3×3	3×3		3×3	3×3	7×7
Stride	1	2	2		2	2	1
Padding	0	1	1		1	1	0
Channel	64	128	256		128	64	3

Table 2. The parameters of the discriminator.

Layer	Conv	Conv	Conv	Conv	Conv
Kernel size	4×4	4×4	4×4	4×4	4×4
Stride	2	2	2	1	1
Padding	1	1	1	1	1
Channel	64	128	256	512 -	1

We utilize adversarial losses [11,43] to train the networks. The adversarial loss of G and D_Y is shown as Eq. (2),

$$L_{Adv}(G, D_Y) = \mathop{\mathbb{E}}_{y \sim p_{clear}(y)}[log D_Y(y)]$$
$$+ \mathop{\mathbb{E}}_{x \sim p_{hazy}(x)}[log(1 - D_Y(G(x)))], \tag{2}$$

where generator G attempts to produce images that look like images in the Y domain, and discriminator D_Y tries to differentiate $G(x)$ and y.

In the same way, the adversarial loss of F and D_X is shown as Eq. (3),

$$L_{Adv}(F, D_X) = \mathop{\mathbb{E}}_{x \sim p_{hazy}(x)}[log D_X(x)]$$
$$+ \mathop{\mathbb{E}}_{y \sim p_{clear}(y)}[log(1 - D_X(F(y)))], \tag{3}$$

where generator F attempts to produce images that look like images in the X domain, and discriminator D_x aims to differentiate $F(y)$ and x.

We utilize the cycle consistency loss [43] to constrain the GAN network, and the cycle consistency loss is shown in Eq. (4),

$$L_{Cycle} = \mathop{\mathbb{E}}_{x \sim p_{hazy}(x)}[||F(G(x)) - x||_1]$$
$$+ \mathop{\mathbb{E}}_{y \sim p_{clear}(y)}[||G(F(y)) - y||_1], \tag{4}$$

To preserve the sharpness of the dehazed images, we follow [8] and use cyclic perceptual-consistency loss to train the model, which is shown in Eq. (5),

$$L_{Per} = ||f(x) - f(F(G(x)))||_2^2$$
$$+ ||f(y) - f(G(F(y)))||_2^2, \tag{5}$$

where f are the features extracted from $relu1_2$, $relu2_2$ and $relu3_3$ of VGG-16 [32].

If the dehazed images have similar properties to the clear images, it indicates that the dehazing effect is better. Therefore, to make the dehazed images have similar properties to the clear images, we introduce the instinct properties of the clear images to further train the image dehazing network, such as the total variation and dark channel prior.

The total variation loss [30] is a gradient prior of dehazed image $G(x)$, which is shown in Eq. (6),

$$L_T = ||\alpha_h G(x)||_1 + ||\alpha_v G(x)||_1, \tag{6}$$

where α_h and α_v are the gradients in the horizontal direction and vertical direction, respectively.

The dark channel prior [12] is shown in Eq. (7), where $\Omega(i)$ represents the local neighborhood centered at pixel i and c represents the color channel.

$$J^{dark}(i) = \min_{j \in \Omega(i)} (\min_{c \in r,g,b} J^c(j)), \tag{7}$$

The dark channel loss [10] is shown in Eq. (8), and we use dark channel loss to constrain network training to obtain better dehazed images.

$$L_{Dark} = ||D(G(x))||_1. \tag{8}$$

For the unpaired training module, the total loss is L, as shown in Eq. (9),

$$L = \lambda_{Adv}(L_{Adv}(G, D_Y) + L_{Adv}(F, D_X)) \\ + \lambda_{Cycle} L_{Cycle} + \lambda_{Per} L_{Per} + \lambda_T L_T + \lambda_{Dark} L_{Dark}, \tag{9}$$

where λ_{Adv}, λ_{Cycle}, λ_{Per}, λ_T and λ_{Dark} are balanced parameters.

3.3 Supervised Training Module

Because real hazy image x does not have a paired haze-free image, supervised training cannot be carried out. How to train the image dehazing model in a supervised manner is a challenging problem. Therefore, we propose a supervised training module in this section. Specifically, we first obtain the dehazed image $G(x)$ from the unpaired training module, and then we use dehazed images as pseudo haze-free images for supervised training to further increase image dehazing performance. We use the commonly used MSE (mean square error) loss function for our supervised training, which can be expressed as:

$$L_{MSE} = \frac{1}{M} \sum_{i=1}^{M} ||x_i - G(x_i)||_2, \tag{10}$$

where M is the number of hazy images.

We also utilize perceptual loss to train the image dehazing model in a supervised manner, which can be expressed as:

$$L_{Per} = \frac{1}{M} \sum_{i=1}^{M} ||f(x_i) - f(G(x_i))||_2^2. \tag{11}$$

For the supervised training module, the total loss is L_s, which is shown in Eq. (12).

$$L_s = L_{MSE} + \lambda_{Sup} L_{Per}, \tag{12}$$

where λ_{Sup} is the balanced parameter.

4   Experimental Results

4.1   Datasets

For our experimental evaluation, we collect and organize a real hazy image dataset from a high-speed railway. We first shot a video of a high-speed train under hazy weather. Then, we take 2,000 training hazy images and 500 test hazy images, and we name this dataset the HRHI (High-speed Railway Hazy Images) dataset. We also collect 2,000 unpaired haze-free images for our experiment. Some samples of hazy images and unpaired haze-free images are shown in Fig. 3.

In addition, to verify the generality of our proposed method, we carry out many experiments on the D-HAZY [2] dataset that is synthesized based on the NYU-Depth [31] dataset and Middlebury [29] dataset. The D-HAZY dataset has 1,449 pairs of hazy images and haze-free images synthesized from the NYU-Depth dataset, but we follow [38] to shuffle randomly to simulate the unpaired images. Some samples of hazy images and haze-free images in this dataset are shown in Fig. 4.

To verify the versatility of our method, we also collect a real High-speed Railway Sandstorm Images (HRSI) dataset. Similar to the collection method of hazy images, we first shot a video of the high-speed train under sandstorm weather. Then, we take 1,700 training images and 200 test images. We also collected 2,000 sandstorm-free images for unpaired training, and some samples of sandstorm images and sandstorm-free images are shown in Fig. 5.

4.2   Implementation Details

To train our model, we use the Adam optimizer and perform 200 epochs. We set the learning rate to 0.0002 and experimentally set $\lambda_{GAN} = 1$, $\lambda_{Cycle} = 10$, $\lambda_{Per} = 1$, $\lambda_T = 0.001$, $\lambda_{Dark} = 0.1$ and $\lambda_{Sup} = 1$ for the HRHI dataset and set $\lambda_{AdvN} = 1$, $\lambda_{Cycle} = 10$, $\lambda_{Per} = 10$, $\lambda_T = 0.0001$, $\lambda_{Dark} = 1$ and $\lambda_{Sup} = 0.1$ for the D-HAZY and HRSI datasets.

Hazy image

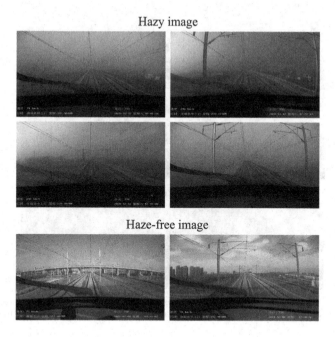

Haze-free image

Fig. 3. Some samples of hazy images and unpaired haze-free images in the HRHI dataset.

Fig. 4. Some samples of hazy images and unpaired haze-free images in the D-HAZY dataset.

Sandstorm image

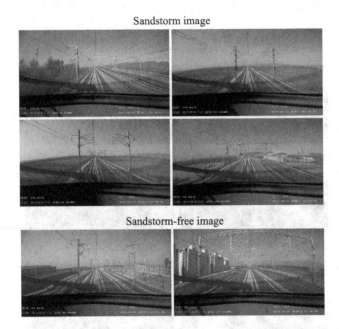

Sandstorm-free image

Fig. 5. Some samples of sandstorm images and unpaired sandstorm-free images in the HRSI dataset.

4.3 Evaluation Metrics

As there are no paired hazy and haze-free images, they cannot be evaluated by commonly used full-reference evaluation metrics, such as the peak signal-to-noise ratio (PSNR) [15] and structural similarity (SSIM) [36]. Therefore, we use no-reference evaluation metrics, such as BLIINDS [28] and NIQE [23], to evaluate image dehazing methods on real hazy images and sandstorm images. In addition, we also use qualitative comparison to compare image dehazing methods.

4.4 Experimental Results on Real Hazy Images

We compare our proposed method with other classic image dehazing methods, including semi-supervised image dehazing methods DA [30] and PSD [6], unsupervised image dehazing method DCP [12], unpaired image translation method CycleGAN [43] and unpaired image dehazing method CycleDehaze [8]. For the semi-supervised image dehazing methods DA and PSD, since it is impossible to train, we use the model trained by the authors to test directly on our test set, and it is the same for Table 5 and Table 7. For the unpaired methods CycleGAN and CycleDehaze, we reimplement the codes and retrain the models on our training set and then test them on our test set. Table 3 shows the experimental results on the HRHI dataset. Although our method does not use paired haze-free images to train the model but uses unpaired haze-free images, it is not only better than the semi-supervised image dehazing methods DA and PSD but also far superior to the unsupervised image dehazing method DCP. It is also better than the unpaired methods based on the BLIINDS metric. The experimental results show the effectiveness of our method.

Table 3. Experimental results on the HRHI dataset.

Method		BLIINDS	NIQE
DA [30]	Semi-supervised	16.29	6.20
PSD [6]		21.11	5.73
DCP [12]	Unsupervised	39.89	7.62
CycleGAN [43]		16.46	4.86
CycleDehaze [8]	Unpaired	15.76	4.83
Ours		13.60	4.98

To verify the validity of each part in our method, we performed ablation experiments on the HRHI dataset, as shown in Table 4. Adv_Cycle trains unpaired module using adversarial loss and cycle consistency loss. Adv_Cycle_Perceptual trains the unpaired module using adversarial loss, cycle consistency loss and perceptual consistency loss. Adv_Cycle_Perceptual_TV denotes using adversarial loss, cycle consistency loss, perceptual consistency loss and total variation loss. Adv_Cycle_Perceptual_TV_DC denotes using adversarial loss, cycle consistency loss, perceptual consistency loss, total variation loss and dark channel loss. Adv_Cycle_Perceptual_TV_DC+Supervised denotes our whole method. From Table 4, it can be seen that the total variation, the dark channel prior and the supervised training module are all helpful for image dehazing.

Table 4. Ablation study on the HRHI dataset.

Method	BLIINDS	NIQE
Adv_Cycle	16.46	4.86
Adv_Cycle_Perceptual	15.76	4.83
Adv_Cycle_Perceptual_TV	15.60	4.88
Adv_Cycle_Perceptual_TV_DC	15.37	4.87
Adv_Cycle_Perceptual_TV_DC+Supervised	13.60	4.98

The qualitative comparison on the HRHI dataset is shown in Fig. 6. The first column is real hazy images, the second to sixth columns are dehazed images generated by using other classic image dehazing methods, and the last column is the dehazed images generated by using our method. From this figure, it can be seen that the dehazed images generated from the semi-supervised image dehazing methods DA and PSD have color distortion. The unsupervised image dehazing method DCP not only has color distortion but also has a poor haze removal effect in the sky area. The dehazed images of our method are clearer and more natural.

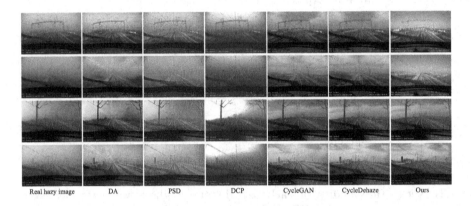

Real hazy image   DA   PSD   DCP   CycleGAN   CycleDehaze   Ours

Fig. 6. Qualitative comparison on the HRHI dataset.

4.5 Experimental Results on Generic Hazy Images

To prove the generality of our method, we carry out an experimental verification on public indoor hazy images of NYU-Depth [31] in the D-HAZY [2] dataset. As hazy images in this dataset have paired haze-free images, we can evaluate them by PSNR and SSIM. We follow CycleDehaze [8] and test our proposed method on all images of NYU-Depth in the D-HAZY dataset. We compare our method with other classic image dehazing methods, including supervised image dehazing methods CAP [44], MSCNN [27] and DehazeNet [5], semi-supervised image dehazing methods DA [30] and PSD [6], unsupervised image dehazing method DCP [12], unpaired image translation method CycleGAN [43] and unpaired image dehazing method CycleDehaze [8]. We copy the experimental results of other methods from reference CycleDehaze [8] except for methods DA and PSD. Table 5 shows the experimental results and we can see that our method is superior to supervised image dehazing methods CAP, MSCNN and DehazeNet, unsupervised image dehazing method DCP, semi-supervised image dehazing method PSD [6], and unpaired methods CycleGAN [43] and CycleDehaze [8]. Compared with the semi-supervised DA method and unpaired PID method, our method also obtains better results based on the PSNR metric and obtains comparable results based on the SSIM metric.

The ablation study on the D-HAZY dataset is shown in Table 6. It can be seen that the total variation, the dark channel prior and the supervised training

Table 5. Quantitative comparison of our method with other classic dehazing methods on the D-HAZY dataset.

Method		PSNR	SSIM
CAP [44]		12.78	0.70
MSCNN [27]	Supervised	12.26	0.70
DehazeNet [5]		12.84	0.71
DA [30]	Semi-supervised	16.21	0.81
PSD [6]		10.93	0.66
DCP [12]	Unsupervised	10.98	0.64
CycleGAN [43]		13.38	0.52
CycleDehaze [8]	Unpaired	15.41	0.66
PID [38]		15.54	0.77
Ours		16.63	0.76

module are beneficial to image dehazing in the D-HAZY dataset. Figure 7 shows the qualitative comparison on the D-HAZY dataset. The first column is the synthetic hazy images, and the second and third columns are the dehazed images generated by the DA and PSD methods. The fourth column shows the dehazed images generated by our method and the last column shows the ground truth haze-free images. From the visualized results, we can see that the dehazed images of our method have better visual effects and are closer to the haze-free images.

Table 6. Ablation study on the D-HAZY dataset.

Method	PSNR	SSIM
Adv_Cycle	14.68	0.60
Adv_Cycle_Perceptual	15.78	0.70
Adv_Cycle_Perceptual_TV	15.88	0.73
Adv_Cycle_Perceptual_TV_DC	16.57	0.76
Adv_Cycle_Perceptual_TV_DC+Supervised	16.63	0.76

4.6 Experimental Results on High-Speed Railways Sandstorm Images

We also carry out experiments on sandstorm images in the HRSI dataset and the experimental results are shown in Table 7, which demonstrates the effectiveness and versatility of our method. Figure 8 is the qualitative comparison on the HRSI dataset, from which we can see that the sandstorm removal effect of DA is not obvious, the color of generated images by the PSD method has changed, and our method produces more natural images.

Fig. 7. Qualitative comparison on the D-HAZY dataset.

Table 7. Ablation study on high-speed railway sandstorm images.

Method	BLIINDS	NIQE
DA [30]	15.06	5.11
PSD [6]	17.73	5.13
Adv_Cycle	16.09	5.22
Adv_Cycle_Perceptual	11.96	5.20
Adv_Cycle_Perceptual_TV	11.75	5.12
Adv_Cycle_Perceptual_TV_DC	14.37	5.08
Adv_Cycle_Perceptual_TV_DC+Supervised	10.78	5.23

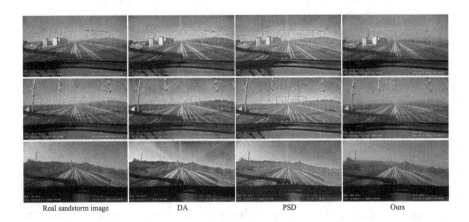

Fig. 8. Qualitative comparison on the HRSI dataset.

5   Conclusion

In this paper, we present an unpaired image dehazing method for real hazy images, which contains the unpaired training module and the supervised training module. For the unpaired training module, we first use CycleGAN to generate the dehazed image. Then, we utilize perceptual loss to make the features of the dehazed image and the unpaired haze-free image more consistent to promote image dehazing performance. Finally, we introduce the instinct properties of the clear images to further promote image dehazing performance. For the supervised training module, we propose constraining the dehazed images generated from the unpaired training module as pseudo haze-free images to conduct supervised training to further increase the performance. We carry out many experiments on real hazy image and public hazy image datasets and experiments on real sandstorm images, which demonstrates the versatility of our method.

Acknowledgement. This work is supported by the Talent Fund of Beijing Jiaotong University (2021RC266), National Natural Science Foundation of China (62106017), Beijing Natural Science Foundation (4232032) and China Postdoctoral Science Foundation (2021M690339, 2022T150042).

References

1. Efficient image dehazing with boundary constraint and contextual regularization. In: IEEE International Conference on Computer Vision, pp. 617–624 (2013)
2. Ancuti, C., Ancuti, C.O., Vleeschouwer, C.D.: D-hazy: a dataset to evaluate quantitatively dehazing algorithms. In: IEEE International Conference on Image Processing, pp. 2226–2230 (2016)
3. Arjovsky, M., Chintala, S., Bottou, L.: Wasserstein GAN (2017)
4. Berman, D., Treibitz, T., Avidan, S.: Non-local image dehazing. In: IEEE Conference on Computer Vision and Pattern Recognition, pp. 1674–1682 (2016)
5. Cai, B., Xu, X., Jia, K., Qing, C., Tao, D.: Dehazenet: an end-to-end system for single image haze removal. IEEE Trans. Image Process. **25**(11), 5187–5198 (2016)
6. Chen, Z., Wang, Y., Yang, Y., Liu, D.: PSD: principled synthetic-to-real dehazing guided by physical priors. In: IEEE Conference on Computer Vision and Pattern Recognition, pp. 7180–7189 (2021)
7. Donahue, J., Krähenbühl, P., Darrell, T.: Adversarial feature learning. arXiv preprint arXiv:1605.09782 (2016)
8. Engin, D., Gen, A., Ekenel, H.K.: Cycle-dehaze: Enhanced CycleGAN for single image dehazing. In: IEEE Conference on Computer Vision and Pattern Recognition Workshops, pp. 825–833 (2018)
9. Fan, G., Hua, Z., Li, J.: Multi-scale depth information fusion network for image dehazing. Appl. Intell. **51**(10), 7262–7280 (2021)
10. Golts, A., Freedman, D., Elad, M.: Unsupervised single image dehazing using dark channel prior loss. IEEE Trans. Image Process. **29**, 2692–2701 (2020)
11. Goodfellow, I.J., Pouget-Abadie, J., Mirza, M., Bing, X., Bengio, Y.: Generative adversarial nets. In: Neural Information Processing Systems, pp. 2672–2680 (2014)
12. He, K., Sun, J., Tang, X.: Single image haze removal using dark channel prior. In: IEEE Conference on Computer Vision and Pattern Recognition, pp. 1956–1963 (2009)

13. He, Z., Patel, V.M.: Densely connected pyramid dehazing network. IEEE Conference on Computer Vision and Pattern Recognition, pp. 3194–3203 (2018)
14. Hong, M., Xie, Y., Li, C., Qu, Y.: Distilling image dehazing with heterogeneous task imitation. In: IEEE Conference on Computer Vision and Pattern Recognition, pp. 3462–3471 (2020)
15. Huynh-Thu, Q., Ghanbari, M.: Scope of validity of PSNR in image/video quality assessment. Electron. Lett. **44**(13), 800–801 (2008)
16. Johnson, J., Alahi, A., Fei-Fei, L.: Perceptual losses for real-time style transfer and super-resolution. In: Leibe, B., Matas, J., Sebe, N., Welling, M. (eds.) Perceptual losses for real-time style transfer and super-resolution. LNCS, vol. 9906, pp. 694–711. Springer, Cham (2016). https://doi.org/10.1007/978-3-319-46475-6_43
17. Li, B., Peng, X., Wang, Z., Xu, J., Dan, F.: AOD-net: All-in-one dehazing network. In: IEEE International Conference on Computer Vision, pp. 4770–4778 (2017)
18. Li, L., Dong, Y., Ren, W., Pan, J., Gao, C., Sang, N., Yang, M.H.: Semi-supervised image dehazing. IEEE Trans. Image Process. **29**, 2766–2779 (2020)
19. Li, R., Pan, J., Li, Z., Tang, J.: Single image dehazing via conditional generative adversarial network. In: IEEE Conference on Computer Vision and Pattern Recognition, pp. 8202–8211 (2018)
20. Liu, M.Y., Tuzel, O.: Coupled generative adversarial networks. In: Advances in Neural Information Processing Systems, vol. 29 (2016)
21. McCartney, E.J.: Optics of the atmosphere: scattering by molecules and particles. New York (1976)
22. Mirza, M., Osindero, S.: Conditional generative adversarial nets. arXiv preprint arXiv:1411.1784 (2014)
23. Mittal, A., Fellow, I.E.E.E., Soundararajan, R., Bovik, A.C.: Making a 'completely blind' image quality analyzer. IEEE Signal Process. Lett. **20**(3), 209–212 (2013)
24. Qin, X., Wang, Z., Bai, Y., Xie, X., Jia, H.: FFA-net: feature fusion attention network for single image dehazing. In: Proceedings of the AAAI Conference on Artificial Intelligence, vol. 34, pp. 11908–11915 (2020)
25. Qu, Y., Chen, Y., Huang, J., Xie, Y.: Enhanced pix2pix dehazing network. In: IEEE Conference on Computer Vision and Pattern Recognition, pp. 8160–8168 (2019)
26. Ren, W., et al.: Gated fusion network for single image dehazing. In: IEEE Conference on Computer Vision and Pattern Recognition, pp. 3253–3261 (2018)
27. Ren, W., Liu, S., Zhang, H., Pan, J., Cao, X., Yang, M.-H.: Single image dehazing via multi-scale convolutional neural networks. In: Leibe, B., Matas, J., Sebe, N., Welling, M. (eds.) ECCV 2016. LNCS, vol. 9906, pp. 154–169. Springer, Cham (2016). https://doi.org/10.1007/978-3-319-46475-6_10
28. Saad, M.A., Bovik, A.C., Charrier, C.: Blind image quality assessment: a natural scene statistics approach in the DCT domain. IEEE Trans. Image Process. **21**(8), 3339–3352 (2012)
29. Scharstein, D., Hirschmüller, H., Kitajima, Y., Krathwohl, G., Westling, P.: High-resolution stereo datasets with subpixel-accurate ground truth. In: German Conference on Pattern Recognition, pp. 31–42 (2014)
30. Shao, Y., Li, L., Ren, W., Gao, C., Sang, N.: Domain adaptation for image dehazing. In: IEEE Conference on Computer Vision and Pattern Recognition, pp. 2808–2817 (2020)
31. Silberman, N., Hoiem, D., Kohli, P., Fergus, R.: Indoor segmentation and support inference from RGBD images. In: Fitzgibbon, A., Lazebnik, S., Perona, P., Sato, Y., Schmid, C. (eds.) ECCV 2012. LNCS, vol. 7576, pp. 746–760. Springer, Heidelberg (2012). https://doi.org/10.1007/978-3-642-33715-4_54

32. Simonyan, K., Zisserman, A.: Very deep convolutional networks for large-scale image recognition. In: International Conference on Learning Representations (2015)
33. Singh, M., Laxmi, V., Faruki, P.: Dense spatially-weighted attentive residual-haze network for image dehazing. Appl. Intell. **52**, 1–15 (2022)
34. Tan, R.T.: Visibility in bad weather from a single image. In: IEEE Conference on Computer Vision and Pattern Recognition, pp. 1–8 (2008)
35. Tarel, J.P., Hautière, N.: Fast visibility restoration from a single color or gray level image. In: IEEE International Conference on Computer Vision, pp. 2201–2208 (2009)
36. Wang, Z.: Image quality assessment: from error visibility to structural similarity. IEEE Trans. Image Process. **13**(4), 600–612 (2004)
37. Wu, H., et al.: Contrastive learning for compact single image dehazing. In: IEEE Conference on Computer Vision and Pattern Recognition, pp. 10551–10560 (June)
38. Yang, X., Xu, Z., Luo, J.: Towards perceptual image dehazing by physics-based disentanglement and adversarial training. In: American Association for Artificial Intelligence, vol. 32 (2018)
39. Yi, Z., Zhang, H., Tan, P., Gong, M.: DualGAN: unsupervised dual learning for image-to-image translation. In: IEEE International Conference on Computer Vision, pp. 2849–2857 (2017)
40. Yu, H., Li, X., Fan, C., Zou, L., Wu, Y.: MSDA: multi-scale domain adaptation dehazing network. Appl. Intell. **53**, 1–14 (2022)
41. Zhang, H., Sindagi, V., Patel, V.M.: Image de-raining using a conditional generative adversarial network. IEEE Trans. Circuits Syst. Video Technol. **30**(11), 3943–3956 (2019)
42. Zheng, Z., et al.: Ultra-high-definition image dehazing via multi-guided bilateral learning. In: IEEE Conference on Computer Vision and Pattern Recognition, pp. 16185–16194, June 2021
43. Zhu, J.Y., Park, T., Isola, P., Efros, A.A.: Unpaired image-to-image translation using cycle-consistent adversarial networks. In: IEEE International Conference on Computer Vision, pp. 2223–2232 (2017)
44. Zhu, Q., Mai, J., Shao, L.: A fast single image haze removal algorithm using color attenuation prior. IEEE Trans. Image Process. **24**(11), 3522–3533 (2015)

Read Pointer Meters Based on a Human-Like Alignment and Recognition Algorithm

Yan Shu[1,2], Shaohui Liu[2(✉)], Honglei Xu[2], and Feng Jiang[2]

[1] State Key Laboratory of Communication Content Cognition,
People's Daily Online, Beijing 100733, China
[2] Computer Science and Technology Department, Harbin Institute of Technology,
Harbin 150001, China
shliu@hit.edu.cn

Abstract. Recently, developing an automatic reading system for analog measuring instruments has gained increased attention, as it enables the collection of numerous types of equipment. Nonetheless, two major obstacles still obstruct its deployment to real-world applications. The first issue is that they rarely take the entire pipeline's speed into account. The second is that they are incapable of dealing with some low-quality images (i.e., meter breakage, blur, and uneven scale). In this paper, we propose a human-like alignment and recognition algorithm to overcome these problems. More specifically, a spatial transformed module (STM) is proposed to obtain the front view of images in a self-autonomous way based on an improved spatial transformer network (STN). Meanwhile, a value acquisition module (VAM) is proposed to infer accurate meter values by an end-to-end trained framework. In contrast to previous research, our model aligns and recognizes meters totally implemented by learnable processing, which mimics human behaviors and thus achieves higher performance. Extensive results verify the robustness of the proposed model in terms of accuracy and efficiency. The code and the dataset is available in https://github.com/shuyansy/Detect-and-read-meters.

Keywords: Analog measuring instruments · Pointer meters reading · Spatial Transformed Module · Value Acquisition Module

1 Introduction

In the complex industrial environment, there are harsh environments such as radiation, toxicity, and high temperature, and it is necessary to inspect the production conditions with the help of instruments to ensure safety [30]. Traditionally acquired data are typically read artificially by humans, who are capable of deriving precise readings from complex meters in a variety of shapes, forms, and styles, despite never having seen the meter in question. However, the manual method is always more labor intensive and time consuming. Therefore, it is

M. Zhang et al. (Eds.): CCF NCCA 2023, CCIS 1960, pp. 162–178, 2024.
https://doi.org/10.1007/978-981-99-8761-0_13

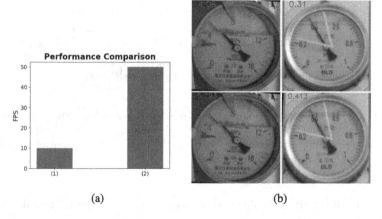

(a)   (b)

Fig. 1. (a) shows the efficiency of our STM (2) for meter alignment, which is 5 times faster than the conventional perspective transform method (1). (b) shows that our VAM (bottom line) can read more accurate values in some low-quality images than prior methods (top line).

of great practical significance to rely on inspection robots and computer vision technology [2,3,20,22] for automatic meter reading.

Substation meters are now classified as digital and pointers. While reading digital meters can be considered an OCR task and is relatively simple to accomplish using text spotting techniques [13,17,19,23], as demonstrated in Appendix A, reading pointer meters presents a different and more difficult problem: there are major visual changes between meter faces, the camera viewpoint has a significant effect on their depicted shape and numbering location, and the existence of shadows, meter breakage, and specular reflections adds to the pointer hands' perplexity. While this issue has been around for a long time, few previous solutions have been capable of reliably obtaining readings from meters, except in extremely limited circumstances. Additionally, it is difficult for researchers to work on this project due to the lack of reliable training and evaluation standards.

Existing automatic meter reading systems [1,8,18,33], according to relevant literature, include the following pipelines. To begin, the meter's pure area is detected using conventional neural network-based detection algorithms or image processing techniques; then, the captured target is aligned to a front view by the perspective transform method. Lastly, meter values can be obtained by meter component (the pointer and the scale) retrieval and meter number recognition. However, most of these methods suffer from two main problems. First, the alignment process is typically time-consuming due to its intricate point-matching steps, which hinders the overall efficiency of the system. Second, their reading model is not robust; it consists of isolated and independent modules for meter component retrieval and number recognition, which are unaware of their interdependence, resulting in poor accuracy. Therefore, "how to design an algorithm

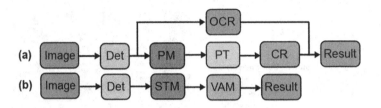

Fig. 2. Overview of previous pointer meter reading pipeline (a) compared to ours(b). "Det", "PM", "PT" and "CR" represent meter detection, point matching, perspective transform and component retrieval. "STM" and "VAM" are our spatial transformed module and value acquisition module.

for efficient alignment and robust recognition of pointer meters" remains largely unsolved.

To address these issues, we propose a novel human-like alignment and recognition algorithm that simplifies the meter reading pipeline, as shown in Fig. 2. To be more precise, we propose a novel spatial transformed module (STM) for alignment via implicitly learning homography transformation, which is heavily inspired by spatial transformer networks (STN) [9]. STM is more efficient at aligning meters than previous morphological conversion methods by discarding the point-matching process. Additionally, a value acquisition module (VAM) is established in a unified framework of meter component retrieval and meter number recognition, simulating the structure of an end-to-end text spotter. By excavating the relationship between the meter component and meter number, VAM can learn a richer representation and thus can read precise meter values from low-quality images. As shown in Fig. 1, on the MC1260 dataset we proposed, the FPS of STM is 50 FPS, which is 5 times faster than the conventional alignment method. Meanwhile, VAM can handle some difficult data, such as meter breakage, blur and uneven scale.

In this paper, we make the following contributions: (i) We design a unified framework involving detection, alignment and recognition stages. The detection can simply be an off-the-shelf object detection model. The alignment stage involves a deep neural network that introduces an improved STN to regress homography transformation parameters implicitly. At the recognition stage, we are the first to establish an end-to-end architecture to tightly couple meter component retrieval and meter number recognition, boosting both the accuracy and efficiency of pointer meter reading.

(ii) We propose a new benchmark dataset called the Meter Challenge (MC1296) which contains 1296 images captured in scene by automatic robots. MC1296 is organized in a tree structure, containing images, annotations and evaluation metrics for different tasks (meter detection, meter alignment, and meter recognition) from top to bottom.

(iii) Extensive experiments verify the effectiveness and robustness of the method we propose.

The rest of this paper is organized as follows. The related background knowledge is provided in Sect. 2, including the previous pointer meter reading pipelines, spatial transformer networks (STN) and end-to-end text spotting methods highly related to our work. Section 3 introduces the implementation process of the proposed method. In Sect. 4, the proposed method is verified by extensive simulation experiments and ablation studies. The conclusions of this paper are summarized in Sect. 5.

2   Related Works

We commence this section by reviewing major pointer meter reading frameworks. Additionally, we discuss the research on STN and end-to-end text spotting methods, which is highly relevant to our work.

2.1   Pointer Meter Reading Frameworks

Numerous advances [1,2,6,8,18,21,32,33] have been made in the reading of pointer meters over the last few years. The existing frameworks are generally divided into three stages: meter detection, meter alignment, and meter recognition. Traditional algorithms [21] such as template matching and the table lookup method are used in meter detection. To address this issue with complex backgrounds, some object detection methods, such as Faster R-CNN [18], have been introduced. To calibrate the camera angle to obtain a front view image, perspective transform techniques [18,33] are applied by calculating the transformation matrix determined by point matching. Image processing methods [27] also propose using the image subtraction method or the Hough transform algorithm to extract the pointer for meter recognition. Additionally, machine learning and deep learning are used to improve reading accuracy. Liu et al. [15] used SVM to separate meters, while He et al. [6] improved the Mask R-CNN [4] method for pointer segmentation. Then, the final values can be determined by calculating the pointer angle and meter number output.

The majority of the aforementioned approaches are able to read pointer meters, but few of them can balance accuracy and speed due to complex postprocessing in meter alignment [18] or inadequate visual representations in meter recognition [15].

2.2   Spatial Transformer Networks (STN)

This is in contrast to the conventional perspective transform method, which explicitly calculates the transformation matrix. STN [9] introduces a novel learnable module that enables spatial manipulation of data within the network. STN is advantageous for a wide variety of computer vision tasks due to its efficiency and flexibility. ASTER [26] consists of a rectification network and a recognition network that can deal with text that is distorted or has an irregular layout.

Lee et al. [11] propose image-and-spatial transformer networks (ISTNs) for downstream image registration optimization. Additionally, Yang et al. [31] introduce a clock alignment architecture based on STN, which motivates us to develop a more efficient meter alignment module.

2.3   End-to-End Text Spotters

To spot texts in images, a straight two-stage idea is proposed to cascade existing detectors and recognizers sequentially. However, due to the lack of complementarity between the detector and recognizer, they suffer from low efficiency and accuracy. To mitigate this problem, an end-to-end trainable neural network for text spotting is attempted, with state-of-the-art performances achieved. Li et al. [12] first built a unified end-to-end work that simultaneously localizes and recognizes text with a single forward pass, with positive results achieved in a horizontal text spotting task. Benefiting from the convolution sharing strategy, FOTS [16] and EAA [7] pool multioriented text regions from the feature map by designing RoI rotate and text-alignment layers, respectively. Unfortunately, few researchers have incorporated end-to-end text spotters into their pointer meter recognition frameworks.

Our work is structured similarly to existing frameworks for pointer meter reading. To increase the applicability of previous work, we replace the traditional perspective transform method with an improved STN and then create an end-to-end meter recognition module for meter component retrieval and meter number recognition.

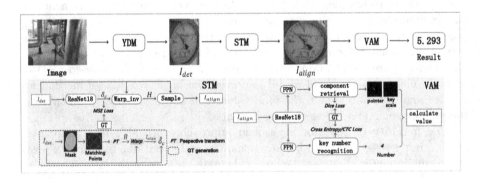

Fig. 3. The proposed framework of the pointer meter recognition. YDM can detect meter targets and crop meter regions into STM, where aligned views can be obtained. VAM can output meter values accurately and efficiently.

3   Methods

The purpose of this paper is to design an algorithm for the efficient alignment and robust recognition of pointer meters. To achieve this goal, we establish a unified framework, which is shown in Fig. 3. Our proposed architecture accepts an image as input and then performs detection, alignment, and recognition sequentially. It is worth noting that our STM (see Sect. 3.2) can directly transform the detected meter into an aligned view without any postprocessing steps. Meanwhile, the VAM (see Sect. 3.3) we proposed can learn rich visual representation by excavating the relationship between component retrieval and number recognition.

3.1 Meter Detection

Cropping meter regions prior to recognition is necessary to eliminate background interference. To accomplish this, some traditional image processing techniques, such as Hough circle detection and template matching, are used, both of which have shortcomings in some low-quality images. At the moment, object detection networks are used to detect and crop the meter, as follows.

$$I_{det} = \Phi_{det}(I; \Theta_{det}) \in \mathbb{R}^{3 \times h \times w} \tag{1}$$

where I is the given unlabelled image, while Φ_{dec} and Θ_{dec} represent the detecting function and learnable parameters, respectively.

The detector, defacto, can be performed using any off-the-shelf object detector. However, to reduce the efficiency cost and handle some small meter targets, we propose a YOLO-based detection module (YDM) based on YOLO-v5 [29], which has achieved state-of-the-art performance in many tasks. To achieve better performance in our tasks where data are scarce and the target is small, we apply a multiscale training strategy and artificially augment the images by copy-pasting some small objects. The performance of YDM can be seen in Sect. 4.

3.2 Meter Alignment

Motivation. The detected pure meter image could be directly passed to a module for reading recognition. This is typically not ideal for two reasons: first, due to the limitations of the localization module; and second, even when the meter is properly localized, it can be hard to read at times due to viewpoint interference. Previous methods apply a direct perspective transform to calibrate the camera angle to obtain a front view image, as shown in the following:

$$(x, y, w') = (u, v, w) \cdot T = (u, v, w) \cdot \begin{bmatrix} a_{11} & a_{12} & a_{13} \\ a_{21} & a_{22} & a_{23} \\ a_{31} & a_{32} & a_{33} \end{bmatrix} \tag{2}$$

$$\begin{aligned} (X, Y) &= (\frac{x}{w'}, \frac{y}{w'}) \\ (U, V) &= (\frac{u}{w'}, \frac{v}{w'}) \end{aligned} \tag{3}$$

where (U, V) represents the coordinate of a point in the original image, (X, Y) is the coordinate of the corresponding point in the transformed image, and (u, v, w) and (x, y, w') are the homogenous space representations of (U, V)

and (X, Y), respectively. By matching four feature points between two images, the transform matrix T is determined. Their methods, however, suffer primarily from complex point matching algorithms, which are time-consuming and not very robust. This drives us to design a more efficient and stronger module for meter alignment.

Revisiting Vanilla STN. Different from the perspective transform which calculates the transformation matrix by point matching, the STN can transform the detected meter to a fronto-paralleled view by learned homography transformation parameters. Specifically, given the output I_{det} of YDM, STN establishes mapping by predicting homography transformation H with 8 degrees of freedom, and ϕ_{sam} represents the Differentiable Image Sampling (DIS) operation to obtain the canonical view of I_{det} by bilinear interpolation:

$$H = \Phi_{stn}(I_{det}) \in \mathbb{R}^{3 \times 3}$$
$$I_{align} = \Phi_{sam}(I_{det}, H) \in \mathbb{R}^{3 \times h \times w} \tag{4}$$

Therefore, how to predict accurate homography transformation H is a key issue.

Spatial Transformed Module (STM). It is a direct idea to regress H given ground truth $\hat{H}$ in a supervised way. Nonetheless, based on our major findings and rigorous testing, the deep network fails to learn the explicit parameter of H for the following reasons: (i) The training data are limited to the deep CNN's huge parameters; (ii) H's parameters have a large range of values, making the regression difficult to optimize. To circumvent these problems, we model the implicit spatial transformation relationship between images instead of regressing H directly.

Specifically, for a $\hat{I}_{det}$ in the training set, we first annotate its inner dial region with a binary mask map. Then, for various meter forms, we match four pairs of feature points to determine the real $\hat{H}$. For an irregular ellipse, the endpoints of the major axis and minor axis are utilized as the initial points, while the corresponding points are defined by the intersection of the major axis, the minor axis, and the circumcircle. For a rectangular shape, the $\hat{H}$ can be calculated by mapping the vertices of the rectangle directly to the vertices of the image. Then, we can obtain the aligned image $\hat{I}_{align}$ by perspective transform:

$$\hat{I}_{align} = warp(\hat{I}_{det}, \hat{H}) \tag{5}$$

The vertex coordinate offsets $\hat{\delta}_c$ between $\hat{I}_{det}$ and $\hat{I}_{align}$ can be obtained, which is the training objective of STM implemented by mean-squared (MSE) loss:

$$L_{align} = \sum_i (\delta_{ci} - \hat{\delta}_{ci})^2 \tag{6}$$

where i is the index of coordinates. Therefore, the STM algorithm can be adjusted as follows:

$$\delta_c = \Phi_{stm}(I_{det}) \in \mathbb{R}^{4 \times 2}$$

$$H = warp\_inv(I_{det}, I_{det} + \delta_c) \in \mathbb{R}^{3 \times 3} \qquad (7)$$

$$I_{align} = \Phi_{sam}(I_{det}, H) \in \mathbb{R}^{3 \times h \times w}$$

In our training process, we use ResNet18 [5] to extract the feature of I_{det}, and by the propagation of the network, accurate H and canonical images can be acquired.

3.3 Meter Recognition

Overall Design. What is the best way to read meters like a human? Key meter elements such as the pointer, scales, and number were predicted in previous methods to achieve this goal. However, they tended to create independent modules to handle different components and numbers, resulting in a suboptimal solution for meter recognition. We propose a unified framework called the value acquisition module (VAM) that consists of a meter component retrieval branch and meter number recognition branch to excavate a deep relationship between them. As illustrated in Fig. 3, we apply ResNet18 as the backbone and create two separate feature merging modules to form a pair of complementary branches. Specifically, upsampling and pixelwise addition are used to fuse intermediate layers of ResNet. VAM allows these two diametrically different tasks to benefit from each other by disentangling weight sharing and introducing a mirror symmetry of FPN [14]. Ablation studies are demonstrated in Sect. 4.

Meter Component Retrieval Branch. We retrieve the meter component (meter pointer and key scales) using semantic segmentation methods that are heavily inspired by the Mask R-CNN [4]. The branch generates two 1-channel segmentation maps, namely, the Pointer Map and the Key Scale Map, by performing two distinct 1×1 convolutional operations on the backbone features. The Pointer Map indicates the location of the meter's pointer, whereas the Key Scale Map indicates its angle. The Pointer Map and Key Scale Map are both trained by minimizing the Dice loss:

$$L_{pm} = 1 - \frac{2 \sum_i P_{pm}(i) G_{pm}(i)}{\sum_i P_{pm}(i)^2 + \sum_i G_{pm}(i)^2}$$

$$L_{ksm} = 1 - \frac{2 \sum_i P_{ksm}(i) G_{ksm}(i)}{\sum_i P_{ksm}(i)^2 + \sum_i G_{ksm}(i)^2} \qquad (8)$$

where pm and ksm represent Pointer Map and Key Scale Map, respectively, and $P_{(.)}(i)$ refers to the value of ith pixel in the predicted result, while $G_{(.)}(i)$ refers to the value of pixel i^{th} in the GT region.

The final loss for the meter component retrieval branch is a weighted combination of the two maps, balanced by $\lambda \in (0, 1)$ as

$$L_{com} = \lambda L_{PointerMap} + (1 - \lambda)L_{KeyScaleMap} \tag{9}$$

In our experiments, we set λ to 0.4, assigning more importance to the key scale map, which is relatively difficult to learn in the training process due to its small spatial occupation.

Meter Number Recognition Branch. Previous methods recognize numbers in meters with another system, which poses severe memory waste and low efficiency. In our VAM, the meter number recognition branch resembles like the standard text spotters, which is mentioned in Sect. 2. To further boost the inference speed, we only detect the key number in the meter, the one closest to the number '0', and then recognize it with the assistance of feature sampling.

The key number detection task is deemed a text classification task, in which one convolution is applied to output dense per-pixel predictions of the key number localization. The key number bounding box can be obtained by the minimum bounding rectangle operation. Meanwhile, to overcome the class imbalance problem, we introduce online hard example mining (OHEM) [28] to better distinguish between number areas and backgrounds, in which the balanced factor is set to 3 in our work. The set of positive elements selected by OHEM in the score map is ω, and the loss function for key number detection can be formulated as:

$$
\begin{aligned}
L_{num\_det} &= \frac{1}{\| \Omega \|} \sum_{x \in \Omega} Cross\_Entropy(p_x, p_x^*) \\
&= \frac{1}{\| \Omega \|} \sum_{x \in \Omega} (-p_x^* log p_x - (1 - p_x^*) log(1 - p_X))
\end{aligned} \tag{10}
$$

where $\| \cdot \|$ means the number of elements in a set, and the p_x and p_x^* are the predicted pixel and the ground truth label, respectively.

The feature sampling layer aims to convert detected feature regions into fixed-size outputs from which an RNN-based sequence recognizer can be established. We introduce RoI rotate in [17] to our work, which can transform the rotated area into a fixed-size region via max-pooling and bilinear interpolation. Similar to but distinguished from STN, RoI rotate gets affine transformation via an unsupervised way, resulting in a more general operation for extracting features for regions of interest. To improve recognition performance, we use only ground truth key number regions during training rather than predicted number regions.

Given the transformed number feature, we first permute key number features $F \in \mathbb{R}^{C \times H \times W}$ into 2D sequence feature $L \in \mathbb{R}^{C \times W}$ in several sequential convolutions, which has the same configurations as CRNN [25]. Then, for each time step $t = 0, 1, \ldots, T + 1$, we feed $l_1, \ldots, l_w \in L$ into bidirectional LSTM, with $D = 256$ output channels per direction, which can be formulated as follows:

$$
\begin{aligned}
h_t' &= f(x_t, h_{t-1}') \\
y_t &= \varphi(h_t') = softmax(W_0 h_t')
\end{aligned} \tag{11}
$$

where $f()$ is the recurrence formulation, h_t is the hidden state at time step t, and the W_0 linearly transforms hidden states to the output space of size 12, including 10 Arabic numerals and a token representing ".", and a special END token. Finally, a CTC layer is applied to align the predicted sequence to the label sequence. Following [25], the recognition loss can be formulated as

$$L_{num\_reco} = -\frac{1}{N} \sum_{n=1}^{N} log p(y_n^* \mid x) \qquad (12)$$

where N is the number of number regions in an input image, and y_n^* is the recognition label.

Training Procedure and Inference. VAM is a unified module that can be trained end-to-end. The overall loss function can be calculated as follows:

$$L = L_{com} + L_{num\_det} + L_{num\_reco} \qquad (13)$$

In our inference process, binarized score maps for pointer and key scale are first obtained by applying the threshold algorithm $\lambda = 0.5$. Then, a thinning algorithm is applied to turn the pointer into a straight line segmentation, and the Hough line transform is used to obtain the position of the pointer. Meanwhile, the key scale centers can be localized by calculating the average pixel position within the closed area. Finally, the meter reading is calculated by the angle method, which is given by

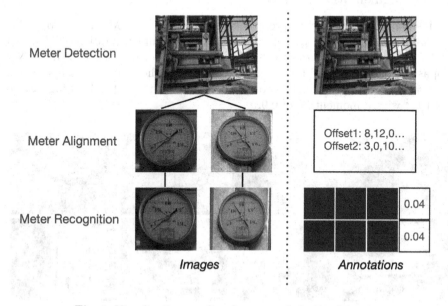

Fig. 4. Visualization results of one sample in the dataset.

$$Result = \frac{\alpha_1}{\alpha_2} \times num\_rec \qquad (14)$$

where α_1 is the angle between the pointer and the zero scale and α_2 is the angle between the zero scale and the key scale. The num_rec is the output of the meter number recognition branch, and then the reading of the meter is completed automatically.

4   Experiments

4.1   Datasets

To our knowledge, there have been no publicly available and appropriate benchmarks for this task. As a result, we created a new dataset called Meter Challenge (MC1296), which contains 1296 images of scenes captured by automated robots. To help the model adapt to its natural environment, the dataset includes complex backgrounds, multiple scales, a variety of viewpoint angles, and a variety of meter shapes. To better fit the meter reading task, we organized the dataset into a tree structure, with each level representing a distinct task (meter detection, meter alignment, and meter recognition), complete with associated images, annotations, and evaluation metrics. Figure 4 illustrates some visualization results, while Table 1 contains summary statistics.

4.2   Implementation Details

In this paper, the system we propose consists of YDM, STM, and VAM. YDM has similar configurations to [29], so we focus on the implementation of STM and VAM. Specifically, for both of modules we use ResNet pretrained in ImageNet [10] as the backbone, and the image size is 640 and the training batch size is 8. We use Adam to optimize the two networks and set the initial learning rate to 1×10^{-4} with a momentum of 0.9.

Fig. 5. Qualitative results of the meter detection, where the yellow bounding box indicates the pointer meter and the green bounding box indicates the digital meter. "ID-num" is the detection confidence. (Color figure online)

Table 1. Statistics of the proposed MC 1260 dataset. "mb", "co", and "psn" represent the meter bounding box, coordinate offsets, and pointer/scale/number mask and number, respectively.

Dataset_task	Train_size	Test_size	Annotations
M_detection	1036	260	mb
M_alignment	1028	247	co
M_reading	739	185	psn

Meanwhile, some basic data augmentation techniques are applied, such as random cropping, random rotation, and brightness contrast. Our experiment is conducted on one general GPU(GTX-1080), with the environment PyTorch 1.5.0.

Table 2. The quantitative results of different methods for meter detection.

Model	AP50 (%)	AP75 (%)	FPS
Liu et al. [18]	91.3	89.5	4.3
YOLO [24]	90.0	88.2	6.7
Ours	98.6	97.1	12.4

Fig. 6. Qualitative results of the meter alignment, where the top row is the original images, and the middle row and the bottom row are the transformed images generated by the STN and STM. Note that the STN cannot handle images with extremely large camera angles.

4.3   Meter Detection Results

To disentangle the effects of YDM, we begin by reporting the dataset's meter detection results. To conform to the object detection literature, we report the average precision (AP) at two different bounding box IoU thresholds, AP50 and AP75. AP50 denotes the average precision for IoU thresholds greater than 0.5, while AP75 denotes the average precision for IoU thresholds greater than 0.75. As shown in Table 2, the meter detection task is relatively successful. To demonstrate the advantages of our method, we compare it to a commonly used YOLO algorithm [24] and the method in [18], which demonstrates that our YDM performs better in terms of accuracy and efficiency. The qualitative results are demonstrated in Fig. 5, which shows that TDM can detect meters with different shapes and sizes.

4.4   Meter Alignment Results

To demonstrate the STM's availability and robustness in the recognition system, we conducted extensive experiments on the validation dataset, comparing it to the traditional perspective transform method and STN. Figure 6 illustrates the qualitative findings. As seen, the image can be easily and automatically transformed into a front-viewing image using STM, regardless of the camera angle. However, due to the limited learning capability of pure STN, it is difficult to align the meter in terms of some extremely large camera angles.

Table 3. The quantitative results of different methods for meter alignment. "rel" is the average relative error, and "ref" is the average reference error.

Method	Rel (%)	Ref (%)	FPS
None	5.91	1.20	–
Perspective transform [18]	1.72	0.23	10
STN [9]	3.40	0.95	44
STM	1.70	0.26	50

Additionally, as shown in Table 3, we conducted ablation studies to demonstrate its superiority by demonstrating inference speed and influence on the meter recognition task. Note that the average relative error and the average reference error are the evaluation metrics used to represent the meter recognition error rate, which will be discussed in detail in Sect. 4.5. It can be seen that STM contributes to reducing the recognition error rate, as it allows meters to be read from various angles and sizes. Our STM also achieves competitive accuracy to perspective transform while increasing inference speed, indicating that STM achieves a more favorable trade-off between accuracy and efficiency.

Table 4. The quantitative results of different methods for meter reading recognition. "Rel" is the average relative error, and "Ref" is the average reference error.

Method	Avenue	Rel (%)	Ref (%)
Zheng et al. [33]	Measurement (2016)	10.32	0.91
Gao et al. [2]	ICRAS (2017)	9.34	0.67
He et al. [6]	ICIST (2019)	1.85	0.30
Liu et al. [18]	Measurement (2020)	1.77	**0.24**
Ours	–	**1.70**	0.26

4.5 Meter Recognition Results

To demonstrate our method's recognition performance, we incrementally compare it to other methods. To minimize interperson variability in readings, the readings obtained by human vision are the average of the results of twenty expert workers. Meanwhile, to make the comparison fairer, we follow similar evaluation metrics as [6]. Specifically, we choose the average relative error $\hat{\Theta}$ and the average reference error $\hat{\Gamma}$ as evaluation indicators, as shown in the following:

Fig. 7. Some visualization results produced by our method. The red line is the predicted pointer line, the blue points are the key scale areas, and the meter reading results are shown in the top left. (Color figure online)

$$\hat{\Theta} = \frac{\sum_{i=1}^{n} \frac{|p_i - g_i|}{g_i}}{n} \times 100\%$$

$$\hat{\Gamma} = \frac{\sum_{i=1}^{n} \frac{|p_i - g_i|}{R}}{n} \times 100\%$$

$$(15)$$

where p_i is the predicted meter value, and g_i is the ground truth value. R represents the meter's range, and n represents the total number of experimental data. As shown in Table 4, our method outperforms previous methods in terms of average relative error and achieves competitive results with [18] in average reference error, indicating that our algorithm has a strong capacity in reading recognition. Additionally, our method can perform inference at a rate of approximately 25 frames per second, demonstrating that it is practical for real-world applications. We show some visualization results in Fig. 7, demonstrating our method's high adaptability to a complex environment with variable illumination, scale, and image tilt.

To disentangle the effects of the unified framework VAM, we conduct ablation studies to investigate the relationships between the meter component retrieval and meter numbering recognition branches. We begin by reporting the full model's end-to-end results in Table 5. Notably, we evaluate pointer/key scale detection and key number recognition using the AP50 and number-level accuracy recognition metrics, respectively. It can be demonstrated that by optimizing all loss functions simultaneously, our model achieves a reasonable level of success in detection and recognition tasks. Additionally, we construct a two-stage model in which the meter component retrieval and meter number recognition branches are trained independently. The meter component retrieval network is built by removing the meter number recognition branch, and similarly, the meter number recognition network is built by removing the meter component retrieval branch from the original network. Our proposed VAM outperforms the two-stage method by a significant margin in both the meter component retrieval and meter number recognition tasks. The results indicate that our joint training strategy accelerated the convergence of the model parameters.

Table 5. Ablation studies on VAM. "MCRB" and "MNRB" represent that we only train the meter component retrieval branch or meter number recognition branch.

Method	pointer_det (%)	key scale_det (%)	key number_reco (%)
VAM	95.6	93.2	88.7
MCRB	93.1	90.5	–
MNRB	–	–	87.2

5 Conclusion

We propose a novel method for accurate and efficient pointer meter reading, which is implemented by the YDM, STM, and VAM equipment. Specifically, STM can obtain the front view of images autonomously with the improved STN, and VAM can recognize meters accurately with unified frameworks with the combination of the meter component retrieval branch and meter number recognition branch. Experiments on the challenging datasets we proposed demonstrate that the proposed method has a strong capacity for pointer meter reading. Currently, the algorithm has been successfully applied to robots performing substation inspections. Future work will concentrate on model acceleration to develop a more efficient framework for video meter reading.

Funding Information. This work was supported in part by the National Key Research and Development Program of China under Grants 2020YFB1406902 and A12003.

References

1. Cai, W., Ma, B., Zhang, L., Han, Y.: A pointer meter recognition method based on virtual sample generation technology. Measurement **163**, 107962 (2020)
2. Gao, J.W., Xie, H.T., Zuo, L., Zhang, C.H.: A robust pointer meter reading recognition method for substation inspection robot. In: 2017 International Conference on Robotics and Automation Sciences (ICRAS), pp. 43–47. IEEE (2017)
3. Guo, R., Han, L., Sun, Y., Wang, M.: A mobile robot for inspection of substation equipments. In: 2010 1st International Conference on Applied Robotics for the Power Industry, pp. 1–5. IEEE (2010)
4. He, K., Gkioxari, G., Dollár, P., Girshick, R.: Mask R-CNN. In: Proceedings of the IEEE International Conference on Computer Vision, pp. 2961–2969 (2017)
5. He, K., Zhang, X., Ren, S., Sun, J.: Deep residual learning for image recognition. In: Proceedings of the IEEE Conference on Computer Vision and Pattern Recognition, pp. 770–778 (2016)
6. He, P., Zuo, L., Zhang, C., Zhang, Z.: A value recognition algorithm for pointer meter based on improved mask-RCNN. In: 2019 9th International Conference on Information Science and Technology (ICIST), pp. 108–113. IEEE (2019)
7. He, T., Tian, Z., Huang, W., Shen, C., Qiao, Y., Sun, C.: An end-to-end textspotter with explicit alignment and attention. In: 2018 IEEE/CVF Conference on Computer Vision and Pattern Recognition, pp. 5020–5029 (2018)
8. Hou, L., Qu, H.: Automatic recognition system of pointer meters based on lightweight CNN and WSNS with on-sensor image processing. Measurement **183**, 109819 (2021)
9. Jaderberg, M., Simonyan, K., Zisserman, A., et al.: Spatial transformer networks. Adv. Neural Inf. Process. Syst. **28** (2015)
10. Krizhevsky, A., Sutskever, I., Hinton, G.E.: ImageNet classification with deep convolutional neural networks. Adv. Neural Inf. Process. Syst. **25** (2012)
11. Lee, M.C.H., Oktay, O., Schuh, A., Schaap, M., Glocker, B.: Image-and-spatial transformer networks for structure-guided image registration. In: Shen, D., et al. (eds.) MICCAI 2019. LNCS, vol. 11765, pp. 337–345. Springer, Cham (2019). https://doi.org/10.1007/978-3-030-32245-8_38
12. Li, H., Wang, P., Shen, C.: Towards end-to-end text spotting with convolutional recurrent neural networks. In: 2017 IEEE International Conference on Computer Vision (ICCV), pp. 5248–5256 (2017)
13. Liao, M., Lyu, P., He, M., Yao, C., Wu, W., Bai, X.: Mask TextSpotter: an end-to-end trainable neural network for spotting text with arbitrary shapes. IEEE Trans. Pattern Anal. Mach. Intell. **43**, 532–548 (2021)
14. Lin, T.Y., Dollár, P., Girshick, R., He, K., Hariharan, B., Belongie, S.: Feature pyramid networks for object detection. In: Proceedings of the IEEE Conference on Computer Vision and Pattern Recognition, pp. 2117–2125 (2017)
15. Liu, K.: Recognition of the analog display instrument based on deep learning. Master's thesis (2017)
16. Liu, X., Liang, D., Yan, S., Chen, D., Qiao, Y., Yan, J.: FOTS: fast oriented text spotting with a unified network. In: 2018 IEEE/CVF Conference on Computer Vision and Pattern Recognition, pp. 5676–5685 (2018)

17. Liu, X., Liang, D., Yan, S., Chen, D., Qiao, Y., Yan, J.: FOTS: fast oriented text spotting with a unified network. In: Computer Vision and Pattern Recognition (2018)

18. Liu, Y., Liu, J., Ke, Y.: A detection and recognition system of pointer meters in substations based on computer vision. Measurement **152**, 107333 (2020)

19. Liu, Y., Chen, H., Shen, C., He, T., Jin, L., Wang, L.: ABCNet: real-time scene text spotting with adaptive Bezier-curve network. arXiv: Computer Vision and Pattern Recognition (2020)

20. Lu, S., Zhang, Y., Su, J.: Mobile robot for power substation inspection: a survey. IEEE/CAA J. Automatica Sinica **4**(4), 830–847 (2017)

21. Mo, W., Pei, L., Huang, Q., Zhang, Y., Fu, W., Zhao, Y.: Development of automatic verification system for high precision pointer instrument based on template. Electr. Meas. Instrum. **54**(12), 100–105 (2017)

22. Park, J.Y., Lee, J.K., Cho, B.H., Oh, K.Y.: An inspection robot for live-line suspension insulator strings in 345-kv power lines. IEEE Trans. Power Delivery **27**(2), 632–639 (2012)

23. Qin, S., Bissacco, A., Raptis, M., Fujii, Y., Xiao, Y.: Towards unconstrained end-to-end text spotting. In: Proceedings of the IEEE/CVF International Conference on Computer Vision (ICCV), October 2019

24. Redmon, J., Divvala, S., Girshick, R., Farhadi, A.: You only look once: unified, real-time object detection. In: Proceedings of the IEEE Conference on Computer Vision and Pattern Recognition, pp. 779–788 (2016)

25. Shi, B., Bai, X., Yao, C.: An end-to-end trainable neural network for image-based sequence recognition and its application to scene text recognition. IEEE Trans. Pattern Anal. Mach. Intell. **39**(11), 2298–2304 (2016)

26. Shi, B., Yang, M., Wang, X., Lyu, P., Yao, C., Bai, X.: ASTER: an attentional scene text recognizer with flexible rectification. IEEE Trans. Pattern Anal. Mach. Intell. **41**(9), 2035–2048 (2018)

27. Shi, J., Zhang, D., He, J., Kang, C., Yao, J., Ma, X.: Design of remote meter reading method for pointer type chemical instruments. Process Autom. Instrum. **35**(5), 77–79 (2014)

28. Shrivastava, A., Gupta, A., Girshick, R.: Training region-based object detectors with online hard example mining. In: Proceedings of the IEEE Conference on Computer Vision and Pattern Recognition, pp. 761–769 (2016)

29. Thuan, D.: Evolution of yolo algorithm and yolov5: the state-of-the-art object detection algorithm (2021)

30. Tsai, M.C., Ko, P.J.: On-line condition monitoring of servo motor drive systems by HHT in Industry 4.0. J. Chinese Inst. Eng. **40**(7), 572–584 (2017). https://doi.org/10.1080/02533839.2017.1372219

31. Yang, C., Xie, W., Zisserman, A.: It's about time: analog clock reading in the wild. arXiv preprint arXiv:2111.09162 (2021)

32. Zhang, X., Dang, X., Lv, Q., Liu, S.: A pointer meter recognition algorithm based on deep learning. In: 2020 3rd International Conference on Advanced Electronic Materials, Computers and Software Engineering (AEMCSE), pp. 283–287. IEEE (2020)

33. Zheng, C., Wang, S., Zhang, Y., Zhang, P., Zhao, Y.: A robust and automatic recognition system of analog instruments in power system by using computer vision. Measurement **92**, 413–420 (2016)

Network Communication and Security

A Prioritized Channel Access and Adaptive Backoff Mechanism for WBAN

Qingling Liu and Qi Wang[✉]

Harbin Engineering University, 145 Nantong Street, Nangang District, Harbin, Heilongjiang, China
wq_5841@163.com

Abstract. The IEEE 8202.15.4 standard, known for its low power consumption and short range communication, is ideally suited for use in wireless body area network (WBAN), which is facing energy scarcity problems. However, it is unable to differentiate data priorities during operation and cannot be adaptively adjusted according to the state of the nodes. Therefore, this paper proposes an alternative combination of priority-based channel access and adaptive backoff mechanism. Firstly, the high-priority data can be accessed after the first clear channel assessment (CCA) without going through two CCAs. Secondly, a fuzzy logic algorithm is used to quantify the state of the nodes based on the node residual energy ratio and the buffer residual space ratio, and the initialisation parameters of the backoff mechanism are adjusted according to the real-time state and priority of the nodes. Simulation results show that the proposed strategy has better performance in terms of network lifetime, throughput, packet delivery rate and average end-to-end delay, and can effectively ensure the transmission of high-priority data.

Keywords: IEEE 8202.15.4 · Wireless Body Area Network · Backoff Mechanism · Clear Channel Assessment

1 Introduction

Population aging is becoming a pressing issue that the world needs to face. According to the projections of the United Nations Department of Economic and Social Affairs (UNDESA), by 2050, people aged 65 and over will account for one-sixth of the world's population [1]. Population aging will not only bring about a shortage of labor force but also have a significant impact on today's medical and social security systems. Due to the deterioration of physical function, older adults are usually more susceptible to chronic non-communicable diseases such as hypertension, heart disease, and diabetes [2]. For chronic diseases, the key is to take reasonable preventive measures based on one's own physical condition. Therefore, there is an urgent need for portable physical health monitoring infrastructure to achieve real-time monitoring of physical condition, detect potential health problems as early as possible, and ensure the health needs of the elderly and chronic disease patients.

With the continuous advancement of microelectronics and sensor technology, WBAN, a subfield of Wireless Sensor Network (WSN), is widely used in the field

© The Author(s), under exclusive license to Springer Nature Singapore Pte Ltd. 2024
M. Zhang et al. (Eds.): CCF NCCA 2023, CCIS 1960, pp. 181–202, 2024.
https://doi.org/10.1007/978-981-99-8761-0_14

of healthcare, where it can work with biosensors attached to the body's surface, outside the body or even implanted inside the body to obtain real-time physiological information such as heart rate, body temperature, blood pressure and EEG. This information is transmitted via wireless channels to healthcare professionals and users to assist them with disease prediction, diagnosis and health assessment, and to prevent accidents from occurring. It enables people to respond to sudden illnesses more quickly, avoiding missing the optimal treatment time, and has great potential for application in the healthcare industry [3].

However, WBAN still faces some issues, one of which is the lack of energy [4]. As WBAN is deployed on the human body, the biometric sensors it uses must be powered by limited batteries. For implanted sensors, replacing the battery is challenging and may cause harm to the body. Accordingly, ensuring the network lifetime of WBAN and improving its energy efficiency as much as possible is a problem that needs to be addressed. In addition, as the number of WBAN users and devices per unit area increases, the collision problem between WBAN devices becomes more severe [5]. Hence, how to schedule channel resources reasonably and ensure the QoS of WBAN is also a problem that needs to be considered. Thus, WBAN requires a suitable MAC mechanism to support its efficient operation.

IEEE 802.15.4 [6] is a communication standard designed for short-range, low-power communication devices. Its superframe can be divided into active and inactive periods, during the inactive periods, devices will enter sleep mode to conserve energy. Additionally, this standard uses a contention-based CSMA-CA mechanism for channel access, which effectively avoids collisions between devices, making it highly suitable for use in WBAN. But the MAC mechanism of IEEE 802.15.4 standard suffers from the inability to prioritise data and to adjust in real-time according to the network situation. Therefore, this paper proposes a differentiated priority MAC mechanism based on the slotted CSMA-CA [7] mechanism in the IEEE 802.15.4 standard beacon mode to accommodate the working requirements of WBAN. The main contributions of this paper are as follows:

Adjustment of channel access mechanism. Using the same scheduling method for different heterogeneous data in the WBAN-oriented IEEE 802.15.4 MAC mechanism may lead to high delay of high-priority data, therefore the channel access mechanism needs to be changed. Let the nodes delivering high priority data access the channel after the first CCA, while nodes transmitting lower priority data must go through two CCAs according to the standard protocol before accessing the channel, in order to reduce the delay of high priority data.

Adjustment of Backoff Mechanism. Firstly, adjust the initial Backoff Exponent (BE) and the maximum number of Backoff attempts (MaxCSMABackoffs) for nodes transmitting high priority data to increase the probability of accessing the channel and avoid loss of high priority data. Secondly, for nodes transmitting normal priority data, use a fuzzy logic algorithm to quantify their status based on the remaining energy and buffer space ratios, and dynamically modify the initial BE and the MaxCSMABackoffs based on the current status, in order to achieve the goals of energy saving and fast congestion relief.

Simulation validation. The performance of the proposed strategy is simulated and validated using a star topology under NS2 software. Performance metrics such as throughput, network lifetime, packet delivery rate and average end-to-end delay of the proposed mechanism are tested at different number of nodes to test the performance of the proposed scheme.

The rest of this paper is organized as follows. Section 2 discusses related works of MAC mechanism for WBAN, Sect. 3 briefly introduces the MAC mechanism of the IEEE 802.15.4 standard. Section 4 describes the proposed method. Section 5 summarizes and analyzes the experimental results, and the conclusion in Sect. 6.

2 Related Works

The tasks of the MAC layer include allocating resources such as communication time and frequency, managing the transmission and reception of data frames, maintaining link relationships between nodes, and implementing security protection mechanisms [8]. In a WBAN system, the MAC layer is responsible for managing and controlling the time spent by a group of biosensor devices accessing a shared communication channel. By optimising the channel resource allocation process, the QoS requirements of WBAN systems in terms of energy efficiency, throughput, fairness and delay can be met [9]. Therefore, the design and optimisation of the WBAN MAC layer is critical to improving network efficiency and reliability. According to the different policies used by MAC protocols, there are three types of MAC protocols, namely scheduling-based MAC protocols, contention-based MAC protocols and hybrid MAC protocols (see Fig. 1).

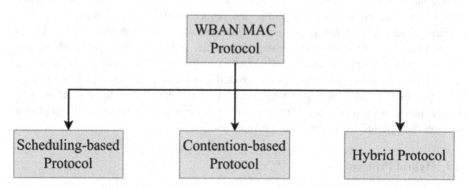

Fig.1. The classification of WBAN MAC protocol.

2.1 A Scheduling-Based Protocol

In a scheduling-based MAC protocol, each device waiting for data transmission at a predefined time slot or based on predicted times without competition to avoid collisions. One of the most used scheduling-based MAC protocols is Time division multiple access (TDMA), which allows multiple biosensor devices to share communication resources on a single communication channel without any form of interference. The HBD-MAC protocol based on the TDMA approach is proposed in [10] to improve the energy efficiency of sensor nodes. The protocol uses the human heartbeat as the synchronisation signal instead of periodic synchronisation beacons to avoid the energy consumption generated by the periodic transmission of the beacons. Although this method has good results in terms of energy saving, it suffers from high delay and is less able to cope with unexpected emergencies. Boudargham et al. [11] proposed a hybrid dynamic TDMA and Code Division Multiple Access (CDMA) technology to meet the transmission needs of different types of data. In this scheme, slots are dynamically allocated to each node using TDMA techniques, while nodes carrying delay-sensitive data are coded differently for them via CDMA techniques, allowing them to share the same slots and ensuring their low latency requirements. Experiments have proven that the proposed strategy has better performance in high traffic scenarios.

2.2 Contention-Based Protocol

A contention-based MAC protocol is a scheme that allows multiple devices to gain access to a radio channel in a competitive manner [12]. A contention-based protocol is more flexible, robust and simple than a scheduling-based protocol. Carrier sense multiple access protocol with collision avoidance (CSMA/CA) [13] and Aloha protocol are typical representatives of this type of protocol. Most existing contention-based MAC protocols are based on the ideas of these two aforementioned protocols. For example, an Aloha-based MAC protocol for wearable monitoring systems is presented in [14], which aims to reduce the frequency of packets sent to save energy and reduce delay. The algorithm uses a sleep and wake mechanism that can effectively reduce synchronisation costs, avoid idle listening and eavesdropping, and reduce implementation complexity, thus ensuring scalability and low packet error rates. In addition, the algorithm is well adapted to the needs of both normal and emergency traffic. In [15], a MAC protocol suitable for WBAN was proposed based on CSMA/CA technology. This protocol controls the number of acknowledgment packets transmitted to achieve a different blocking strategy from CSMA/CA. Additionally, during operation, the protocol classifies nodes based on their contention window size and transmission power to identify nodes with urgent data to meet the demand for urgent data transmission.

2.3 Hybrid Protocol

The hybrid MAC protocol is a combination of a scheduling-based MAC protocol and a contention-based MAC protocol [16]. In [17], the authors proposed a new MAC protocol for WBAN by combining TDMA and CSMA/CA. Under this protocol, two modes of operation are defined for the biosensor and the coordinator, one for receiving and the other for transmitting. When a biosensor is in the transmit mode, it competes for channel through CSMA/CA mechanism. The mode transition of the biosensor is controlled by a beacon frame sent by the coordinator to reduce energy consumption. It was estimated to improve the energy efficiency to some extent, however network scalability is still an issue to be considered. The Hybrid Multichannel MAC (HMC-MAC) protocol proposed by the authors [18] aims to reduce the possible interference and collisions between WBANs.

By using a mixture of CSMA/CA and TDMA protocols, the protocol allows different WBAN devices to transmit data simultaneously on different radio channels, thus reducing the possibility of collisions. Also, the protocol provides an efficient channel selection scheme to achieve low energy consumption and high throughput. The channel-aware polling-based MAC protocol (CPMAC), proposed by Yu et al. [19], aims to address the shortcomings of the sleep-wake scheduling mechanism used in traditional static sensor networks and to improve the efficiency of its application in WBANs. The CPMAC is implemented by adjusting the superframe polling cycle to accommodate complex traffic and channel fluctuations to maximise energy efficiency. However, the simple wake-up strategy of CPMAC can not ensure fast and reliable data transmission and may lead to delays and instability in data transmission.

3   IEEE 802.15.4 MAC Mechanism Overview

The IEEE 802.15.4 standard is a low-data-rate protocol that supports group data transmission rates between 20 kbps to 250 kbps and can operate in multiple frequency bands to meet different application requirements. Devices in a network that employs the IEEE 802.15.4 mechanism can be divided into two types: Full Function Devices (FFD) and Reduced Function Devices (RFD). In each network that operates under this standard, an FFD must be included as a network coordinator. The IEEE 802.15.4 MAC layer has two optional modes for controlling channel access: beacon-enabled mode and non-beacon-enabled mode [20]. This paper mainly focuses on the beacon-enabled mode.

3.1 Superframe Structure

In beacon-enabled mode, the network coordinator divides the channel into time slots within each superframe, which is a periodic frame with a start and end marked by beacon frames, serving as a delimiter between adjacent superframes. Each superframe consists of two parts: an active part and an inactive part. Sensor nodes only transmit data during the active part while they go into sleep mode to conserve energy during the inactive part. The active part of the superframe can be further divided into the contention access period (CAP) and contention-free period (CFP), the latter being optional and immediately following the CAP, consisting of two guaranteed time slots (GTS) with a maximum of seven time slots (see Fig. 2).

The superframe is defined by two parameters: the beacon order (BO) and superframe order (SO). The duration between two consecutive beacon frames, also known as the beacon interval (BI), is determined by BO and can be calculated by Eq. 1. The duration of the active part of the superframe, also known as the superframe duration (SD), can be calculated by Eq. 2 and its length depends on the value of SO. The duty cycle of the superframe is defined as the ratio of the active part to the total length of the superframe, which is the ratio of SD to BI, and can be represented by Eq. 3. Therefore, the duty cycle can be changed by adjusting the values of SO and BO, both of which are less than or equal to 14 in the IEEE 802.15.4 standard, with BO being necessarily not more than to SO.

$$BI = aBaseSuperFrame \times 2^{BO} \qquad (1)$$

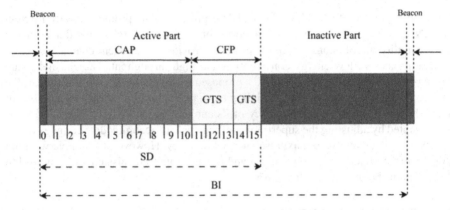

Fig. 2. The structure of superframe.

$$SD = aBaseSuperFrame \times 2^{SO} \tag{2}$$

$$DutyCycle = \frac{SD}{BI} \tag{3}$$

3.2 Slotted CSMA-CA Mechanism

In beacon-enabled mode, CAP uses the slotted CSMA-CA protocol. In slotted CSMA-CA, the node needs to maintain three parameters: Number of Backoffs (NB), Contention Window (CW) and Backoff exponent (BE). Before accessing the channel, the three parameters are first initialized, generally CW is initialized to 2, NB has an initial value of 0, and BE is relatively complex, when Battery Life Extension (BLE) flag is set to true, the initial value of BE will choose the smaller of 2 and macMinBE, and when BLE is set to false it is set to macMinBE. Afterwards When the node competes for the channel, it needs to choose a random number based on the value of BE to perform backoff. After completing backoff, the sensor node will perform CCA to check if the channel is idle, and if the channel is idle, it will subtract CW by one and perform CCA again, and if the channel is found to be occupied in either of the two CCAs, it will reset the value of CW and increase the NB and BE to perform backoff again until the channel is successfully accessed or the BE and NB reach the maximum value. For the IEEE 802.15.4 standard, the maximum value of NB is typically 5, which means that a device can perform up to 5 CSMA/CA processes in a single channel access attempt. The upper limit of BE, aMaxBE, also has a value of 5. Then, when BLE is false, the optional backoff periods available to the node during each round of backoff are 0–7, 0–15, 0–31, 0–31, and 0–31, which indicates that the optional backoff periods during the last three rounds of CSMA-CA are the same.

3.3   Channel Access Mechanism

The MAC mechanism in the IEEE 802.15.4 standard uses two consecutive CCAs for channel condition detection, which we refer to as the channel access mechanism. The CCA mechanism in the IEEE 802.15.4 standard uses energy detection, carrier sensing or a combination of both to detect whether the channel is busy. The two CCAs are achieved by decrementing CW. If the channel is detected to be idle after the first CCA, the node performs a second CCA to ensure that the transmission channel is completely idle. In this paper, CW decreases from 2 to 1 for the first stage CCA, and when CW decreases from 1 to 0 for the second stage CCA, the channel can only be occupied for data transmission when both stage CCAs detect that the channel is idle. With this channel access mechanism, nodes perform two consecutive channel detections before accessing the channel, minimising the possibility of collisions. However, successive CCAs also increase packet transmission delays and affect channel utilisation, which is not suitable for delay-sensitive data.

4   Proposed Work

WBAN acquires physiological data from the human body through biosensors. The data acquired by different sensors is heterogeneous and has varying degrees of importance. Therefore, different resource allocation methods need to be employed to ensure the transmission of high-priority data. In response to the problem that the IEEE 802.15.4 MAC mechanism for WBAN cannot differentiate data priority and cannot adaptively adjust according to network conditions, this paper proposes a channel access mechanism that distinguishes priority and an adaptive backoff mechanism.

4.1   Prioritised Channel Access Mechanism

Before accessing the channel under the slotted CSMA-CA mechanism, two CCA checks are required, which means that the channel must be detected as idle twice by the nodes before they can access the channel. Studies have shown that performing multiple channel checks has a positive effect on improving network throughput, but it also increases data delay. This is not a problem for regular priority data, but high priority data requires low delay. Therefore, to achieve a balance in network performance and maximize the transmission of high priority data, different scheduling and channel access mechanisms should be used for different priority levels of data.

This paper only considers the classification of WBAN data into high priority and regular priority. High priority data is more delay-sensitive than regular priority data. To ensure low-delay transmission of high priority data, the source node responsible for transmitting high priority data will immediately seize the channel if it detects the channel is idle after the first CCA. Regular priority data, on the other hand, needs to access the channel after two CCA stages using the original algorithm. The channel access mechanism that distinguishes data priority is implemented by first determining the data type before initializing the value of CW. If the data type is high priority, the initial value of CW is set to 1 to ensure its low-delay requirements. Conversely, if it is regular priority data, CW is initialized to 2 according to the original algorithm. Table 1 shows the initialization of CW for different priority data.

Table 1. CW values for data of different priorities.

Priority	Value of CW
High priority	1
Regular priority	2

4.2 Adaptive Backoff Mechanism

In the MAC mechanism of the IEEE 802.15.4 standard, the traditional backoff mechanism is based on exponential backoff, with the backoff range being from 0 to, and the range of BE values is between macMinBE and aMaxBE. Generally, the value of macMinBE is 3 and the value of aMaxBE is 5. When BE reaches the maximum value, it no longer increases unless the backoff count reaches MaxCSMABackoffs, in which case packet loss will be chosen. Research has shown that the channel access probability of nodes is negatively correlated with macMinBE. When the number of nodes in the network is constant, the smaller the macMinBE, the higher the probability of nodes accessing the channel, and the delay will be relatively smaller. In addition, the larger the MaxCSMABackoffs, the smaller the probability of data being discarded. Therefore, this paper proposes an adaptive backoff mechanism by taking into account the differences in network performance requirements for different priority data to achieve energy efficiency, rapid congestion relief, and ensure the transmission of high-priority data.

For High Priority Data. High priority data has high requirements for delay and packet delivery rate, so it needs to access the channel with shorter delay and higher probability. Additionally, it is necessary to minimize packet loss. Therefore, nodes carrying high-priority data require a larger number of backoff retries, which means that smaller values of macMinBE and larger values of MaxCSMABackoffs should be selected. In the improved backoff mechanism described in this paper, different values of macMinBE and MaxCSMABackoffs are set first according to the priority level of the data. For high priority data, the value of macMinBE is set to 0 to ensure the highest probability of accessing the channel, and to achieve a high packet delivery rate, the maximum number of backoff retries, MaxCSMABackoffs, is set to the default value plus 1.

For Regular Priority Data. Regular priority data is less delay demanding and accepts some degree of packet loss, therefore, our goal for transmitting regular priority data is to achieve energy efficiency and enable the MAC mechanism to adjust adaptively according to the network status. When initializing the backoff parameters for nodes that carry regular priority data, the current state of the regular priority node will be quantified based on the remaining energy and congestion level of the node. Different values of macMinBE and MaxCSMABackoffs will be assigned based on the node's state to achieve adaptive adjustment of the backoff mechanism, thereby achieving the goal of energy efficiency and rapid congestion reduction. Fuzzy logic algorithm [21] is used to implement the quantification of the state of regular priority data nodes. As shown in Fig. 3, this is a schematic diagram of a commonly used two-input single-output fuzzy controller. Before using the fuzzy controller, it is necessary to determine the input variables, output variables, fuzzy rules between the inputs and outputs, and the membership functions for each input and output variable based on the labels in the diagram.

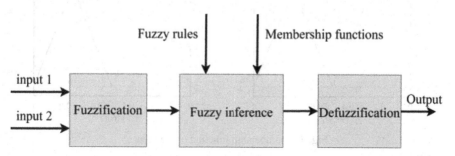

Fig. 3. Fuzzy controller diagram.

Inputs. In this paper, energy and congestion level of nodes are chosen as inputs for fuzzy control to achieve quantification of node status, and to achieve the goals of energy conservation and fast congestion relief. Since different nodes in a WBAN may have different hardware characteristics, these two parameters need to be normalized first to ensure fairness in scheduling different nodes. Normalization of the two parameters is performed by Eqs. 4 and 5, respectively.

$$E_r(i) = \frac{RE(i)}{IE(i)} \tag{4}$$

In the Equation, $RE(i)$ represents the current remaining energy of the node i, while $IE(i)$ represents the initial energy of the node i, which is the total energy allocated at the beginning. $E_r(i)$ represents the current remaining energy ratio, which serves as the input 1 of the fuzzy controller.

$$Br(i) = \frac{L_{init}(i) - L_{cur}(i)}{L_{init}(i)} \tag{5}$$

In Eq. 5, $L_{init}(i)$ refers to the maximum capacity of the buffer, $L_{cur}(i)$ refers to the current queue length of the buffer, and $Br(i)$ represents the normalized congestion level, which we call the buffer remaining space ratio. $Br(i)$ is the input 2 of the fuzzy controller.

Fuzzification. In fuzzy control, it is necessary to fuzzify the input precise data. Fuzzification is the process of converting clear and accurate data into fuzzy and inaccurate data. In the fuzzification process, precise data needs to be mapped to one or more fuzzy subsets for fuzzy logic operations. Fuzzification can be achieved through some membership functions, such as triangle functions, trapezoidal functions, Gaussian functions, etc. These functions can transform actual data into a membership degree between 0 and 1, indicating the degree to which the data belongs to a fuzzy subset. In this paper, we adopt the triangle membership function to fuzzify the remaining energy ratio of nodes and the remaining buffer space ratio (see Fig. 4), which displays the membership functions of the two inputs.

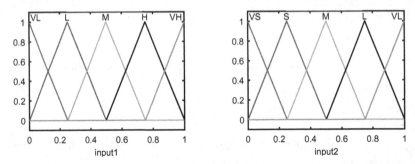

Fig. 4. Membership function of the input.

In the figure, five fuzzy sets are defined for each input, namely, Very Low (VL), Low (L), Medium (M), High (H), and Very High (VH) for the remaining energy ratio, and Very Small (VS), Small (S), Medium (M), Large (L), and Very Large (VH) for the fuzzy sets of remaining buffer space. Fuzzification involves taking two precise numerical inputs and calculating the degree of membership for each fuzzy set using a membership function.

Fuzzy Inference. Fuzzy inference refers to the process of inferring the output variable based on fuzzy rules between input and output variables, considering the membership of each fuzzy set. Prior to conducting fuzzy inference, fuzzy rules describing the logical relationship between input and output variables need to be defined. Table 2 shows the fuzzy rules used in this paper, which is composed of fuzzy subsets of inputs and output.

As shown in the table, there are five output fuzzy subsets: VB, B, M, G, and VG, which represent very bad, bad, moderate, good, and very good node status, respectively. Fuzzy rules can be described in natural language, for example, when the remaining energy and remaining space are both very low, the node condition is very bad. When the node condition is very bad, the values of macMinBE and MaxCSMABackoffs need to be reduced to save energy and ease congestion. This rule corresponds to the first column of the second row in the Table 2.

After defining fuzzy rules, fuzzy inference is required. In this paper, the Mamdani method is used for fuzzy inference, which uses the minimum operator to calculate the output membership degrees. For instance, if the membership degrees of two input parameters on fuzzy subsets VL and VS are 0.3 and 0.6 respectively, the membership degree of the output on VB is 0.3. In the Mamdani inference method it is necessary to take the union of all output fuzzy subsets and their affiliation values to obtain the result of the whole fuzzy inference (see Fig. 5). In the figure, the corresponding membership degrees of the input 1 on fuzzy subsets M and H, after fuzzification, are 0.75 and 0.25, denoted as M(0.75) and H(0.25), respectively. After fuzzification of the input 2, S(0.4) and M(0.6) are obtained. Based on the fuzzy rules, when input 1 is M(0.25) and input 2 is M(0.75), the output is M(0.6), which is represented in the figure as taking the height of

Table 2. Fuzzy rules.

Input1 Input 2	VL	L	M	H	VH
VS	VB	VB	B	B	M
S	VB	B	B	M	M
M	B	B	M	G	G
L	B	M	G	G	VG
VL	M	M	G	VG	VG

0.6 and cutting off the top of the membership function corresponding to the fuzzy subset M, and taking the shaded part. For other input combinations, the output membership degrees are M(0.25), B(0.4), and G(0.25), respectively, and their corresponding shaded blocks are obtained. Finally, the union of all results of fuzzy inference is taken to obtain the complete result.

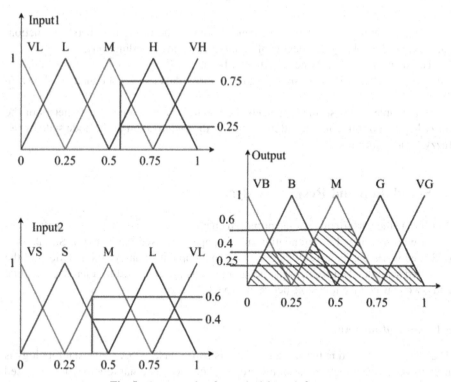

Fig. 5. An example of mamdani fuzzy inference.

Defuzzification. The result of fuzzy inference must be transformed into precise quantities in order to be used as instructions for the controller. In this paper, this means obtaining specific quantized values for the node state. The centroid method is a commonly used method for defuzzification, which uses the horizontal coordinate value of the centroid of the shaded area in Fig. 5 as the result of defuzzification. Mathematically, the centroid method is to calculate the weighted average of the membership function as the clear value of the output, as shown in Eq. (6).

$$v_0 = \frac{\int v\mu_v(v)dv}{\int \mu_v(v)dv} \tag{6}$$

In the Equation, v_0 is the precise result of the output after resolving ambiguity, and $\mu(v)$ is the membership function. Equation (6) can be discretized to Eq. (7) for ease of calculation.

$$v_0 = \frac{\sum\limits_{j=1}^{n} v_j\mu(v_j)}{\sum\limits_{j=1}^{n} \mu(v_j)} \tag{7}$$

In the equation, v_j represents the central point value of the membership function, and $\mu(v_j)$ is the value of the degree of membership corresponding to v_j.

The quantized value of node state can be obtained by fuzzy logic algorithm, and the adaptive backoff mechanism of regular priority data can be obtained, as shown in Table 3.

In the table, the first line represents the update of the two input parameters of the fuzzy logic algorithm, the second line refers to the quantization of the node state by the fuzzy logic algorithm.

5   Simulation and Results Analysis

To validate the performance of the proposed channel access and adaptive backoff mechanism with prioritized differentiation in this paper, we used the Network Simulator 2 (NS2) network simulation software to perform comparative analysis simulations of the proposed scheme, the original scheme, and the scheme proposed in reference [22] that adds two consecutive idle slots between two CCA stages.

5.1   Simulation Setup

The NS2 version used in the simulation in this paper is NS2.35, and the star topology is used to verify the effectiveness of the proposed method. The star topology is composed of a network coordinator node and several sensor nodes, among which the coordinator node is the sink node in WBAN. The topology diagram is shown in Fig. 6.

In the simulation, the initial energy of each sensor node is set to 50 J, while the initial energy of the coordinator node is set to 100 J because it needs to undertake more

Table 3. The adaptive backoff mechanism of regular priority data.

1: Update the RE(i) and Br(i);
2: Sta(i)=Fuzzy(RE(i),Br(i));
3: if (Sta(i)<=0.25)
4:    macMinBE=1;
5:    MaxCSMABackoffs-=2;
6: else if (0.25<Sta(i)<=0.45)
7:    macMinBE=2;
8:    MaxCSMABackoffs-=1;
9: else
10:    macMinBE=3;
11:    MaxCSMABackoffs=5;
12: endif

tasks. Due to the limited bandwidth resources available for the WBAN, conflicts may occur when devices per unit area increase, resulting in decreased network performance. Therefore, in order to verify the effectiveness of the proposed mechanism, this paper takes the number of sensor nodes in the network as variables, and sets the number of sensor nodes as 4, 6, 8, 10 and 12 respectively to conduct simulation experiments to test the performance of three different MAC mechanisms. In addition, set the size of node packets to 1000 bytes, WBAN-oriented IEEE 802.15.4 network coordinator to start receiving packets after the network initialization of 20 s, set both BO and SO to 4, and simulation time to 250 s. Due to the randomness of channel access and backoff mechanism, there are many irregularity in wireless media. The simulation is carried out for many times, and the results are averaged. Some other simulation parameters are shown in Table 4.

5.2 Simulation Results and Analysis

This paper compares the performance of the three MAC mechanisms from the aspects of network lifetime, network throughput, packet arrival rate and average end-to-end delay, and focuses on the comparison of packet arrival rate and average end-to-end delay of high-priority data, so as to verify the adaptability of the method proposed in this chapter to heterogeneous data transmission.

Network Lifetime. Network lifetime is the time when the energy of the first node is exhausted, which also becomes the stable period of the network [23]. The later the first

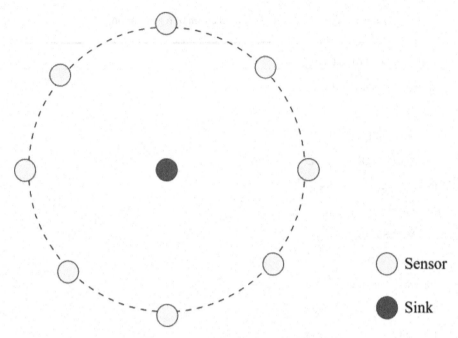

Fig. 6. Star Topology Diagram Used in Simulation.

Table 4. Parameters used during simulation.

Parameter	Value
Radio band	2.4 GHz
Network interface type	WirelessPhy
IfqType	Queue/DropTail/PriQueue
IfqLen	50
Data generation interval	0.05 s
Traffic Generator	CBR
Transmission power	0.9 J
Receiving power	0.5 J
Idle power	0.2 J
Sleeping power	0.05 J
aUnitBackoffPeriod	20Symbols

node dies, the more stable the network will be. Figure 7 shows the discounted graph of the network lifetime changing with the number of nodes obtained from the analysis of trace files after simulation, where the horizontal axis is the number of nodes and the vertical axis is the network lifetime.

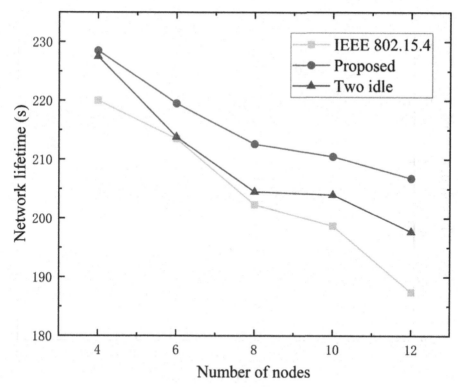

Fig. 7. The simulation results of network lifetime.

Proposed in the figure refers to the strategy proposed in this paper, and Two idle refers to the scheme of inserting two idle slots between two CCA stages. As can be seen from the figure, no matter which mechanism is used, when the number of nodes increases, the nodes tend to die earlier. This is because when there are more nodes, due to the limited spectrum resources, the intensity of competition between nodes will increase, and more collisions and retransmissions will occur, thus consuming more energy. However, no matter how many nodes there are, the mechanism proposed in this paper always performs better than the other two in terms of network lifetime. This is because the mechanism proposed in this paper firstly schedules data of different priorities differently, which reduces conflicts to a certain extent. Secondly, when nodes are low in energy and high in congestion, the scheduling mode is changed to save energy. The premature death of the node is avoided.

Network Throughput. Throughput refers to the amount of data successfully received by the sink node within a unit time. Figure 8 shows the simulation result of network throughput.

From the graph, it can be seen that as the number of nodes increases, the network throughput of all three mechanisms first increases and then decreases. The reason for the initial increase in network throughput is that as the number of nodes increases, the number of source nodes in the network also increases, resulting in an increase in throughput.

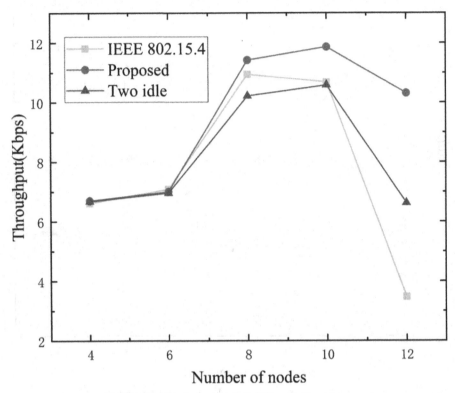

Fig. 8. The simulation results of network throughput.

However, when the number of nodes reaches a certain amount, the increase in collisions causes many data packets to be unable to access the channel due to competition, leading to a decrease in throughput. However, the mechanism proposed in this paper, except for a slightly weaker performance or no significant difference in throughput compared to the other two mechanisms with fewer nodes, shows significantly better throughput than the other two mechanisms as the number of nodes increases. Moreover, when the number of nodes grows even larger, the decrease in throughput is not as drastic as with the other two mechanisms. This is because the differentiated priority scheduling alleviates the severity of competition to some extent, reduces packet loss, and the adaptive backoff mechanism adjusts the backoff method based on the node's state, allowing nodes with a larger occupancy rate of buffer data packets to access the channel first, further avoiding packet loss and reducing the severity of the decrease in throughput.

Packet Delivery Rate. The packet arrival rate refers to the proportion of packets successfully reaching the destination node that were sent from the source node. Figure 9 shows a simulation data analysis graph of the packet arrival rate for three different MAC mechanisms.

As can be seen from the figure, the packet delivery rate of the three different mechanisms is negatively correlated with the number of nodes. The reason for this is that when the number of nodes increases, due to the limited channel resources, more nodes will

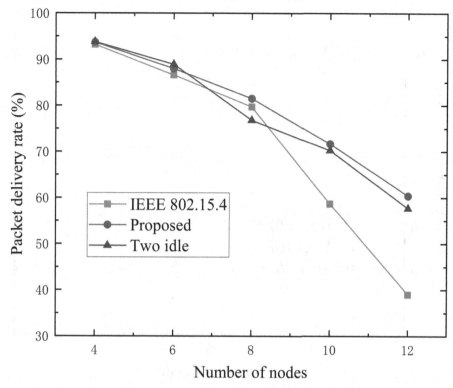

Fig. 9. The simulation results of packet delivery rate.

participate in the channel access competition. In each channel contention, only one node will win, and many packets will be discarded due to channel contention failure. However, it can be seen from the figure that the packet delivery rate of the proposed mechanism is only slightly lower than or approximately equal to the other two mechanisms when the number of nodes is small. When the number of nodes increases and channel contention is intensified, the packet delivery rate of proposed mechanism declines more gently than the other two mechanisms due to the use of priority scheduling mechanism and adaptive retreat mechanism, and the packet arrival rate performs better than the other two mechanisms.

For high priority data in WBAN, it is often physiological data closely related to human health, which plays a more important role in disease prevention, treatment, and prediction. Therefore, it is important to ensure that high priority data has a higher packet delivery rate. Figure 10 shows the packet delivery rate of high priority data under three mechanisms.

Firstly, a comparison of the packet delivery rate of high priority data among the three mechanisms reveals that the proposed mechanism outperforms the other two mechanisms significantly in terms of packet delivery rate of high priority data when there are more nodes. However, when there are fewer nodes, its performance is not inferior to the other two mechanisms. In addition, a comparison of Fig. 10 and Fig. 9 shows that, regardless

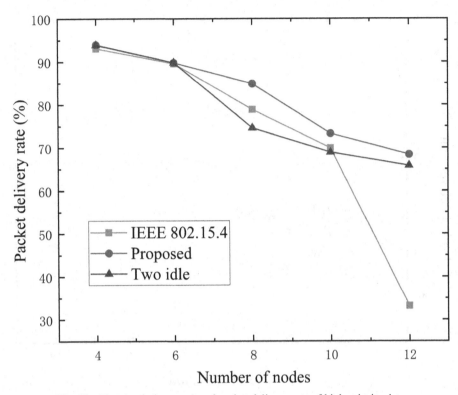

Fig. 10. The simulation results of packet delivery rate of high priority data.

of the number of nodes, the packet delivery rate of high priority data in the proposed mechanism is better than that of all data shown in Fig. 9, while the other two mechanisms exhibit some randomness due to the lack of differentiated scheduling for different priority data. This is because the proposed mechanism gives priority to the transmission of high priority data.

Average End-to-End Delay. Delay refers to the time it takes for a data packet to travel from the source node to the destination node, while average end-to-end delay refers to the average delay of all successfully received data. Figure 11 shows the simulation results of the average end-to-end delay of three MAC mechanisms.

As can be seen from the Fig. 11, the delay of all three mechanisms increases as the number of nodes increases. This is because as the number of nodes increases, the channel competition becomes more intense, and each node has to wait longer when sending data, resulting in an increase in average delay. However, the figure clearly shows that regardless of the number of nodes, the mechanism proposed in this paper performs better in terms of average end-to-end delay than the other two mechanisms. Moreover, as the number of nodes increases, the degree of delay deterioration of the proposed mechanism is smaller. This is because the paper first classifies data priorities and schedules different

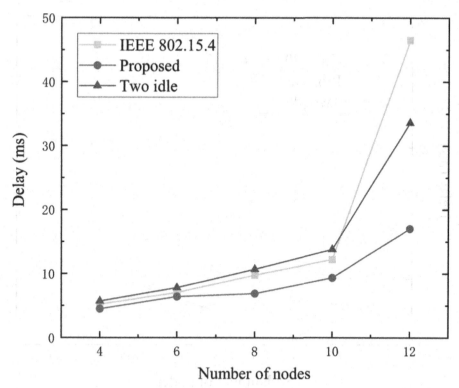

Fig. 11. The simulation results of end-to-end delay.

priority data separately, which alleviates competition to some extent. In addition, when nodes cannot access the channel for a long time, causing data congestion, the adaptive backoff mechanism will change the backoff parameters, increasing the probability of nodes accessing the channel and thus reducing delay.

The Fig. 12 shows the end-to-end delay of high priority data under three different mechanisms. As can be seen from the figure, the mechanism proposed in this paper performs significantly better in terms of high priority data delay than the other two MAC mechanisms. Additionally, comparing Fig. 12 and Fig. 11, it can be observed that under the proposed mechanism, the delay of high priority data is better than the overall delay. This is because the modified channel access mechanism and backoff mechanism increase the probability of high-priority data accessing the channel and reduce the waiting time for backoff, resulting in low-delay transmission of high priority data.

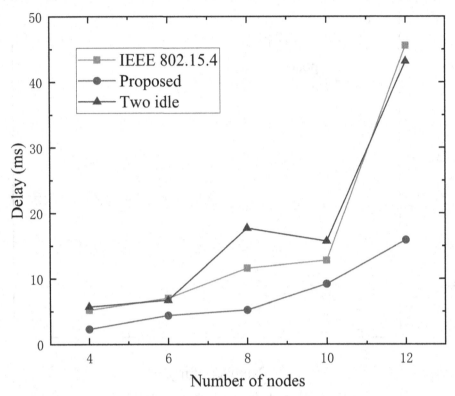

Fig. 12. The simulation results of end-to-end delay of High priority data.

6 Conclusion

This paper proposes a priority-based channel access mechanism and an adaptive backoff mechanism to address the shortcomings of the IEEE 802.15.4 MAC layer mechanism for WBANs, which cannot differentiate data priority for scheduling and cannot adaptively adjust based on the status of nodes in the network.

Firstly, the mechanism that requires two consecutive CCA checks for accessing the channel by high priority data has been modified to only require one CCA, thereby increasing channel utilization and reducing transmission delays for high priority data. Secondly, the initialization parameters for the high priority data backoff mechanism have been adjusted to increase the probability of high priority data accessing the channel relative to regular priority data. In addition, the node residual energy ratio and buffer residual space ratio are used as the input of fuzzy controller to realize the quantization of the real-time state of the node. According to the quantized state, the parameters of the conventional priority data backoff mechanism are adjusted to realize the adaptive backoff mechanism, which can save energy and relieve congestion quickly. The simulation results of NS2.35 software show that the proposed mechanism has better performance in the aspects of network lifetime, network throughput, packet delivery rate and average end-to-end delay. The proposed mechanism has better adaptability to the scenario with a large number of nodes and can better ensure the transmission of high priority data.

References

1. Mahmood, M.N., Dhakal, S.P.: Ageing population and society: a scientometric analysis. Qual. Quant. **2022**, 1–18 (2022)
2. Thiyagarajan, J.A., et al.: The UN decade of healthy ageing: strengthening measurement for monitoring health and wellbeing of older people. Age Ageing **51**(7), afac147 (2022)
3. Yessad, N., et al.: QoS-based routing in wireless body area networks: a survey and taxonomy. Computing **100**(2018), 245–275 (2018)
4. Rahangdale, H.: A review on WMSN (Wireless Medical Sensor Networks) for health monitoring systems. ECS Trans. **107**(1), 1973 (2022)
5. Masud, F., et al.: Traffic adaptive MAC protocols in wireless body area networks. Wirel. Commun. Mobile Comput. **2017**, 1–14 (2017)
6. Infrastructure, Low-Energy Critical, and Monitoring LECIM Physical Layer. IEEE standard for low-rate wireless networks. IEEE Stand 2015, 1-708 (2015)
7. Mkongwa, K.G., Liu, Q., Wang, S.: An adaptive backoff and dynamic clear channel assessment mechanisms in IEEE 802.15. 4 MAC for wireless body area networks. Ad Hoc Netw. **120**, 102554 (2021)
8. Olatinwo, D.D., Abu-Mahfouz, A.M., Hancke, G.P.: Towards achieving efficient MAC protocols for WBAN-enabled IoT technology: a review. EURASIP J. Wirel. Commun. Netw. **2021**(1), 1–47 (2021)
9. Gopalan, S.A., Park, J.-T.: Energy-efficient MAC protocols for wireless body area networks: survey. In: International Congress on Ultra Modern Telecommunications and Control Systems. IEEE (2010)
10. Li, H., Tan, J.: Heartbeat driven medium access control for body sensor networks. In: 1st ACM SIGMOBILE International Workshop on Systems and Networking Support for Healthcare and Assisted Living Environments, pp. 25–30. Association for Computing Machinery, New York (2007)
11. Boudargham, N., et al.: Performance of low level protocols in high traffic wireless body sensor networks. Peer-to-Peer Netw. Appl. **13**, 850–871 (2020)
12. Kaur, M., Bajaj, R., Kaur, N.: A review of mac layer for wireless body area network. J. Med. Biol. Eng. **2021**, 1–38 (2021)
13. Achroufene, A., Chelik, M., Bouadem, N.: Modified CSMA/CA protocol for real-time data fusion applications based on clustered WSN. Comput. Netw. **196**, 108243 (2021)
14. Li, N., et al.: Design and implementation of a MAC protocol for a wearable monitoring system on human body. In: 11th international conference on ASIC (ASICON), pp. 1–4. IEEE, Chengdu, China (2015)
15. Shah, A.M., et al.: eHealth WBAN: energy-efficient and priority-based enhanced IEEE802. 15.6 CSMA/CA MAC protocol. Int. J. Adv. Comput. Sci. Appl. **9**(4) (2018)
16. Javadpour, A., et al.: Toward a secure industrial wireless body area network focusing MAC layer protocols: an analytical review. IEEE Trans. Ind. Inform. **19**(2), 2028–2038 (2022)
17. Yang, X., Wang, L., Zhang, Z.: Wireless body area networks MAC protocol for energy efficiency and extending lifetime. IEEE Sens. Lett. **2**(1), 1–4 (2018)
18. Le, T.T.T., Moh, S.: Hybrid multi-channel MAC protocol for WBANs with inter-WBAN interference mitigation. Sensors **18**(5), 1373 (2018)

19. Yu, J., et al.: Cor-MAC: contention over reservation MAC protocol for time-critical services in wireless body area sensor networks. Sensors **16**(5), 656 (2016)

20. Khan, Z.A., et al.: Effect of packet inter-arrival time on the energy consumption of beacon enabled MAC protocol for body area networks. Procedia Comput. Sci. **32**, 579–586 (2014)

21. Bouazzi, I., et al.: A new medium access control mechanism for energy optimization in WSN: traffic control and data priority scheme. EURASIP J. Wirel. Commun. Networking **2021**(1), 1–23 (2021)

22. Sahoo, P.K., Pattanaik, S.R., Wu, S.-L.: A novel IEEE 802.15. 4e DSME MAC for wireless sensor networks. Sensors **17**(1), 168 (2017)

23. Mateen Yaqoob, M., et al.: Adaptive multi-cost routing protocol to enhance lifetime for wireless body area network. Comput. Mater. Continua **72**(1), 1089–1103 (2022)

Frontier and Comprehensive
Applications

Precision Seeding Monitoring System for Cooperative Operation of Multicast Lines

Fangwei Peng[1]([✉]) [iD], Xiang Li[1,2], Yong Fan[3], Wen Liao[1] [iD], Weile Zhang[1] [iD], and Ziyi Zhang[1] [iD]

[1] East China University of Technology, Nanchang 330013, China
Shepherd_p@163.com
[2] Jiangxi Research Center of Nuclear Geo-Data Science and System Engineering, East China University of Technology, Nanchang 330013, China
[3] Geely Automobile Research Institute, Ningbo 315336, China

Abstract. In the operation process of traditional air-suction seeders, the phenomenon of missing seeding and reseeding is often caused by the blockage of the seed guide tube, the lack of a seed box and mechanical failure. If it is not found in time, it may lead to the phenomenon of a large area of missing seeding or reseeding, which will affect the crop yield. To solve the above problems, the team designed and developed a precision seeding monitoring system that can support the cooperative operation of up to 24 seeding lines. The system includes the design of an infrared photoelectric monitoring unit, a speed monitoring unit, a controller unit, a central control instrument unit and a fault alarm unit. The results of the bench test show that the designed monitoring system can monitor the cooperative operation of 24 seeding lines in real time, identify the seeding line number in time and accurately when the phenomenon of missing or rebroadcasting occurs, and give fault alarm. The alarm success rate reaches 100%, and the average response time is less than 0.5 s. The results of field experiments showed that the average accuracy of the system was over 98.5%, and the average accuracy of the pass rate, miss rate and replay rate was over 96.6%, 97.4% and 98.8%, respectively, under the normal operation speed of 4–12 km/h. It is of great significance to improve seeding quality and reduce production cost.

Keywords: seeding monitoring · Missed seeding · Multicast cooperation · Infrared photoelectric sensor · Speed sensor · Suction seeder

1 Introduction

As an important link in agricultural production, sowing quality has a direct impact on crop yield. The traditional air-suction seeder [1, 2] is often affected by problems such as plugging of the seed guide tube, lack of seeds in the seed box and mechanical failure in the operation process. If it is not found in time, a large area of miss sowing or replay sowing phenomenon may occur, thus affecting crop yield. With the rapid development of agricultural machinery intelligence, precision seeding monitoring technology has become the mainstream research direction of agricultural machinery intelligence. It

M. Zhang et al. (Eds.): CCF NCCA 2023, CCIS 1960, pp. 205–224, 2024.
https://doi.org/10.1007/978-981-99-8761-0_15

is helpful to improve seeding quality and reduce production costs to realize accurate monitoring of the seeding operation of seeders.

At present, the technical methods of precision seeding monitoring mainly include capacitive [3], high-speed photography [4], piezoelectric [5], machine vision [6], photoelectric [7, 8], etc. Borja et al. [9] designed a control system with machine vision and mechatronics technology to accurately monitor seeding conditions, but the operating speed of the system was limited by the limitations of mechatronics drive torque generation and the delay of camera image capture. Zhang, Y. et al. [10] designed a seeding monitoring system based on linear array CMOS, which used high-frequency linear array CMOS image sensors to detect seed fall, but it was difficult to guarantee the image quality in the field operating environment with complex light.

In recent years, many scholars have conducted in-depth studies on the precise monitoring of individual seeding [11–24]. Zhao, Z. et al. [6] used a machine vision algorithm for image analysis and processing to identify the seeding situation of hole disks, but the disadvantage was that the cost of image acquisition equipment was high. Zhou, L. et al. [3] monitored the discharge amount by using the principle that the capacitance changes with the change in the capacitor plate relative to the medium, but the capacitor sensor was easily interfered with by the change in temperature. Niu, K's team [25] adopted two pairs of laser beam sensors and contact travel switch sensors to detect missed potato sowing.

In addition, it is important to monitor seeding failures, such as blocked seed tubes or missing seed boxes. Raheman's team [26] noted that if the seeder was not equipped with monitoring equipment, the driver could not observe the actual seeding situation during the seeding process, nor could he know the seeding situation on the cultivated land passed by the seeder. Caner C [27] noted that the two main reasons for the lack of seeds in the seed ditch were the failure of the seed discharge device or the seed was blocked in the seed guide tube and failed to fall into the seed ditch. To solve this problem, Kumar and Raheman [28] developed an embedded system for monitoring information about seeds in seed tubes. The system is equipped with a buzzer and light-emitting diode that alerts the driver with sound and visual signals if the seed has fallen into the seed ditch.

The photoelectric type mainly uses the photoelectric sensor to detect the light signal when the seed falls, generates an electrical signal and forms a pulse signal that can be recognized by the controller after processing. The controller further collects and analyses the pulse signal to realize seeding monitoring. With the advantages of strong optical signal transmission stability, fast response and high recognition rate, it has become the most widely used precision seeding monitoring method at present. Therefore, this study designed a precision seeding monitoring system according to the structural characteristics of precision air-suction seeders. The infrared photoelectric sensor is installed in the seed guide pipe and combined with the single chip microcomputer to realize the man-machine interaction function, achieve high precision sowing quality monitoring, and further improve the intelligent level of agricultural machinery operation.

2   System Structure and Working Principle

2.1   System Structure

In this paper, a precision seeding monitoring system for precision air-suction seed dispersers was designed, including an infrared photoelectric monitoring unit, vehicle speed monitoring unit, controller unit, central control instrument unit and fault alarm unit.

2.2   Working Principle

Working Principle of Precision Air-Suction Seeder

When the seeding device is working, the sowing fan is started first to generate negative pressure in the pipeline. Then, the seeding controller drives the sowing plate to rotate and store seeds. In addition, the system calculates the real-time speed according to the parameters measured by the speed sensor, and the sowing controller precisely controls the seeder according to the sowing parameters set by the user. When it reaches the predetermined soil position, seed once.

Working Principle of Precision Seeding Monitoring System

The infrared photoelectric sensor installed on the seed guide tube forms a light path after being energized. When the seed particle falls, it will block the light path. At this time, the infrared photoelectric sensor will generate pulse signals. The IO pin of the controller is connected with the signal line of the sensor, the pulse signal is captured in real time, and parameters such as the time interval, frequency and total number of seeds are calculated through corresponding processing. At the same time, the vehicle speed sensor is used to obtain the forward speed of the seeder in real time, and the controller calculates the actual seeding distance, seeding area and other parameters after collecting the speed parameters and calculates the seeding parameters such as the miss rate and replay rate according to the theoretical grain distance set by the user. The monitoring information is further transmitted to the central control instrument through the CAN communication protocol, and the precision seeding information is displayed in real time. In addition, in the monitoring of miss sowing or replay sowing phenomena, sound and light alarms provide timely reminders to drivers. The system uses an independent power supply and is completely separated from the tractor and seeder to avoid interference and facilitate installation and disassembly. The structure of the precision seeding monitoring system is shown in Fig. 1.

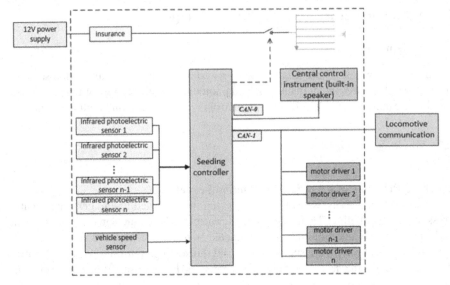

Fig. 1. Structure diagram of the system

3   Design of Precision Sowing Monitoring System

The precision sowing monitoring system is composed of a central control instrument man-machine interaction system unit, controller unit, vehicle speed sensor unit and infrared photoelectric sensor monitoring unit.

3.1   Design of Infrared Photoelectric Monitoring Unit

In this study, an infrared through-beam sensor was designed for monitoring the requirements of crop seeding of different sizes. The transmitter of the sensor adopts three infrared transmitting tubes to emit infrared signals, and the receiving end adopts three photosensitive diodes to receive infrared signals. The infrared light path formed by this sensor can cover the cross section of the whole seed guide tube, realizing no blind area monitoring. In addition, the modulation tube is used to modulate the emission frequency of the infrared transmitter tube, which can improve the anti-dust interference ability of the system and realize the monitoring of crop seeding with different particle sizes. Figure 2 shows the physical shape of the infrared photoelectric sensor.

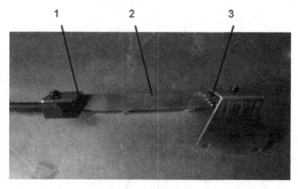

Fig. 2. Infrared photoelectric sensor. 1. Transmitting end; 2. Bracket; 3. Receiving end.

In the normal operation process, when the seed particle passes through the monitoring unit, it will block the infrared light path. At this time, the light source signal received by the photosensitive diode will change. When the signal intensity is lower than the set threshold, the detection circuit will form a pulse signal and transmit it to the controller. The model of the infrared photoelectric monitoring unit is shown in Fig. 3.

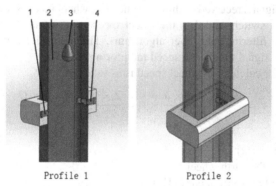

Profile 1   Profile 2

Fig. 3. Infrared photoelectric monitoring unit model. 1. Transmitting end; 2. Seed guide tube; 3. Crop seed; 4. Receiving end.

3.2 Design of Vehicle Speed Monitoring Unit

The speed monitoring unit adopts the NJK-5002C DC three-wire NPN normally open Hall proximity switch as the speed detection sensor. The sensor is installed on the motor cover of the wheel, the induction block is fixed on the clip, and then two screws are used to fix the clip on the rotating shaft as the measuring point and adjust the distance between the patch and the rotating shaft to 2–3 mm. The vehicle speed detection unit model is shown in Fig. 4.

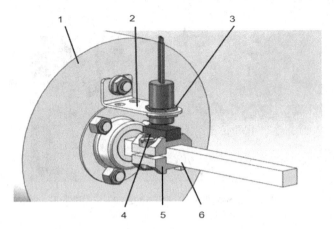

Fig. 4. Vehicle speed detection unit model. 1. Wheel motor; 2. Fixed support; 3. Hall proximity switch; 4. Induction block; 5. Clamping plate; 6. Rotating shaft.

According to the Hall effect principle, when the iron plate approaches the Hall proximity switch, the Hall proximity switch will generate pulse signals and transmit them to the controller. The controller obtains the pulse frequency by calculating the number of pulse signals received within the time. The wheel motor speed is captured by the Hall proximity switch, and then the wheel speed pulse signal is formed by outlier elimination, pulse filtering and other algorithms. The controller further collects and analyses the pulse signal to achieve speed monitoring [29, 30].

The formula for calculating wheel speed is as follows:

$$v = \frac{2 \times \pi \times R \times u}{K} \times f = \frac{2 \times \pi \times R \times u \times Q}{K \times \Delta T} \tag{1}$$

where:

R – wheel radius (m)

u – Slip rate of the earth wheel

f – wheel speed pulse frequency (Hz)

K – the tooth ratio of the gear ring

Q – Number of wheel speed pulses in time(s)

V – Speed (m/s).

The calculation of the pulse frequency is completed through pulse input capture, and the pulse time and number are recorded. Generally, the larger the cycle is, the more accumulated pulses will be captured and the smaller the calculation error will be, but the worse the real-time performance will be at the same time. The planter mainly focuses on the update frequency of the low-speed zone, and a lower value, such as the update cycle of 500 ms, is preferred.

When the displayed speed is inconsistent with the actual speed, the monitoring system needs to adjust the value of parameter C. "C" represents the number of pulses sent out by the speed sensor every 100 m travelled. The controller will calculate the accumulated number of sowing areas through parameter C. Table 1 is the reference of common "C" values obtained by testing different types of planters.

Table 1. "C" values refer to the table.

A	B	Tyre size				
		5.00–15	6.5/80–15	6.5/80–15	7.50–16	20 * 8.00–10
23	23	49	47	45	41	48
20	20					
23	16	70	68	65	58	68
16	23	34	33	31	28	33

For example, if the number of transmission teeth B is 16, the number of rim teeth A is 23, and the specification of the tires is 7.50–16, then C is 58. When the detected speed is consistent with the actual speed, parameter "C" is the correct setting. To calculate the sowing area more accurately, parameter "C" can also be set through the automatic calibration program. Its principle is to make the planter travel 100 m before stopping, and the pulse number is recorded as "C".

3.3 Design of the Controller Unit

The controller is the core of signal acquisition and parameter calculation. Two main chips (AT89S52-24U-TW and STC15F2K60S2-28I LQFP44) are created in the controller unit of this system. The circuit diagram of the controller terminal is shown in Fig. 5.

STC15F2K60S2-28I LQFP44 is the main control chip, and its main function is to upload operation information (such as working area and sowing number, etc.) to the background through a CAN message and store each operation information. Pin P3.7/INT3/TxD_2/CCP2/CCP2_2 has write protection. When the pin is in high voltage mode, data cannot be written. When the pin is in low voltage mode, data can be written. The CANINTE register contains the interrupt enable bits that enable each interrupt source. Signals 1–6 are used to configure the CAN controller. The CANINTF register contains interrupt flag bits for each interrupt source. When an interruption occurs, the INT pin is pulled to a low level and remains low until the interrupt is cleared. An interrupt is cleared only after the corresponding interrupt condition has disappeared.

AT89S52-24U-TW is a CMOS 8-bit microcontroller. Where the (INT0) P3.2 pin is used to receive the speed signal of the body. It is low when there is no signal and high when there is a signal. (T0) P3.4 Pin is used for detecting PWM waves, such as measuring how many PWM waves there are in 100 m when the speed is constant.

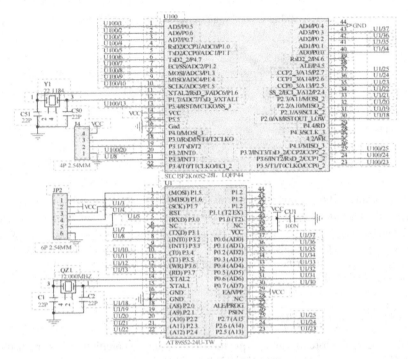

Fig. 5. Controller terminal circuit diagram

3.4 Design of the Sowing Parameter Calculation Program

Seeding parameters such as the seeding amount, miss seeding rate and repeat seeding rate can be calculated according to the standard proposed in GB/T6973-2005 "Test Method for Single Seed (Precision) Planter" [31]. When the actual sowing grain spacing is greater than 1.5 times the theoretical grain spacing, it is judged to be missed sowing; when it is less than or equal to 0.5 times the theoretical grain spacing, it is judged to be repeated.

Planting Area and Sowing Amount

1. Start the calculation condition

    When the wheel speed pulse changes and any seeding row falls are detected, the controller starts the cumulative calculation of the operating area.
2. Calculation method

    Partial operation area = number of rows * row width * distance travelled.
3. Theoretical seeding quantity

    Let us assume that the driving distance S is calculated correctly, $S = v * t$.

    At present, if the grain distance is set at L, the theoretical sowing amount is the number of seeds that should be sown within the driving distance S.
4. Calculate the theoretical sowing quantity N_t

After the sowing operation time t, the driving distance S and the theoretical sowing quantity N_t = S/L. For ease of calculation, S was taken as an integer multiple of the grain distance L; for example, missed seeding evaluation was performed after every 100 seeds were sown.

5. Calculate the actual sowing quantity

The number of seeds N_r was obtained by counting the pulse signals generated by the accumulated infrared photoelectric sensor.

6. Actual grain distance calculation

The actual seed spacing of sown crops is calculated by the actual sowing quantity at time t and the driving distance of the seeding vehicle at time t.

Calculation of Miss Rate

Comprehensive analysis of several ways:

1. The ratio between the total sowing amount and the expected total amount within a certain time interval;
2. If the time difference between two adjacent seeds is too large, it is considered to be missed seeding; if it is within the time difference, it is considered to be repeated seeding. The missed seeding number/(normal seeding number + missed seeding number + replay number) is the missed seeding rate;
3. The results were calculated in real time according to the national standard method, counting the results every 250 seeds and calculating the ratio of the actual time difference between the current two seeds and the current expected time difference * the ideal grain distance.

Replay Rate Calculation

$$A = \frac{n_0}{N} \times 100\% \tag{2}$$

$$D = \frac{n_1}{N} \times 100\% \tag{3}$$

$$M = \frac{n_2}{N} \times 100\% \tag{4}$$

where:

n_0 – qualified sowing quantity;
n_1 – number of replays;
n_2 – the number of missed seeding;
N – actual sowing quantity;
A – Conformity index;
D – replay index;
M – leakage index.

3.5 Design of Central Control Instrument Unit

After the system is powered on, the system enters startup mode. All components of the central control instrument light on and sound signals (buzz) sound. Long press the Programming (PROG) key to enter the setting mode. When "C–" appears, press PROG to select the parameters to be set. Use the "+" and "–" keys to modify the parameters. After the parameters are set, hold down the PROG key to save the parameters and exit the setting mode (approximately 5 s). The seed distance button was pressed each time to display the seed distance in a cycle, and a black box was used to display the percentage difference between the actual seed distance and the set seed distance in the display area. When the percentage error of a seeding line exceeds the set range, the black box of the corresponding row will blink, and there will be a sound alarm to remind the driver to check whether the seeder of the corresponding seeding line is faulty. The sowing density can be displayed by pressing the sowing density button (the number of seeds sown per square meter). In the display area, the effective sowing rows are represented by black squares to represent the percentage difference between the actual seed density and the set seed density. Press the speed button each time: the speed button indicator light, at the same time in the lower right corner of the screen shows the speed (km/h), the driver needs to confirm whether the displayed speed and the actual speed is consistent, if not, it needs to set the parameter C (the parameter C has been introduced above); press the total area key, the screen displays the total area, unit: hectare; press the total distance key, and the screen will display the total distance, in meters; press the partial area key, and the screen displays the partial area, unit: hectare. The central control interface is shown in Fig. 6.

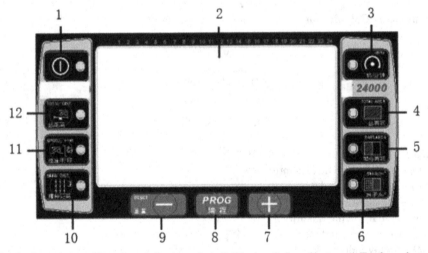

Fig. 6. Central control interface. 1. Power switch; 2. Display; 3. Speed button; 4. Total area button; 5. Part of the area key; 6. Sowing density key; 7. "Plus" key; 8. Programming (PROG) key; 9. "Reduce" key; 10. Seed spacing key; 11. Speed button; 12. Total distance button

3.6 Design of Fault Alarm Unit

Fault alarms are a very important function in precision seeding monitoring systems, especially for large farm seeding work, and fault alarm functions are essential. Precision air-suction seeders in the operation process are often due to the plug of the seed guide tube, lack of seed in the seed box, mechanical failure and other problems caused by misses and replay, if not found in time, may lead to a large area of leakage or replay phenomena and affect crop yield. In this study, the alarm function of missing broadcasts and replay broadcasts was realized. When the sowing distance of a seeding line exceeds the set range, the black box of the corresponding line on the central control instrument will flash, and the buzzer will issue an alarm sound to remind the driver to check the missing seed of the seeder of the corresponding seeding line. Similarly, when the seeding distance of a seeding line is less than the set range, the central control instrument and buzzer will give an alarm. The software control flow chart is shown in Fig. 7.

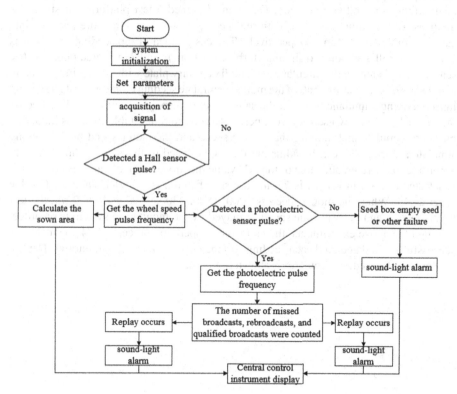

Fig. 7. Software control flow chart.

4 Performance Experiment of Precision Seeding Monitoring System

To verify the performance of the precision seeding monitoring system for the cooperative operation of multicast rows, bench simulation and field seeding experiments were conducted. It includes the precision test of simulated vehicle speed monitoring, the simulation of the multiseeding line cooperative operation monitoring performance test, the reliability test of fault alarm and the field seeding test for real-time monitoring of seeding parameters.

4.1 Precision Test of Simulated Vehicle Speed Monitoring and Monitoring Performance Test of Simulated Multicast Line Collaborative Operation

To verify the system reliability of the precision seeding monitoring system in the process of multiline cooperative operation. Our team designed a test platform for simulated multicast row seeding operation with the seeding simulator as the core and multiple auxiliary modules working cooperatively. The design idea of the seeding simulator is to use a controllable motor to simulate turbine rotation, install 24 infrared photoelectric sensors equidistant on the circular base, and fix a rotary plate with 24 fine irons equally equidistant on the rotating shaft of the motor to simulate seeding monitoring of 24 seeding lines operating simultaneously. At the same time, two speed sensors were installed on the motor base, and two screws were perforated on the rotary table to act as induction blocks to simulate and monitor the turbine speed and the motor speed of the seeding simulator. During the test, by adjusting the motor speed of the seeding simulator and according to the reference table of the "C" value mentioned above, transmission gear B is selected as 23, rim gear A is 23, the tire specification is 6.5/80-15, and the C value is set as 45. When the motor speed is 1200, 1800, 2400, 3000 and 3600 r/h, the test is carried out, and the real-time speed displayed by the monitoring system is recorded. Through the above experiments, the cooperative operation process of 24 channels was successfully simulated, and each seeding parameter was effectively monitored. The test platform of the seeding simulator is shown in Fig. 8.

4.2   Reliability Test of Fault Alarm

To verify the reliability of the fault alarm function of the precision seeding monitoring system, the team built a bench test platform with a precision air suction seed discharge device as the core and tested it with a controllable seeding fan. The test platform is shown in Fig. 9.

Fig. 8. Seeding simulator test platform. 1. Motor speed controller; 2. Sound and light alarm; 3. Speed sensor; 4. Infrared optoelectric sensor; 5. Motor and motor base; 6. Power; 7. Data box; 8. Controller

To verify the reliability of the fault alarm function of the precision seeding monitoring system, this experiment mainly simulated the failure of the seed box and the blockage of the seed guide tube, which occurred most frequently in the operation process of the seeder. First, by controlling the start and stop button of the seeding fan to control the work of the air-suction seed drainer, an artificial missing seed phenomenon is caused, and the lack of seed drainer fault is simulated. Second, the seed guide tube was artificially blocked in the process of seeding so that the seeds could not fall, and the blockage of the seed guide tube was simulated. During the test, the team members, through coordination and cooperation, artificially created seeding faults while observing whether the monitoring system correctly sent an alarm when seeding faults occurred, recorded the response time of the system, and obtained the response speed of the system. The two methods were repeated 100 times.

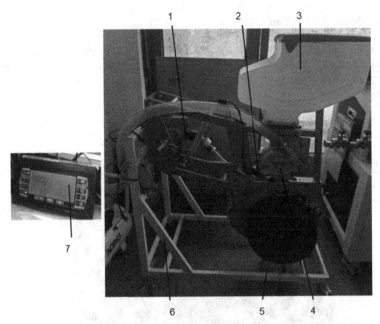

Fig. 9. Test platform. 1. Speed sensor; 2. Infrared photoelectric sensor; 3. Seeding box; 4. Air-suction seed separator; 5. Seed collection box; 6. Bracket; 7. Controller.

4.3 Field Sowing Experiment

To verify the monitoring performance of the designed precision seeding monitoring system under real seeding operation conditions, the team conducted field seeding experiments. Sixteen rows of precision air suction seeders were used to carry out the sowing operation test. The grain spacing was 0.3 m, and the sowing distance was 75 m. The test was repeated 5 times for 5 different operating speeds, such as 4.0, 6.0, 8.0, 10.0 and 12.0 km/h, and the test results were averaged. The test arrangement conforms to Chinese national standard GBT 6973-2005 "Test Method for Single Seed (Precision) planter" [31]. The test scenario is shown in Fig. 10.

Fig. 10. Field seeding picture.

5   Analysis of Test Results

The performance of the system was comprehensively and accurately verified by bench simulation experiments and field seeding experiments. The test results are analysed as follows:

5.1   Analysis of Monitoring Accuracy Test of Simulated Vehicle Speed and Monitoring Performance Test Results of Collaborative Operation of Simulated Multicast Lines

Through 5 tests at motor speeds of 1200, 1800, 2400, 3000 and 3600 r/h, according to the turbine speed formula mentioned above, without considering the slip rate of the ground wheel, the actual speed under 5 kinds of motor speeds is calculated and compared with the real-time detection speed shown by the recorded monitoring system. As shown in Table 2, the actual speed is completely consistent with the speed monitored by the system, with no difference. The accuracy of the velocity measurement function of the monitoring system designed in this study is verified. At the same time, in the monitoring performance test simulating the cooperative operation of multicast lines, when the parameter "C" is correctly set, the system can display the sowing grain spacing of each line in a cycle and display the percentage difference between the actual grain spacing and the set standard grain spacing with black squares in the display area. Each column of black squares represents a sowing row. The test interface is shown in Fig. 11. It can be seen from the figure that the actual grain spacing of each line is accurately monitored to be equal to the theoretical grain spacing, and the displayed percentage is 100%. At the same time, the phenomenon of missing seeding and replay was successfully simulated by adjusting the motor speed of the seeding simulator, and the percentage error of the seeding line exceeded the set range. At this time, the black box of the corresponding line flashed, and the buzzer sounded alarm. Through the above experiments, the reliability of the monitoring performance of multicast line cooperative operation is verified.

Table 2. Vehicle speed detection table

Rotate speed (r·h − 1)	Locomotive speed (km·h − 1)	
	Actual velocity	Detection speed
1200	3.1	3.1
1800	4.7	4.7
2400	6.2	6.2
3000	7.7	7.7
3600	9.3	9.3

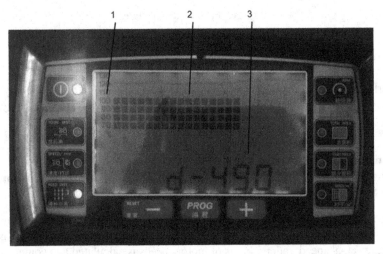

Fig. 11. Test interface. 1. Actual grain distance percentage to standard grain distance; 2. Black displays block; 3. Actual grain distance.

5.2 Seeding Fault Alarm Reliability Test Results and Analysis

Through the reliability test, the leakage phenomenon caused by the failure of the seed box and the blockage of the seed guide tube is simulated successfully, and the time interval of the system alarm is recorded, ignoring the delay of manual timing. The test results show that the precision seeding monitoring system has 100% monitoring accuracy and alarm success rate for these two kinds of faults, and there are no missing alarm accidents.

This result successfully verifies the reliability of the fault alarm function of the system. Figure 12 shows a scatter plot of the system fault alarm response time. As seen from the figure, the response time range of the system is relatively stable, with an average error of less than 0.5 s. The system can respond to the fault alarm quickly and accurately and meet the actual work requirements.

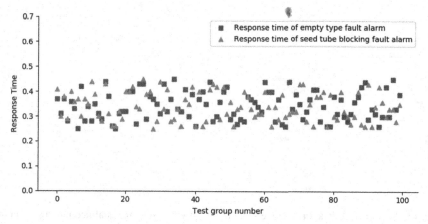

Fig. 12. Scatter plot of the response time of the monitoring system fault alarm.

5.3 Analysis of Field Seeding Experiment Results

Aiming at four different grain sizes of corn, soybean, cotton and sugar beet, the theoretical seed number of each experiment can be calculated as 250 grains under the seeding parameters of 0.3 m standard grain distance and 75 m sowing length. In addition, considering whether the operation speed would affect the monitoring accuracy, seeding experiments were carried out at seeding speeds of 4.0, 6.0, 8.0, 10.0 and 12.0 km/h, and the actual number of seeds was manually counted. The average statistical results are shown in Fig. 13.

It can be seen from the figure that the average monitoring accuracy of the qualified rate, the miss rate and the replay rate of crop seeding monitoring of different sizes exceeds 96.6%, 97.4% and 98.8%, respectively, with small errors and no large fluctuations in the monitoring accuracy within the range of common operation speed, which proves that the monitoring accuracy of the system can meet the requirements of actual operation and has high reliability.

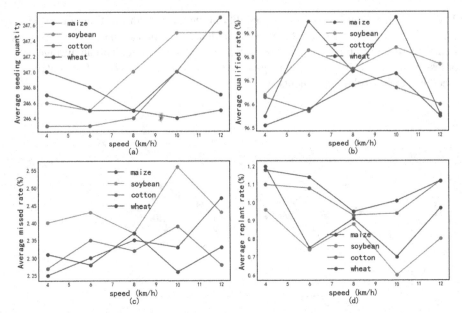

Fig. 13. Seeding test data. (a)Average seeding quantity; (b) Average qualified rate; (c) Average missed rate; Average replant rate.

6   Conclusion

In this paper, a precision seeding monitoring system is designed and developed for the cooperative operation of multicast lines. The system uses an infrared photoelectric sensor and vehicle speed sensor to capture signals and realizes effective monitoring of seeding parameters such as seeding area, missing seeding rate, replay rate and qualified rate. At the same time, when seeding failure occurs, it can be reported in time to avoid the loss caused by the phenomenon of missing data or replay. The conclusions are as follows:

1. To verify the coordination and consistency of software and hardware, a seeding simulator supporting 24 channels of seeding line cooperative operation monitoring was designed. This solves the problems of test site limitation and energy consumption cost, improves the convenience of development and testing, and verifies the accuracy of the vehicle speed monitoring function and the reliability of the monitoring performance of multicast line cooperation.
2. The average response time of the fault alarm of the monitoring system is less than 0.5 s, and the success rate of the alarm is 100%. The fault alarm response time of the system is fast, and it can alarm accurately and timely to meet the actual work needs.
3. The results of field experiments showed that the monitoring accuracy of the monitoring system for the seeding number of different grain sizes was more than 98.5% on average, and the monitoring accuracy of the qualified rate, the missing rate and the reseeding rate were more than 96.6%, 97.4% and 98.8%, respectively, under sowing speeds of 4–12 km/h. The accuracy of the monitoring system is relatively stable for

different sizes of crop seeds, and the seeding speed has little effect on the monitoring accuracy, which can meet the monitoring needs of precision seeding operations. Please help me revise this paragraph to make it more smooth and concise.

Author Contributions. Conceptualization, F.P. (Fangwei Peng); Writing, reviewing and editing, Y.F.; Verification, X.L. (Xiang Li); Supervision, W.Z.; Formal Analysis, W.L.; Data Management, Z.Z.; All authors have read and agreed to the published version of the manuscript.

Funding. This work was supported by the Key Laboratory of Cyberspace Security of Jiangxi Province, No. JKLCIP202205.

Institutional Review Board Statement: Not applicable.

Informed Consent Statement: Not applicable.

Data Availability Statement. Not applicable.

Conflicts of Interest. The authors declare no conflicts of interest.

References

1. Zhao, M.Q., Liu, Y.Q., Hu, Y.W.: An airflow field finite element analysis of the seed adsorption hole of pneumatic seeder. Appl. Mech. Mater. **117–119**, 1810–1815 (2011). Trans Tech Publications
2. Gaikwad, B.B., Sirohi, N.: Design of a low-cost pneumatic seeder for nursery plug trays. Biosys. Eng. **99**(3), 322–329 (2008)
3. Zhou, L., Wang, S., Zhang, X., Yuan, Y., Zhang, J.: Seed monitoring system for corn planter based on capacitance signal. Nongye Gongcheng Xuebao/Trans. Chin. Soc. Agric. Eng. **28**(13), 16–21 (2012)
4. Chen, J., Bian, J., Li, Y., Zhao, Z., Wang, J.: Performance detection experiment of precision seed metering device based on high-speed camera system. Trans. Chin. Soc. Agric. Eng. **25**(9), 90–95 (2009)
5. Qiu, Z., Zhang, W., Jin, X., Ji, J., Xing, F.: Design and experiment of the fertilizer monitoring system based on piezoelectric film. Int. Agric. Eng. J. **27**(3), 87–96 (2018)
6. Zhao, Z., Liu, Y., Liu, Z., Gao, B.: Performance detection system of tray precision seeder based on machine vision. Nongye Jixie Xuebao/Trans. Chin. Soc. Agric. Mach. **45**, 24–28 (2014)
7. Xie, C., Zhang, D., Yang, L., Cui, T., He, X., Du, Z.: Precision seeding parameter monitoring system based on laser sensor and wireless serial port communication. Comput. Electron. Agric. **190**, 106429 (2021)
8. Zhang, J., Chen, H., Ouyang, B., Ji, W.: Monitoring system for precision seeders based on a photosensitive sensor. Qinghua Daxue Xuebao/J. Tsinghua Univ. **53**(2), 265–268+273 (2013)
9. Borja, A.A., Amongo, R., Suministrado, D.C., Pabico, J.P.: A machine vision assisted mechatronic seed meter for precision planting of corn. In: 2018 3rd International Conference on Control and Robotics Engineering (ICCRE) (2018)
10. Zhang, Y., Zhao, L., Ai, X.: Design of seeding measurement system based on linear array CMOS. Foreign Electron. Meas. Technol. **38**(12), 50–55 (2019)

11. Wang, G., Sun, W., Zhang, H., Liu, X., Zhu, L.: Research on a kind of seeding-monitoring and compensating control system for potato planter without additional seed-metering channel. Comput. Electron. Agric. **177**(2), 105681 (2020)
12. Bai, J., Hao, F., Cheng, G., Li, C.: Machine vision-based supplemental seeding device for plug seedling of sweet corn. Comput. Electron. Agric. **188**, 106345 (2021)
13. Dong, W., Ma, X., Li, H., Tan, S., Guo, L.: Detection of performance of hybrid rice pot-tray sowing utilizing machine vision and machine learning approach. Sensors **19**(23), 5332 (2019)
14. Xia, H., Zhen, W., Liu, Y., Zhao, K.: Optoelectronic measurement system for a pneumatic roller-type seeder used to sow vegetable plug-trays. Measurement **170**(3), 108741 (2020)
15. Besharati, B., Navid, H., Karimi, H., Behfar, H., Eskandari, I.: Development of an infrared seed-sensing system to estimate flow rates based on physical properties of seeds. Comput. Electron. Agric. **162**, 874–881 (2019)
16. Ding, Y., Yang, J., Zhu, K., Zhang, L., Liao, Q.: Design and experiment on seed flow sensing device for rapeseed precision metering device. Trans. Chin. Soc. Agric. Eng. **33**(9), 29–36 (2017)
17. Bracy, R.P., Parish, R.L.: Seeding uniformity of precision seeders. HortTechnology **8**(2), 182–185 (1998)
18. Zhang, X., Zhao, B.: Automatic reseeding monitoring system of seed drill. Trans. Chin. Soc. Agric. Eng. **24**, 119–123 (2008)
19. Pizarro, A., Sasso, S., Manfreda, S.: Refining image-velocimetry performances for streamflow monitoring: seeding metrics to errors minimization. Hydrol. Process. **34**, 5167–5175 (2020)
20. Tang, Y., Ji, C., Fu, W., Chen, J.: Design of seeding monitoring system for corn precision seeder. J. Agric. Mechanization Res. (2020)
21. Yang, C., Meng, Z., Mei, H., Luo, C., Dong, J., Fu, W.: Design and test of corn precision seeding monitoring system. J. Agric. Mech. Res. (2019)
22. Chen, T.: Design and realization of seeding quality monitoring system for air-suction vibrating disc type seed meter. Processes **10**, 1745 (2022)
23. Marrion, C.C., et al.: System and method for three-dimensional alignment of objects using machine vision. US (2013)
24. Lan, Y., Kocher, M.F., Smith, J.A.: Opto-electronic sensor system for laboratory measurement of planter seed spacing with small seeds. J. Agric. Eng. Res. **72**(2), 119–127 (1999)
25. Niu, K., Zhou, L., Yuan, Y., Liu, Y., Fang, X.: Design and experiment on automatic compensation system of spoon-chain potato metering device. Trans. Chin. Soc. Agric. Mach. **47**, 76–83 (2016)
26. Raheman, H., Singh, U.: A sensor for seed flow from seed metering mechanisms (2003)
27. Çuhac, C., Virrankoski, R., Hänninen, P., Elmusrati, M.: Seed flow monitoring in wireless sensor networks (2012)
28. Kumar, R.: Detection of flow of seeds in the seed delivery tube and choking of boot of a seed drill. Comput. Electron. Agric. **153**, 266–277 (2018)
29. Qin, Z.K., Li, S.Y., Wang, C.W., Ma, Z.P.: An improved hall vehicle speed sensor detection system. Appl. Mech. Mater. **423–426**, 2334–2337 (2018). Trans Tech Publications
30. Pattakos, P., Angelopoulos, S., Katsoulas, A., Ktena, A., Hristoforou, E.: Magnetic harvester for an autonomous steel health monitoring system based on Hall effect measurements. Micromachines **14**(1), 28 (2022)
31. China National Standard, 2005. Standardization Administration of the PR China and General Administration of Quality Supervision, Inspection and Quarantine of the PR China. Testing methods of single seed drills (precision drills). In: GB/T 6973-2005 (2005)

A Survey of Control Flow Graph Recovery for Binary Code

Qianjin Wang, Xiangdong Li$^{(\boxtimes)}$, Chong Yue, and Yuchen He

Henan Key Laboratory on Public Opinion Intelligent Analysis, ZhongYuan University of Technology, Zhengzhou, China
`lixiangdong2510@126.com`

Abstract. With the rapid development of Internet applications, the study of software security has received increasing attention. The recovery of control flow graphs, as one of the fundamental tasks in software security analysis, is essential to understand the structure and flow of program execution. The accuracy of control flow recovery is crucial to security techniques such as vulnerability mining and code similarity comparison, which are based on control flow graphs. In the field of reverse analysis, the recovery of the control flow graph for binary code has become a hot research topic. In this paper, we review the methods of control flow graph construction of binary code, including static analysis, dynamic analysis, and hybrid analysis, and compare their advantages and disadvantages. After that, we discuss the difficult problems in control flow graph construction and summarize the research progress of the indirect jump problem in recent years. Finally, the focus and outlook of future research in this area are summarized and discussed.

Keywords: Binary analysis · Control flow graph (CFG) · Indirect jump

1 Introduction

Software security has always been an important part of network security, and network attacks caused by software vulnerabilities are one of the most important risks facing networks today. Especially in recent years, with the rapid development and wide application of the Internet of Things, mobile Internet, and industrial Internet, the amount of software and firmware has grown dramatically. At the same time, the software is gradually becoming more varied, and vulnerabilities are increasingly numerous [1,2]. Over the last five years, NIST (National Institute of Standards and Technology) has found an average of nearly 17,000 software vulnerabilities per year, with the number of vulnerabilities found increasing each year since 2016 [3]. As a result, higher demand is put forth for security analysis approaches. However, the analysis of programs requires the understanding of high-level semantics such as the data structure and control

---

The original version of the chapter has been revised: A typo error in the title has been corrected. A correction to this chapter can be found at
https://doi.org/10.1007/978-981-99-8761-0_19

© The Author(s), under exclusive license to Springer Nature Singapore Pte Ltd. 2024, corrected publication 2024
M. Zhang et al. (Eds.): CCF NCCA 2023, CCIS 1960, pp. 225–244, 2024.
https://doi.org/10.1007/978-981-99-8761-0_16

structure of programs [4]. Thus, recovering the control flow graph of programs is the basis for upper-level security analysis.

Since its introduction by Frances E. Allen [5] in 1970, control flow graphs (CFGs) have been frequently used in program analysis and optimization techniques. Examples include malware analysis [6–8], vulnerability detection [9,10], code similarity analysis [11,12], and other related applications. CFGs represent all possible paths a program may take during execution. Accurate CFGs can help security researchers understand the construction of programs to accomplish professional review and analysis. Therefore, how to quickly recover accurate CFGs is a field of greater interest to current researchers.

Although significant progress has been made in source-code-oriented control flow graph recovery, source code is not always available. For example, some companies rely on third-party code and components (e.g., frameworks, databases) to create their applications. However these COTS (Commercial Off The Shelf) are usually not source code. In addition, the semantics of the actual executed binary program may differ from the source code through the compilation and optimization process of the compiler [13]. Vulnerabilities are even introduced during the compilation process. The binary-oriented analysis approach allows us to directly analyse the actual code running on the system [14]. Therefore, control flow graph recovery based on binary code is essential.

Some well-known binary analysis tools, such IDA Pro [15] and Angr [4], already offer CFG recovery. IDA Pro is a powerful professional disassembler that is widely used in the field of disassembly and code analysis. The core component of IDA Pro is a recursive traversal disassembler. It creates control flow graphs and function call graphs by applying heuristics to find missing code during recursive traversal. Angr is a binary analysis tool that automates the analysis of binary files and identifies vulnerabilities. Finding and exploiting vulnerabilities in binary code is a very challenging task for analysis tools. The advantage of Angr is that it uses symbolic execution to precisely recover data structures and control flow information from binary.

However, the method of recovering CFG based on binary code still needs to be improved. First, there is the problem of completeness. Due to special code structures such as indirect jumps and tail calls, general recovery methods cannot accurately identify them, resulting in incomplete control flow graphs. In addition, the effectiveness of control flow graph generation is constrained by the constraints of dynamic analysis approaches such as symbolic execution. At the same time, the advent of code obfuscation, handwritten assembly, and malicious code makes it more difficult to extract high-level semantic information from binary code.

This paper gives a survey of the control flow graph recovery for binary code and makes a comprehensive analysis and summary of the related technical achievements. First, it details the manifestation, the basic concepts of the control flow graph, and the existing control flow graph analysis along with the specific implementation of these methods. Then, the differences between methods and their respective advantages and disadvantages are analysed. After that, it discusses the difficulties that need to be overcome to recover accurate control flow graphs and collects relevant literature to organize the methods used in them. Finally, the limitations and challenges of the current work are concluded, and future research directions are elaborated.

2   Methods of Control Flow Graph Recovery

The CFG shows all the paths a program could execute as a directed graph, where the nodes represent basic blocks and the directed edges between the nodes represent the relationship between branch sources and branch targets [5,16]. Each basic block is a sequential instruction sequence with atomicity. By executing one instruction in the block, all instructions are executed with no other internal branches or interrupts [17].

For the control flow, the instructions that actually control the connection relationships in program execution can be simply classified into two types of instructions. One is fall-through instructions, which do not change the sequential control flow, and the other is jump instructions, which change the sequential control flow. Jump instructions are used to transfer the execution flow by changing the PC register to a specified value. The classification of jump instructions can be divided into direct and indirect jumps, conditional and unconditional jumps [18].

The difference between direct and indirect jumps is that the jump target of a direct jump is encoded as part of the instruction. However the jump target of an indirect jump is kept in a register or memory and needs to be computed when the program is run dynamically.

A conditional jump executes a jump to a specified location only when a specific condition holds; otherwise, it changes the PC register to instruct the CPU to execute the next instruction. In contrary, an unconditional jump transfers the program jump directly to the specified location. Their relationship and example instructions in x86 are shown in Table 1.

Table 1. Classification of jump instructions

	Direct	Indirect
Unconditional	jmp 0x004006D4	jmp eax
Conditional	je 0x004006D4	je eax

From the software operation point of view, the CFG recovery methods for binary can be classified into three categories: static analysis, dynamic analysis, and hybrid analysis.

2.1   Static Analysis

Static analysis refers to the analysis of a program based on disassembly techniques without executing the program. After the binary is disassembled, the assembly code is parsed, and only then can the control flow information be extracted. The CFG recovery method using static analysis has three main steps: static disassembly, basic block division, and basic block association [19]. In some cases, intermediate representation(IR) [4,20] generation is added after static disassembly, and static analysis can be split into four steps (see Fig. 1).

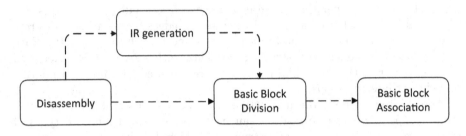

Fig. 1. Steps of static analysis.

Disassembly. Disassembly is the process of recovering assembly instructions from binary. Common static disassembly strategies are classified into two categories [21,22]: linear scan strategies and recursive traversal strategies. To obtain a more accurate control flow graph, some heuristics are usually combined with these disassembly strategies.

(1) Linear sweep. The main idea of the linear sweep strategy is to scan the entire code segment in a linear pattern starting from the first byte and disassemble each instruction encountered during the scan, one by one, in sequence, until the end of the entire segment. Although this method guarantees that maximum coverage is attained, recovering the code so blindly is bound to misidentify data in the segment or padding characters used for alignment as instructions, thus generating errors. Such errors are backwards-propagating and can cause cumulative errors for subsequent instruction recovery [17].

Therefore, the key point of the linear scan strategy is how to correctly separate instructions from data and how to perform error detection. Mainstream disassembly tools usually apply heuristics for error detection. For example, OBJ-DUMP skips the bytes when it encounters an invalid opcode. PSI has a richer error-handling function. When PSI identifies an invalid opcode, it goes back to the previous step along the recovered control flow, replaces the padding after the jump instruction with a nop instruction, and then reassembles the disassembly [21].

(2) Recursive traversal. The main idea of the recursive traversal strategy is to use the control flow information to determine the next instruction to be disassembled. The code is disassembled, and each possible execution path is scanned according to the actual possible execution paths of the code [23,24]. Compared to the linear scanning strategy, the recursive traversal strategy will

be more accurate due to the combination of control flow information. However, the disadvantage arising from such selective recovery instructions is that it is difficult to cover the entire code due to special structures such as indirect calls and non-return functions.

Therefore, existing tools using recursive traversal strategies usually combine heuristics to improve coverage, such as BAP [25], Dyninst [26], Ghidra [27], and radare2 [28]. These tools use function prologues and epilogues to search for function entry points. When a new function entry is discovered, the tools treat it as a new beginning point for disassembly.

In addition, some tools convert the assembly code into an intermediate representation. Intermediate representation (IR) [29–31] is a low-level programming language that is closer to machine code and does not depend on the architecture. It can also express control flow information. Therefore, IR is an important method for solving heterogeneous problems, both for source-code-based analysis and binary-based analysis.

Basic Block Division. After disassembly, the basic blocks need to be identified. As the basic unit of program analysis, many techniques and algorithms are designed and implemented based on the concept of basic blocks.

The principle of classifying basic blocks is that one basic block contains only one single entry point and one single exit point. The entry point corresponds to the first instruction within the basic block, meaning that no code within it is the destination of a jump instruction anywhere in the program. The exit point is the last instruction in the basic block or a jump instruction in the basic block (e.g., conditional branch, return instruction).

According to this principle, the following steps can be used to divide basic blocks:

(1) Find all program entry points, including the program start address and the entry points of other subroutines.
(2) Starting from the program's beginning, scan the instructions in order, and divide the consecutive instructions into a basic block until a jump instruction is encountered.
(3) If a jump instruction is encountered, use the instruction before the current instruction as a basic block and use that instruction as the entry point of a new basic block.

Then, repeat step 2 until all instructions have been traversed.

Basic Block Association. Control flow recovery can start after gathering some parameters, such as the starting address and size of the fundamental blocks.

The edges in the control flow graph indicate the possible jump relationships between basic blocks. Linking basic blocks is essentially finding a pointer to a basic block, which can be found in the operand of a jump instruction, address constants, and global data stored in jump tables or function pointers [20].

Basic block associations are usually of two types:

(1) Boundary associations. In the code order, $block_b$ follows $block_a$, and $block_a$ does not contain an unconditional jump statement.
(2) Control association. $block_a$ has a jump statement to $block_b$.

When the basic block satisfies either of these cases, an edge from $block_a$ to $block_b$ is added.

In practice, however, this information we gathered before recovery is not enough to recover an accurate CFG. The main challenge is handling instructions related to indirect jumps. In general, it is impossible to enumerate all indirect jump targets. The address of targets could be the result of complex calculations and may not even be traceable [20].

Typical tools for static analysis include IDA Pro [15], BINCOA [32], and Jakstab [33]. Although static analysis has the advantages of high coverage and low time overhead, it is not good at recovering control flow when faced with complex codes with missing debugging information in the case of indirect jumps and calls.

2.2 Dynamic Analysis

In contrast to static analysis, dynamic analysis requires running the program in a real or simulated environment. By inputting test cases and analysing the corresponding paths in the running program, we can trace the specific state of the program when the code is executed and thus obtain the CFG.

From the perspective of execution mode, dynamic analysis can be classified into two categories: concrete execution and forced execution.

Concrete Execution. Concrete execution executes the program using carefully generated test cases and constructs a program control flow graph by recording control flow information [34]. To generate such input, fuzz testing is usually used.

Fuzzing is a common vulnerability mining method, and the basic idea is to provide unexpected or random data as input, monitor the program for anomalies, and record the input data that cause the anomalies. Then, the bug report is then manually analysed to further locate vulnerabilities in the software.

Forced Execution. Forced execution tracks conditional branch instructions during program execution dynamically and saves the current program state at each branch point before continuing execution. With the execution of a test case, the program executes along a single path. Afterward, forced execution resumes the execution at a branch point, enforcing a specific sequence of code and operations for the other path of the branch [14]. By employing this approach, each branch of a branch point can be explored efficiently, and indirect branches can be resolved dynamically to construct an accurate CFG.

Currently, most of the dynamic analyses for control flow graphs are built on emulators or fine-grained frameworks. Whether the method is based on interpretation or simulation, on actual execution, or on enforcement, the aim is to trace the program execution. The most commonly used dynamic analysis frameworks include Pin [35], QEMU [36], and Valgrind [29].

Pin is a dynamic binary instrumentation tool. It uses just-in-time (JIT) compilation to dynamically insert arbitrary code (C/C++) into any location during runtime. Pin offers comprehensive APIs that abstract the underlying instruction set features and enables the injection of code with context-sensitive information, such as the process register data. When instrumenting a branch, Pin automatically stores and resets the registers overwritten by the injected code, compiles and executes the instrumentation code, and then restores the previously saved runtime information to allow the program to continue running.

QEMU is a fully virtualized system emulator, a multiplatform-supported and widely used open-source virtual machine software. QEMU has an instruction level-based emulation capability that works at the basic block level of granularity and tracks the CPU instructions executed in a virtual machine. With this feature, users can understand the actual sequence of instructions executed in the virtual machine and perform related debugging and analysis.

Additionally, Valgrind is a dynamic instrumentation framework for binary that uses JIT-based compilation. Unlike Pin, Valgrind uses a heavyweight instrumentation technique for more complex memory debugging, memory leak detection, and performance analysis. Valgrind can perform dynamic binary translation of the target binary file to obtain an architecture-independent intermediate representation (VEX), insert its monitoring code into the translated intermediate representation, and finally compile. The modified VEX is then compiled into the machine code for execution, allowing instruction-level monitoring, and the target program is running on a virtual CPU. However, Valgrind does not provide a programming interface for users and thus cannot meet their specific needs.

The accuracy of dynamic analysis is generally higher than that of static analysis, and indirect call information can be obtained to improve the CFG. However, the dynamic analysis also suffers from low path coverage and relies heavily on the program's test cases [37]. At the same time, the computational overhead is high, and it does not run as efficiently as static analysis.

2.3 Hybrid Analysis

Currently, an increasing number of tools focus on reconstructing CFGs using hybrid analysis because both static and dynamic analysis have drawbacks that are difficult to remedy. Although static analysis has high coverage and fast generation, it is still a challenge to solve the issue of indirect jumps. Dynamic analysis can solve the indirect jump problem to a certain extent, but the low efficiency seriously affects the ease of use and applicability of dynamic analysis tools. Therefore, existing practices usually require a combination of techniques to improve the integrity and efficiency of recovering CFGs. Different techniques have their advantages and disadvantages, and a mixture of different techniques can compensate for each other's shortcomings and provide more technical options for recovering CFGs [38]. The general process of hybrid analysis is shown in Fig. 2.

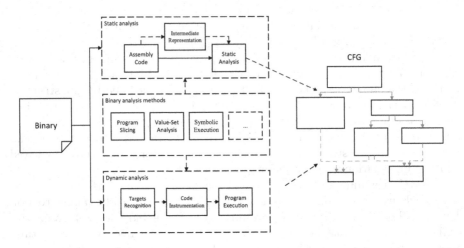

Fig. 2. General process of hybrid analysis.

In hybrid analysis, analysis techniques such as program slicing, value set analysis, and symbolic execution are usually combined. The related techniques are briefly described below, and the details can be found in the related literature [26, 39–42].

Program Slicing. Program slicing is a technique that cuts the execution of a program into smaller parts, generating subsets of the program called slices that contain a particular behavior or property of the program [43]. Program slicing can help developers or testers quickly locate and diagnose defects or problems in a program and is mainly used in areas such as code optimization and security analysis.

In control flow analysis, it can be used not only to reduce the complexity of program analysis by limiting the target to specific subcomponents of the program and removing paths in the program that are not of interest to us but also to supplement and guide the analysis of control flow with additional data information (e.g., variable, the condition of a branch statement).

Value-Set Analysis. Value-set analysis (VSA) is a technique for statically analysing assembly code or instruction traces based on abstract interpretation to infer the set of possible variables in a program [40]. To represent the variables in an executable program, VSA first builds a Value-Set Abstract domain, recovers the variables within it, and represents them using abstract addresses. Then, the set of potential values that each instruction's abstract address contains is calculated.

Value-set analysis is context-sensitive and supports interprocedural analysis [44]. It can calculate the possible targets of indirect jumps or possible targets of memory operations. Therefore, a wide range of uses of VSA exists in the field of recovering control graphs.

Symbolic Execution. Classical symbolic execution is used in analytic techniques to obtain input for the execution of a particular region, originally proposed by King JC [41] at ACM in 1976. When encountering a branch statement, it explores each branch, adding the branch condition to the corresponding path constraint. If the constraint is solvable, then the path is reachable.

With the development of symbolic execution, dynamic symbolic execution, also known as concolic execution, has emerged that mixes the advantages of both concrete execution and symbolic execution [42]. The main concept is to execute the program with specific inputs and search the program path sequentially by collecting path constraints using program staking during the program run. The constraint solver is employed to solve the collected set of constraints to obtain the specific input to reach this path [48]. When the execution of the program encounters a branch point, concolic execution selects one of the branch judgment points for constraint inversion and then solves it with the constraint solver to obtain a test case for executing another path. By iterating this way, we can avoid executing duplicate paths and thus achieve high test coverage with few test sets.

3 Problems of Control Flow Graph Recovery

As one of the fundamental techniques in software security analysis, control flow analysis has made great progress after many years of development. Although different analysis methods have their advantages and disadvantages, the main problem of CFG recovery is to accurately identify indirect jumps, which is a challenge that all analyses have to solve. Other problems are discussed, which include instruction set differences, code obfuscation strategies, and a dynamic examination of how these elements affect control flow graph recovery.

3.1 Main Problem

This paper reviews three types of *indirect jumps*: indirect jumps/calls, tail calls, and non-return functions. For simplicity, we use the term *indirect jumps* to represent both indirect jumps and indirect calls [45].

Indirect jumps. Indirect jumps are generated because the target addresses of jump/call instructions are stored in registers or memory cells and need to be computed when the program is executing. Indirect jumps are mainly derived from jump tables, which are usually compiled from *switch-case* and *if-else* statements. Indirect calls are mainly compiled from function pointers and C++ virtual functions, which are mostly used to implement program polymorphism [46,47]. Most current disassembly tools support the recovery of jump tables, which usually represent in-process control flow, and their precise parsing is essential for applications such as binary rewriting [16] and control flow integrity [67].

Figure 3 shows a simple example to explain what is an indirect jump, in which subfigures (a,b) give its source code and CFG, respectively.

In function *func*, *cal* is a function pointer that allows passing functions as variables to other functions. If $a > num$(line 10), *cal* points to *add*, otherwise *cal* points to *sub*. Accordingly, the input to the program or the intermediate variables of the program influences the change in the function pointer. Finally, when the function *cal* is called, there is an indirect call. In Fig. 3(b), the dotted line indicates the indirect jump relationship. The path selection of the program depends on the value of the incoming function, and for CFG recovery, the general method cannot analyse all possible paths.

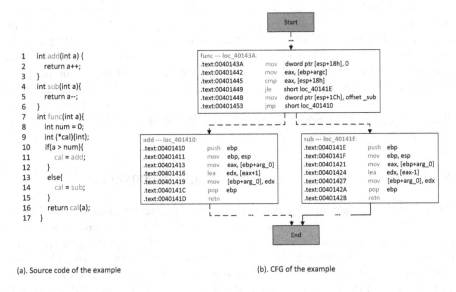

(a). Source code of the example   (b). CFG of the example

Fig. 3. Example of indirect jump.

Tail calls. Tail calls appear as a result of compiler optimization and refer to the last statement of a function returning a call to the next function. This call is usually optimized and compiled as an indirect jump instruction, avoiding the overhead of creating a new stack frame and thus improving the execution efficiency of the program [49]. If the binary analysis tool does not recognize the tail call, the control flow from the tail call instruction will be marked as in-process and incorrectly analysed.

Non-return functions. A return-free function, i.e., a function with no return value, is usually obtained by compiling a void function, where the return statement does not need to be explicitly defined [50]. Tools either assumed that all functions return to their calling location or used simple name-matching to identify non-return functions. The correct identification of non-return functions affects the function boundaries of the recovered assembly code and thus the connection of edges in the control flow recovery.

3.2   Other Problems

Instruction Set Differences. Different CPU architectures have different instruction sets, especially x86 and x64 platforms that use variable length instruction (VLE) encoding architecture, which makes it more difficult to distinguish code from data. Therefore, building a common CFG recovery tool or binary analysis platform needs to overcome many difficulties of instruction set differences. To overcome the problem of instruction set differences, the existing common practice is to first convert assembly code of different architectures into a uniform representation, the Intermediate Representations. Analysing tools can overcome the heterogeneity of the code and examine it on the IR.

Code Obfuscation. Code obfuscation is a software protection technique that can effectively increase the attackers' cost of reverse analysis and attacks. This technique is usually performed by changing the internal structure and logic of a program to make the code more difficult to analyse while keeping the semantics of the program intact. Software developers use code obfuscation to build defenses for their software, and attackers use code obfuscation to try to get their malware to bypass security reviews. In any case, obfuscation against control flow reduces program readability by changing the order and flow of the program and inhibits proper disassembly and control flow extraction [51,52]. The most common obfuscation used for binaries is the control flow spreading algorithm. This algorithm disrupts the original control logic of a program and uses the switch-case pattern to replace the nesting and looping structure in the program. The goal is to guarantee that each basic block has unique predecessors and successors. The switch module is located in the decision module, which dynamically decides which basic block the control flow is shifted to based on the value of the dispatch variable [53].

Path Explosion. The path explosion problem is an important factor that limits the recovery of control flow graphs. When there are a large number of branches and loop structures in the program, a large number of execution paths are generated, resulting in excessive time and space overhead for recovery and an increased error rate in graph generation [54,55]. The result is that the structure of the control flow graph becomes very complex. The path explosion problem is also a major constraint to the implementation of symbolic execution in control flow recovery. This is because during symbolic execution, the branch will be divided into two symbolic instances. With an increase in branch paths, the amount of symbolic data that must be saved grows exponentially [41]. Constraint solving is the basis of symbolic execution, and many studies have made significant progress. In recent years, the capability of constraint solving and its inherent limitations are still the primary obstacle to improving the usability of symbolic execution as far as they are concerned.

4   Solutions and Comparisons

This section mainly reviews the solutions for control flow graph recovery and their shortcomings in recent literature and summarizes them in Table 2.

Meng and Miller proposed Dyninst [26], a binary staking tool that supports dynamic and static staking, in which CFG recovery is handled using static analysis. For jump table recovery, Dyninst models the jump table and transforms it into a univariate function. It also obtains the instruction slice for each indirect jump and uses data flow analysis to parse slices to complete jump tables. To find non-return functions, an interprocedural analysis is designed to detect the cyclic dependencies of the functions.

Alessandro [20] classifies indirect control instructions into three categories: all indirect jump instructions generated by the compiler, reasonable handwritten assemblies, and indirect function calls, while the proposed REV.NG is designed to handle the first two cases. Based on the conversion of binary code into LLVM IR with the help of the QEMU platform, two methods for recovering indirect jumps are performed: Simple Expression Tracker and OSR analysis (a data flow analysis), focusing on the values stored in instructions and the jump targets generated by switch instructions.

Razor [45] recovers the control flow graph dynamically, using Dynamorio and Pin for instruction instrumentation and Intel PT to record changes in flow information in hardware. It obtains an accurate instruction address and function boundary from the execution trace. Razor is designed to perform code reduction for deployed binaries, so it recovers only part of the control flow graph.

Xu et al. [14] developed a control flow graph construction tool called FXE based on the QEMU emulator. FXE uses the idea of dynamic coercion and does not depend on specific inputs for the execution of the driver. It does not provide any specific input to the program but uses random data in memory when input is needed. In contrast to constraint solving, this may lead to programs that are often in an inconsistent state. The authors argue that the results of the analysis are available even if there is a situation in which the intermediate states are incorrectly calculated in the program run, as long as the indirect jump target is resolved. Code coverage can be improved by the combination of execution and rollback. For jump table recovery, FXE uses simple pattern-matching to locate the start address at the indirect instruction.

X-Force also uses the enforced execution approach. Peng et al. [56] implemented X-Force to perform coercion only in the branching part of the predicate, defining functions of different fitness (Fitness) to control the range to be explored and combining it with taint analysis to reduce the search range.

Problems with the forced execution approach are that it does not accurately approximate the control flow, enforces infeasible edges, and leads to an algorithm that is not guaranteed to finish in a limited time. It is very computationally intensive, and saving a large amount of intermediate state during program execution is also very memory intensive.

Zhu et al. [59], on the other hand, use fuzzing for CFG recovery, and CFGConstructor uses a strategy of static generation followed by dynamic optimization.

To solve the indirect jump, the set of test cases is generated by variation-based fuzzing, and the binary is guided to execute specifically. Moreover, the jump address is established by staking indirect call instructions, and the statically acquired CFG is improved by dynamically recognized indirect call associations. In subsequent work, they introduced directed gray-box fuzzing (DGF) instead of the previous coverage-based fuzzing, implementing DGF-CFGConstructor [39] based on AFLGO. DGF-CFGConstructor uses indirect call instructions as target points, combined with a distance-based fitness function that prioritizes seeds with closer variance by computing the distance between the seed and the target point. Such an approach makes fuzzing "directed" in nature. In addition, a feedback mechanism that iteratively improves input generation is incorporated with this. This mechanism primarily solves the "undirected" and "unsustainable" issues that arise when fuzzing is applied to control flow analysis.

Both CFGConstructor and DGF-CFGConstructor rely on fuzzing tools, so the integrity and efficiency of control flow recovery depend on the selection of test cases and the performance of the fuzzing tools themselves.

CFGCombine [60] also uses static generation followed by a dynamic optimization approach and combines backwards slicing and symbolic execution. Backwards slicing starts at the indirect jump of the solution to be solved and goes up to the start of the previous basic block. The purpose is to address a situation where a function uses a pointer as a function variable and the pointer is used as the indirect jump address of the function.

CFGgrind [51] extends the range of coverage for a test case based on Dyninst. In addition, it refines the formal definition of CFG, adding phantom nodes and OS signals. These two structures are used to accommodate special structures such as handling indirect jumps when dynamically recovering control flow graphs. In particular, for unconditional jump instructions, CFGgrind chooses to execute the next instruction sequentially by skipping to explore more unvisited paths.

Angr [4], proposed by Shoshitaishvili et al., is a very well-known framework for binary analysis and provides two CFG recovery schemes in terms of CFG recovery: CFGFast and CFGAccurate. CFGFast uses recursive disassembly combined with heuristics (alias analysis, dataflow tracing, and predefined policies). Fast generation of CFGs has high coverage but misses most of the indirect control flow. To obtain a more precise CFG, CFGAccurate uses a constraint solver to precisely calculate the potential values of the indirect jump target address after pushing the execution to explore more paths. There are still some unresolvable jump cases using symbolic execution that may be implemented in a context-insensitive way. For example, when a function accepts a pointer as an argument and that pointer is subsequently utilized as the destination for an indirect jump, the analysis will not be able to solve it. CFGAccurate mode computes the target address from the beginning of the previous call context to an unresolved jump.

Thomas [18] adds two algorithms for alternate control flow recovery to Jakstab. The goal is to keep track of the propagation of constants through the program and the multiple program locations contained in registers or memory locations recorded in the step-interval analysis, providing locations for directed symbol execution that require parsed symbols. However, the algorithms for alternate control flow reconstruction are still very memory intensive, and step interval analysis cannot find all paths in a reasonable amount of time.

Table 2. Comparison of CFG recovery tools

Category	Tool name	Integrity	Efficiency	multi-arch	Open sourced	Base tool	Benchmarks
Static analysis	Dyninst	Low	High	✗	✔	–	SPECint 2006, real programs
	REV.NG	Medium	High	✔	✔	QEMU	GNU Core Utilities
Dynamic analysis	FXE	High	Low	✗	✔	QEMU	Siemens Test Suite, CINT2000
	X-Force	High	Low	✗	✗	Pin	SPECint 2000
	Razor	Low	Low	✗	✔	Dynamorio, Pin, Intel PT	SPECint 2006, CHISEL paper, 2 real programs
Hybrid analysis	Angr(CFGAccurate)	Medium	Low	✔	✔	Valgrind	CGC binaries
	CFGCombine	Medium	Low	✗	✗	–	CGC binaries
	CFGConstructor	Medium	Low	✗	✗	AFL, Pin	CGC binaries
	Jakstab	Medium	Medium	✗	✔	Manticore	GNU Core Utilities
	CFGgrind	Medium	Low	✗	✔	Valgrind	Collective Benchmark, SPEC CPU2017
	DGF-CFGConstructor	High	Medium	✔	✗	AFLGO	8 real programs

In this paper, we summarized CFG recovery tools and compared them in terms of the recovery method, analysable architecture, open source, base tool, and benchmark. As shown in Table 2, a brief evaluation is also presented in terms of both integrity and efficiency dimensions. Some binary analysis tools have not been developed for recovering control flow graphs alone.

Of the eleven tools, nearly half employ a hybrid analysis, with Angr also offering a static analysis for binary.

For the architectures that the tools can analyse, all tools can analyse executable programs compiled on the x86 architecture. REV.NG and Angr can analyse multiplatform programs with the help of the IR, which is converted to an intermediate language after the program has been disassembled. It avoids the impact of instruction differences between architectures and allows the tool to analyse programs compiled for different architectures, improving the applicability of the tool.

For the evaluation of the experiment, there is no general approach to evaluate CFG recovery tools in this research area. Regarding the completeness of CFGs, the literature often takes coverage such as the number of found functions, basic blocks and instructions, as well as statistics on the number of indirect jumps solved, and compares them with some well-known tools such as IDA Pro.

The efficiency of recovering CFGs is measured by two metrics: binary size and time cost. Tools that employ dynamic analysis (including concolic execution) will always lag behind non-dynamic analysis, and generally, these tools are also difficult to apply to large programs.

The datasets used to verify the validity of the tools are broadly divided into six types: SPECint [61], GNU Core Utilities [62], Siemens Test Suite [63], CGC binaries [64], Collective Benchmark [65], CHISEL paper [68] and some real programs. All of them are benchmark suites with C/C++ code. In addition, the CGC binaries are focused on verifying the finding and exploitation of vulnerabilities.

5   Conclusion

CFG recovery of binary code is an important part of software reverse analysis work, a prerequisite and guarantee for correct interpretation of software code, and an important technical means to realize program security testing and intellectual property protection. Therefore, in software security testing and binary vulnerability mining, the control flow graph recovery of binary is of great significance.

Current techniques related to binary control flow graph recovery have made some progress in static analysis, dynamic analysis, and hybrid analysis. Among them, static analysis can efficiently solve part of the indirect jump problem and has the advantage of high coverage for code analysis. However, static analysis still lacks effective heuristics when facing complex indirect jumps and indirect calls. For dynamic analysis, there are many well-established tools and systems, but the execution efficiency in dealing with large programs seriously affects the wider application of dynamic analysis. Hybrid analysis, which improves the overall efficiency and accuracy of analysis by combining different heuristics or techniques with conventional methods, has become more popular in recent years. Moreover, the problem of recovering a completely accurate CFG is undeterminable, which means that we can only expect to obtain approximate solutions.

A summary of related studies shows that in the field of control flow graph recovery of binary, there is a need to optimize basic work such as disassembly or code staking on the one hand and to propose more general schemes or systems on the other.

Acknowledgements. This work is supported by Key Science and Technology Program of Henan Province under Grant No. 182102210130, No. 232102210134, No. 232102211088. We would like to thank the anonymous reviewers for valuable comments on this paper.

References

1. Wurm, J., et al.: Security analysis on consumer and industrial IoT devices. In: 2016 21st Asia and South Pacific Design Automation Conference (ASP-DAC), pp. 519–524. IEEE (2016). https://doi.org/10.1109/ASPDAC.2016.7428064
2. Bogart, C., et al.: When and how to make breaking changes: policies and practices in 18 open source software ecosystems. ACM Trans. Softw. Eng. Methodol. 30(4), 1–56 (2021). https://doi.org/10.1145/3447245
3. NIST. National Vulnerability Dtabase (2023). https://nvd.nist.gov. Accessed 26 Apr 2023
4. Shoshitaishvili, Y., et al.: SOK: (state of) the art of war: offensive techniques in binary analysis. In: 2016 IEEE Symposium on Security and Privacy (SP), pp. 138–157. IEEE (2016). https://doi.org/10.1109/SP.2016.17
5. Allen, F.E.: Control flow analysis. ACM Sigplan Notices 5(7), 1–19 (1970). https://doi.org/10.1145/390013.808479
6. Sun, Q., et al.: Leveraging spectral representations of control flow graphs for efficient analysis of windows malware. In: Proceedings of the ACM on Asia Conference on Computer and Communications Security, 2022, pp. 1240–1242 (2022). https://doi.org/10.1145/3488932.3527294
7. Wu, C.Y., et al.: IoT malware classification based on reinterpreted function-call graphs. Comput. Secur. 125, 103060 (2023). https://doi.org/10.1016/j.cose.2022.103060
8. Herath, J.D., et al.: CFGExplainer: explaining graph neural network-based malware classification from control flow graphs. In: 2022 52nd Annual IEEE/IFIP International Conference on Dependable Systems and Networks (DSN), pp. 172–184. IEEE (2022). https://doi.org/10.1109/DSN53405.2022.00028
9. Cao, S., et al.: Bgnn4vd: constructing bidirectional graph neural-network for vulnerability detection. Inf. Softw. Technol. 136, 106576 (2021). https://doi.org/10.1016/j.infsof.2021.106576
10. Cheng, X., et al.: Path-sensitive code embedding via contrastive learning for software vulnerability detection. In: Proceedings of the 31st ACM SIGSOFT International Symposium on Software Testing and Analysis, pp. 519–531 (2022). https://doi.org/10.1145/3533767.3534371
11. Xu, X., et al.: Neural network-based graph embedding for cross-platform binary code similarity detection. In: Proceedings of the ACM SIGSAC Conference on Computer and Communications Security, 2017, pp. 363–376 (2017). https://doi.org/10.1145/3133956.3134018
12. Wang, H., et al.: jTrans: Jump-Aware Transformer for Binary Code Similarity. arXiv preprint arXiv:2205.12713 (2022). https://doi.org/10.48550/arXiv.2205.12713
13. Balakrishnan, G., Reps, T.: Wysinwyx: what you see is not what you execute. ACM Trans. Prog. Lang. Syst. 32(6), 1–84 (2010). https://doi.org/10.1145/1749608.1749612
14. Xu, L., Sun, F., Su, Z.: Constructing Precise Control Flow Graphs from Binaries. University of California, Davis, Tech. Rep. 28 (2009)
15. Hex-Rays. IDAPro Disassembler. https://www.hex-rays.com/. Accessed 24 Feb 2023
16. Wenzl, M., et al.: From hack to elaborate technique-a survey on binary rewriting. ACM Comput. Surv. 52(3), 1–37 (2019). https://doi.org/10.1145/3316415

17. Wang, J., et al.: Survey on application of machine learning in disassembly on x86 binaries. Netinfo Security **22**(6), 9–25 (2022). https://doi.org/10.3969/j.issn.1671-1122.2022.06.002

18. Peterson, T.: Alternating Control Flow Graph Reconstruction by Combining Constant Propagation and Strided Intervals with Directed Symbolic Execution (2019). http://kth.diva-portal.org/smash/record.jsf?pid=diva2%3A1416002

19. Zhang, B., Li, Q.-B., Cui, C.: Dynamic control flow recovery algorithm based on automatic path driven. Comput. Eng. **39**(8), 77–82 (2013). https://doi.org/10.3969/j.issn.1000-3428.2013.08.016

20. Di Federico, A., Payer, M., Agosta, G.: rev. ng: a unified binary analysis framework to recover CFGs and function boundaries. In: Proceedings of the 26th International Conference on Compiler Construction, pp. 131–141 (2017). https://doi.org/10.1145/3033019.3033028

21. Pang, C., et al.: SoK: all you ever wanted to know about x86/x64 binary disassembly but were afraid to ask. In: 2021 IEEE Symposium on Security and Privacy (SP), pp. 833–851. IEEE (2021). https://doi.org/10.1109/SP40001.2021.00012

22. Pang, C., et al.: Ground truth for binary disassembly is not easy. In: 31st USENIX Security Symposium (USENIX Security 22), pp. 2479–2495 (2022). https://www.usenix.org/conference/usenixsecurity22/presentation/pang-chengbin

23. Dai, C., et al.: Research on disassembly against the Malware obfuscated with embedded code. J. Inf. Eng. Univ. **19**(3), 347–352 (2018). https://doi.org/10.3969/j.issn.1671-0673.2018.03.018

24. Flores-Montoya, A., Schulte, E.: Datalog disassembly. In: Proceedings of the 29th USENIX Conference on Security Symposium, pp. 1075–1092 (2020)

25. Brumley, D., Jager, I., Avgerinos, T., Schwartz, E.J.: BAP: a binary analysis platform. In: Proceedings of the Computer Aided Verification-23rd International Conference, CAV 2011, Snowbird, 14–20 July 2011, pp. 463–469 (2011). https://doi.org/10.1007/978-3-642-22110-137

26. Meng, X., Miller, B.P.: Binary code is not easy. In: Proceedings of the 25th International Symposium on Software Testing and Analysis, pp. 24–35 (2016). https://doi.org/10.1145/2931037.2931047

27. NSA. Ghidra Software Reverse Engineering Framework. National Security Agency (2022). https://github.com/NationalSecurityAgency/ghidra. Accessed 24 Feb 2023

28. Radare 2 (2023). https://rada.re. Accessed 24 Feb 2023

29. Nethercote, N., Seward, J.: Valgrind: a framework for heavyweight dynamic binary instrumentation. In: Proceedings of the ACM SIGPLAN 2007 Conference on Programming Language Design and Implementation, PLDI 2007, p. 100. ACM (2007). https://doi.org/10.1145/1273442.1250746

30. Lattner, C., Adve, V.: LLVM: a compilation framework for lifelong program analysis and transformation. In: International Symposium on Code Generation and Optimization, CGO 2004, pp. 75–86. IEEE (2004). https://doi.org/10.1109/CGO.2004.1281665

31. Naus, N., Verbeek, F., Walker, D., Ravindran, B.: A formal semantics for P-code. In: Lal, A., Tonetta, S. (eds.) Verified Software. Theories, Tools and Experiments. VSTTE 2022. LNCS 13800, pp. 111–128. Springer, Cham (2023). https://doi.org/10.1007/978-3-031-25803-9_7

32. Bardin, S., et al.: The BINCOA framework for binary code analysis. In: CAV 2011, pp. 165–170. https://doi.org/10.1007/978-3-642-22110-1

33. Kinder, J., Veith, H.: Jakstab: a static analysis platform for binaries: tool paper. In: Gupta, A., Malik, S. (eds.) Computer Aided Verification. CAV 2008. LNCS

5123, pp. 423–427. Springer, Heidelberg (2008). https://doi.org/10.1007/978-3-540-70545-140

34. Song, D., et al.: BitBlaze: a new approach to computer security via binary analysis. In: Sekar, R., Pujari, A.K. (eds.) ICISS 2008. LNCS, vol. 5352, pp. 1–25. Springer, Heidelberg (2008). https://doi.org/10.1007/978-3-540-89862-7_1

35. Luk, C.K., et al.: Pin: building customized program analysis tools with dynamic instrumentation. ACM Sigplan Notices **40**(6), 190–200 (2005). https://doi.org/10.1145/1064978.1065034

36. Bellard, F.: QEMU, a Fast and Portable Dynamic Translator. In: Proceedings of the USENIX Annual Technical Conference, pp. 41–46 (2005)

37. Nataraj, L., et al.: A comparative assessment of malware classification using binary texture analysis and dynamic analysis. In: Proceedings of the 4th ACM Workshop on Security and Artificial Intelligence, pp. 21–30 (2011). https://doi.org/10.1145/2046684.2046689

38. Liu, Z., et al.: Automated binary analysis: a survey. In: Meng, W., Lu, R., Min, G., Vaidya, J. (eds.) Algorithms and Architectures for Parallel Processing. ICA3PP 2022. LNCS, 13777, pp. 392–411. Springer, Cham (2023). https://doi.org/10.1007/978-3-031-22677-9_21

39. Zhu, K., et al.: Constructing more complete control flow graphs utilizing directed gray-box fuzzing. Appl. Sci. **11**(3), 1351 (2021). https://doi.org/10.3390/app11031351

40. Balakrishnan, G., Gruian, R., Reps, T., Teitelbaum, T.: CodeSurfer/x86—a platform for analyzing x86 executables. In: Bodik, R. (ed.) CC 2005. LNCS, vol. 3443, pp. 250–254. Springer, Heidelberg (2005). https://doi.org/10.1007/978-3-540-31985-6_19

41. King, J.C.: Symbolic execution and program testing. Commun. ACM **19**(7), 385–394 (1976). https://doi.org/10.1145/360248.360252

42. Godefroid, P., Klarlund, N., Sen, K.: DART: directed automated random testing. In: Proceedings of the ACM SIGPLAN conference on Programming Language Design and Implementation, 2005, pp. 213–223 (2005). https://doi.org/10.1145/1065010.1065036

43. Weiser, M.: Program slicing. IEEE Trans. Softw. Eng. **4**, 352–357 (1984). https://doi.org/10.1109/TSE.1984.5010248

44. Lin, J., et al.: A value set analysis refinement approach based on conditional merging and lazy constraint solving. IEEE Access **7**, 114593–114606 (2019). https://doi.org/10.1109/ACCESS.2019.2936139

45. Qian, C., et al.: RAZOR: a framework for post-deployment software debloating. In: USENIX Security Symposium, pp. 1733–1750 (2019)

46. Hao, Q., et al.: A hardware security-monitoring architecture based on data integrity and control flow integrity for embedded systems. Appl. Sci. **12**(15), 7750 (2022). https://doi.org/10.3390/app12157750

47. Altinay, A., et al.: BinRec: dynamic binary lifting and recompilation. In: Proceedings of the Fifteenth European Conference on Computer Systems, pp. 1–16 (2020). https://doi.org/10.1145/3342195.3387550

48. Ye, Z.-B., Yan, B.: Survey of symbolic execution. Comput. Sci. **45**(6A), 28–35 (2018). https://doi.org/10.11896/j.issn.1002-137X.2018.Z6.005

49. Garcia, R.: Proper Tail Calls (2015)

50. GNU. Gnulib Manual. https://www.gnu.org/software/gnulib/manual/html_node/Non_002dreturning-Functions.html. Accessed 26 Apr 2023

51. Rimsa, A., Nelson Amaral, J., Pereira, F.M.Q.: Practical dynamic reconstruction of control flow graphs. Softw. Pract. Exp. **51**(2), 353–384 (2021). https://doi.org/10.1002/spe.2907
52. He, X., et al.: BinProv: binary code provenance identification without disassembly. In: Proceedings of the 25th International Symposium on Research in Attacks, Intrusions and Defenses, pp. 350–363 (2022). https://doi.org/10.1145/3545948.3545956
53. Linn, C., Debray, S.: Obfuscation of executable code to improve resistance to static disassembly. In: Proceedings of the 10th ACM Conference on Computer and Communications Security, pp. 290–299 (2003). https://doi.org/10.1145/948109.948149
54. Steinhöfel, D.: Symbolic execution: foundations, techniques, applications, and future perspectives. In: Ahrendt, W., Beckert, B., Bubel, R., Johnsen, E.B. (eds.) The Logic of Software. A Tasting Menu of Formal Methods. LNCS, vol. 13360, pp. 446–480. Springer, Cham (2022). https://doi.org/10.1007/978-3-031-08166-8_22
55. Vinçont, Y., Bardin, S., Marcozzi, M.: A tight integration of symbolic execution and fuzzing (Short Paper). In: Aimeur, E., Laurent, M., Yaich, R., Dupont, B., Garcia-Alfaro, J. (eds.) Foundations and Practice of Security. FPS 2021. LNCS, vol. 13291, pp. 303–310. Springer, Cham (2022). https://doi.org/10.1007/978-3-031-08147-7_20
56. Peng, F., et al.: X-Force: force-executing binary programs for security applications. In: 23rd USENIX Security Symposium (USENIX Security 14), pp. 829–844 (2014)
57. Bernat, A.R., Miller, B.P.: Structured binary editing with a CFG transformation algebra. In: 2012 19th Working Conference on Reverse Engineering, pp. 9–18. IEEE (2012). https://doi.org/10.1109/WCRE.2012.11
58. Di Federico, A., Agosta, G.: A jump-target identification method for multiarchitecture static binary translation. In: Proceedings of the International Conference on Compilers, Architectures and Synthesis for Embedded Systems, pp. 1–10 (2016). https://doi.org/10.1145/2968455.2968514
59. Zhu, K., Lu, Y.U., Huang, H., et al.: Construction approach for control flow graph from binaries using hybrid analysis. J. ZheJiang Univ. (Eng. Sci.) **53**(5), 829–836 (2019). https://doi.org/10.3785/j.issn.1008-973X.2019.05.002
60. Ye, Z., Jiang, X., Shi, D.: Combined method of constructing binary-oriented control flow graphs. Appl. Res. Comput. **35**(7), 2168–2171 (2018). https://doi.org/10.3969/j.issn.1001-3695.2018.07.060
61. SPEC CPU. Standard Performance Evaluation Corporation. https://www.spec.org/. Accessed 25 Apr 2023
62. GNU Core Utilities. Free Software Foundation: Coreutils. https://ftp.gnu.org/gnu/coreutils/. Accessed 25 Apr 2023
63. Hutchins, M., et al.: Experiments on the effectiveness of dataflow-and control-flow-based test adequacy criteria. In: Proceedings of 16th International Conference on Software Engineering, pp. 191–200. IEEE (1994). https://doi.org/10.1109/ICSE.1994.296778
64. DARPA. DARPA cyber grand challenge. https://github.com/CyberGrand. Challenge . Accessed 25 Apr 2023
65. The CTuning Foundation. Collective Benchmar. https://ctuning.org/. Accessed 25 Apr 2023
66. Zhao, Y.J., Tang, Z.Y., Wang, N., Fang, D.Y., Gu, Y.X.: Evaluation of code obfuscating transformation. J. Softw. **23**(3), 700–711 (2012)

67. Kumar, S., Moolchandani, D., Sarangi, S.R.: Hardware-assisted mechanisms to enforce control flow integrity: a comprehensive survey. J. Syst. Architect. **130**, 102644 (2022). https://doi.org/10.1016/j.sysarc.2022.102644

68. Heo, K., et al.: Effective program debloating via reinforcement learning. In: Proceedings of the ACM SIGSAC Conference on Computer and Communications Security, 2018, pp. 380–394 (2018). https://doi.org/10.1145/3243734.3243838

An Architectural Design of Urban Road Transport of Dangerous Goods Based on the DoDAF

Caixi Luo[1]([⊠]) and Xiaohong Liu[2]

[1] Tianjin Renai College, Tianjin 301636, China
luocaixi@tjrac.edu.cn

[2] Tianjin Hedong District Workers and Staff's College, Tianjin 300161, China

Abstract. By investigating and analysing the management of the safety of road freight transport of dangerous goods in City A, this paper presents an architecture framework of urban road freight transport of dangerous goods based on the DoDAF (Department of Defense Architecture Framework) in accordance with *the Measures for the Administration of Road Transport Safety of Dangerous Goods* and other related laws and regulations. The top-level design involves a brief introduction, standards and specifications, capability, procedure, data, models, etc. Thus, 8 viewpoints are created. The paper is expected to offer a systematic, normative approach to architecture implementation of urban road freight transport of dangerous goods.

Keywords: dangerous goods · safety of road transportation · DoDAF · 8 viewpoints · architecture framework

1 Background

China is a major country that produces and uses dangerous goods such as dangerous chemicals explosive and radioactive substances [1]. China is also a country with a large transport capacity for dangerous goods. In recent years, the management of road transport of dangerous goods has become increasingly standardized and presents a better tendency. However, frequent accidents expose some bugs and problems in its management.

The transport of dangerous goods is the main supervised domain of road freight transport. It directly offers service to all kinds of fields from industry to agricultural production, from national defense sci-tech to people's life. Thus, it plays an important role in supporting economic development and serving the people [2].

The supervision and research in this aspect could be dated back to the 1950s in developed countries when the UN began to establish the UNCETDG (United Nations Committee of Experts on the Transport of Dangerous Goods). Since then, extensive research on the global transport safety of dangerous goods has been conducted [3].

To thoroughly implement the deployment requirements of the CPC Central Committee and the State Council, six ministries jointly issued *Measures for the Administration of*

Road Transport Safety of Dangerous Goods (hereinafter referred to as *Measures*). (The six ministries are Ministries of Transport and Communications, Industry and Information Technology, Public Security, Ecology and Environment, Emergency Management and Market Supervision.) The other purpose of *Measures* is to reinforce its management, prevent transport accidents, protect the environment and safeguard people's lives and property against dangers. *Measures* are expected to compensate for the deficiency of related regulations and focus on constructing a more effective system of managing road transport of dangerous goods. In this system, the market entities are operated standardly, and the government sectors supervise thoroughly to ensure that all the factors of transportation are safe and controllable [4].

Requirements related to road freight transport of dangerous goods are listed in the *Measures*. It also clarifies the duties and requirements of corresponding ministries, government sectors, manufacturers and transport enterprises. However, how to address the coordination and management among all these ministries and related businesses is the prime focus facing the government sectors at all levels.

However, in terms of the urban road freight transport safety of dangerous goods, top-level design has obviously been lacking until now. At present, there are various problems. For example, certain functional departments deal with it according to its process, dependency or a certain focus in different provinces. Although they created many information management systems, questions such as data inconformity and disorder when shared arose frequently due to a lack of integrated planning and top-level design. Some even more operated independently and formed data islands [5]. Therefore, these systems cannot meet the practical needs of supervision during the entire process [6] in this situation.

This paper presents a top-level design [8] of urban road freight transport of dangerous goods based on DoDAF 2.0 [7] and an operation management mechanism in which not only is the safety of dangerous goods managed intelligently, dynamically and visually, but also multisectors can coordinate and link with one another. Thus, a system that includes all factors, periods, processes, and entities is established to provide measures for dealing with the urban road freight transport of dangerous goods.

2 Introduction of DoDAF 2.0

2.1 Overview of DoDAF 2.0

An architecture framework (abbreviated as AF), a method to describe an architecture to a certain specification [9], is the basis of classifying and organizing its information as well as the principles and guidelines for developing products. AF plays an important role in developing integrated electronic information systems. Since the 1990s, the US army has conducted research on AF and successively issued several versions of AF. To date, DoDAF 2.0 [10] of the US Department of Defense has been the top-level all-around framework and conceptional model of architecture.

DoDAF depicts a universal developing method tested by practice, which can be widely applied in architecture development after relatively simple adjustment and be helpful to architects and development teams. It is not product-centric but data-centric.

It stresses the relationship among data and ensures the capture of all the needed data to support analysis to realize data consistency in different viewpoints.

DoDAF 2.0 includes 8 viewpoints [11], as follows:

1. All viewpoint (AV): AV depicts all the viewpoints.
2. Capability viewpoint (CV): CV clarifies the capabilities requirements, delivery timing and deployment.
3. Data and Information Viewpoint (DIV): DIV describes the relations among data and the alignment of data structures to meet the demands of capability, operation and process of systems engineering.
4. Operational Viewpoint (OV): OV provides the operational scenarios, activities and demands that can support its functions.
5. Project Viewpoint (PV): PV describes the relationship between the demands of operation and capability and the ongoing project. PV also specifies in detail the interdependence of the operational and capability requirements in the process of the Defense Acquisition System, system engineering, system design and service design.
6. Services Viewpoint (SvcV): SvcV is used to design a resolution that clearly depicts the performers, activities, services and swaps by providing for or supporting operation and capability.
7. Standards Viewpoint (StdV): StdV describes applicative operation, business, techniques and industry strategies, standards, guidance, constraints and predictions.
8. Systems Viewpoint (SV): SV is to design a resolution that clearly depicts the systems, composition, interconnectivity and context to provide for or support operation and capability.

2.2 Design Method of DoDAF2.0

There are six steps in the process of architecture design.

Step 1. Determine the expected uses of architecture

According to the principle of applicable purpose, the purpose and expected uses are described, as are the result guidance, the development method and the measure of its indicators.

Step 2. Determine its scope

The scope indicates the depth and width of architecture and shows the difficulties of establishing architecture. It is helpful to describe the relationship among the viewpoint products and the levels of detailed content.

Step 3. Determine the needed data that support development

Levels of details acquired for data items are determined by repeated process analysis in Step 2, including the determination of data that are needed for the procedure and the other data needed to realize changes in the current step. These items will determine the types of data collected in Step 4 and have a relationship with the architecture and depth of details needed.

Step 4. Collect, organize, correlate and save data

For the purpose of expression and policy-making, viewpoints are usually used to describe the collected and organized data.

Step 5. Analyse the tasks that support architecture

That the managerment of the process needs to be classified into different levels is determined by data analysis. This step may be helpful to identify the other steps and demands of data collection. Thus, its application will be better promoted.

Step 6. Achieve results consistent with the requirements of the policymaker

The last step is to build a viewpoint to find the hidden data. To meet the demands of different users, data of one kind usually must be converted into a different type.

3   Architecture Design of Urban Road Freight Transport of Dangerous Goods [12]

The viewpoints are a set of selected data that are organized in an understandable way to be more intuitive. There are different ways to be intuitive, such as dashboards, text and combined images, which symbolize the collected data and output information during the development of architecture. Let us analyse them one by one.

3.1   Viewpoint of Urban Road Freight Transport of Dangerous Goods

Below is a panoramic view of urban road freight transport of dangerous goods. It describes the architecture from 8 aspects (All Viewpoints, Capability Viewpoint, Operational Viewpoint, Services Viewpoint, Systems Viewpoint, Data and Information Viewpoint, Project Viewpoint and Standards Viewpoint) and their interrelation (Fig. 1).

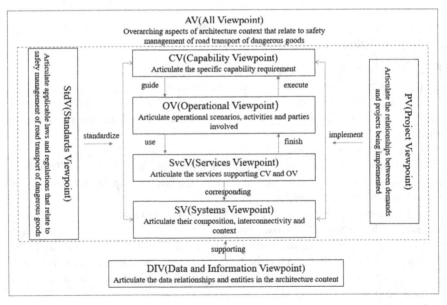

Fig. 1. A panorama of urban road freight transport of dangerous goods

As we can see, this architecture is supposed to provide a universal and normative analysis of its general view from different aspects. All Viewpoints (abbreviated as AV) in

DoDAF provides a model to solve the above questions. AV mainly describes information related to top-level design and is the leading guide of the architecture.

Capability Viewpoint (abbreviated as CV) articulates the specific demands of capabilities. It guides OV to complete its procedures, activities and participants.

Operational Viewpoint (abbreviated as OV) articulates the operational scenarios, procedures, activities and participants in this field. It utilizes the service in SvcV to complete the relative operation procedures and activities.

Services Viewpoint (abbreviated as SvcV) articulates the services concerned to support CV and OV.

Systems Viewpoint (abbreviated as SV) articulates the components, interrelation and environment requirements of the system. It corresponds to SvcV.

Data and Information Viewpoint (abbreviated as DIV) articulates the data entities for top-level design and their relation. It provides data and a model for the architecture.

Project Viewpoint (abbreviated as PV) articulates the relation between the demands in this field and developing projects. It is an important part of the implementation of the architecture.

Standards Viewpoint (abbreviated as StdV) articulates the laws and norms that may be considered. It provides basic information such as data, terms, information, management methods and legal basis for CV and other viewpoints. It also lists the regulations for urban road freight transportation. Therefore, it is an important part of the architecture.

The above eight viewpoints conduct a full range of planning and design for urban road freight transport of dangerous goods from aspects of general view, standards and norms, capability requirements, operation procedures and activities, supporting services, components of system and environment, data entity and their relationships, and relationships between projects being implemented.

3.2 CV-1 Capabilities Vision

CV-1 [13] provides a strategic context and a high-level view for the capabilities described in the architecture. The CV-1 here is, by architectural design of urban road freight transport of dangerous goods, to describe a top-level design idea in terms of 8 viewpoints. An operation management mechanism based on DoDAF 2.0 is given in which not only is the safety of dangerous goods managed intelligently, dynamically and visually, but also multisectors can coordinate and link with one another. Thus, a system that includes all factors [14], periods, processes and entities is established to provide measures to address the urban road freight transport of dangerous goods and create a cloud platform for the security management of road freight transport of dangerous goods (Fig. 2).

3.3 CV-2 Capability Taxonomies

In DoDAF, CV-2 captures capability taxonomies. The model presents a hierarchy of capabilities that specifies the capabilities needed currently and in the future.

According to *the Measures* and the laws and regulations concerned, we propose an overall capability taxonomy in dangerous chemicals trade management as follows:

As we can see from the above diagram, there are 9 capabilities, namely, safe production, consignment, exception and limited quantities, carriage, loading and unloading,

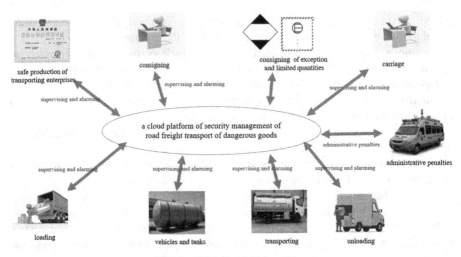

Fig. 2. CV-1 Capabilities vision

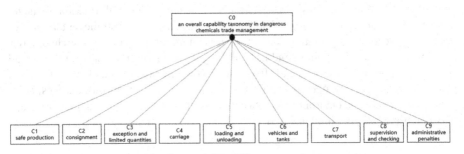

Fig. 3. CV-2 Capability taxonomies

vehicles and tanks, transportation, supervision and checking and administrative penalties (see Fig. 3).

CV-2 focuses on the nine above-mentioned capabilities. Among them, the first is the basis and requisite, the last two are means of administrative supervision and the left are the core of urban road freight transport of dangerous goods. All together constitute the capabilities of CV-2.

3.4　CV-4 Capabilities Phasing and Dependencies

The following is the diagram of capabilities phasing and dependencies on urban road freight transport of dangerous goods. It describes the phasing-in or phasing-out of capabilities during transport and dependencies between each other (Fig. 4).

As seen from the above diagram, the capabilities concerned with the urban road freight transport of dangerous goods can be grouped into basic, supporting and controlling capabilities. Basic capabilities refer to the capabilities of exceptions/limited quantity consignment, carriage, loading and unloading, transport, and detection of vehicles and tanks. It is the basic element of urban road freight transport and the base of road

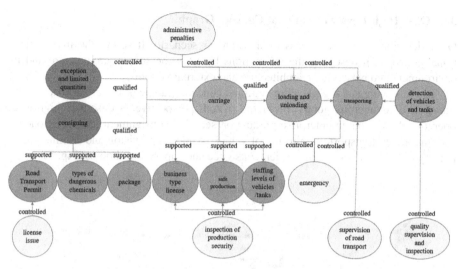

Fig. 4. CV-4 Capabilities phasing and dependencies

freight transport of dangerous goods. Supporting capabilities mainly refer to the capabilities of Road Transport Permit, types of dangerous chemicals, packaging, business-type licences, safe production, staffing levels of vehicles/tanks, etc. It is the supporting element of urban road freight transport of dangerous goods. This guarantees the security management of road freight transport of dangerous goods. Its operating entities are enterprises producing, storing, consigning, loading and unloading, transporting and disposing dangerous goods. The controlling capabilities refer to the capabilities of administrative penalty, licence issue, inspection of production security, emergency, supervision of road transport, quality supervision and inspection, etc. It is the controlling element and plays a monitoring and controlling role in the security management of road freight transport of dangerous goods. It is done by administrative supervisory bodies, quality inspection and supervision bureaus at all levels.

We can also see from this diagram that the basic capabilities are basic and essential components of road transport of dangerous goods. They are also the basis of urban road freight transport of dangerous goods. Meanwhile, to meet the demands of management and ensure security, enterprises must be qualified with capabilities of operation licence, staffing, production security and road transport when they produce, store, package, load and unload, transport dangerous chemicals, manufacture vehicles/tanks, etc. Finally, security management is supported as a system and supervisory management by controlling capabilities, such as issuing enterprise operation licences, supervision and inspection of production security, road transport, the quality of vehicles/tanks, administrative penalties, and emergency disposal.

3.5 OV-1 High-Level Operational Concept Graphic

OV-1 describes a mission, class of mission, or scenario. It shows the main operational concepts. It describes the interactions between the subject architecture and its environment and between the architecture and external systems.

The following is a high-level operational concept graphic of the urban road freight transport of dangerous goods. From the overall perspective, it describes high-level operational concepts in enterprise production security, consignment, carriage, loading and unloading, transport, monitoring of vehicles/tanks, supervision and administrative penalty in terms of consignor, carrier, consignee and supervisory bodies (Fig. 5).

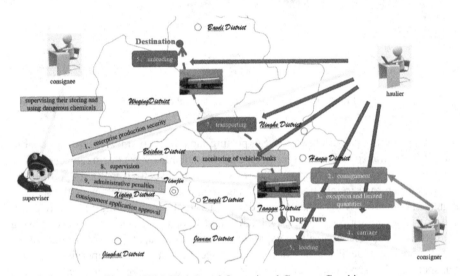

Fig. 5. OV-1 High-Level Operational Concept Graphic

3.6 OV-2 Operational Resource Flows

OV-2 may be used to depict flows of information, funding, personnel or materials. A definite application of OV-2 is to describe the logical model of resource flows whose main characteristic is operational resource flows and the location of operational facilities (or locations/environment).

The following depicts the operational resource flow of urban road freight transport of dangerous goods. It shows the operational resource flows of enterprises, supervisors and other bodies concerned with dangerous goods.

Figure 6 shows that the information flow of enterprises and supervisory bodies concerned with dangerous goods mainly includes enterprise records, production, storage supervision, operation records, consumables, road transport, inspection of vehicles/tanks, etc. Via the specified network platform, such information can be transmitted to corresponding supervisory bodies who have access to the platform according to their administrative rights. They can obtain information about enterprises connected with

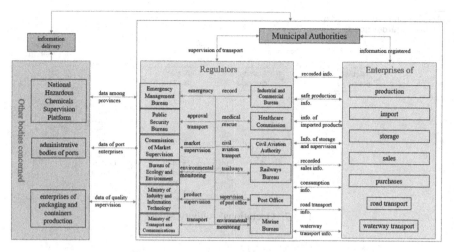

Fig. 6. OV-2 Operational resource flows

dangerous goods: production security, enterprise records, transport approval, market supervision, environment monitoring, inspection of vehicles/tanks, medical aid, road transport, etc. They can exchange these data with the National Hazardous Chemicals Supervision Platform via interprovincial information exchange.

3.7   OV-5b Operational Activity Model

OV-5b [15] describes the context of capabilities and activities and their relationships among activities, inputs and outputs; additional data can show cost, performers, or other pertinent information.

The following is the operational activity model of road transport of dangerous goods. It depicts five types of activities: consigning, carriage, loading and unloading, transporting and supervising. They follow the process—consigning, carriage, loading, transporting, and unloading. Supervision runs throughout the whole process. Loading refers to loading dangerous goods before transport, while unloading refers to unloading goods at the destination. Therefore, transport occurs after loading and before unloading (Fig. 7).

3.8   OV-6c Event-Trace Description

Different modelling techniques [16] can be adopted to extend and refine the operational viewpoint of architectural description, so OV can fully describe the dynamic activities and temporal properties. The OV-6 model of DoDAF includes OV-6a (Operational Rules Model), OV-6b (State Transition Description), and OV-6c (Event-Trace Description). OV-6c enables the tracing of actions in a scenario or sequence of events [17].

The following figure shows the operational event/trace descriptions of the urban road freight transport of dangerous goods. It focuses on road freight transport of dangerous goods, describing a sequence of events ranging from consignment to the end. Road Transport Permit, consignment, carriage, transport approval, loading, transporting, supervision and unloading are all involved (Fig. 8).

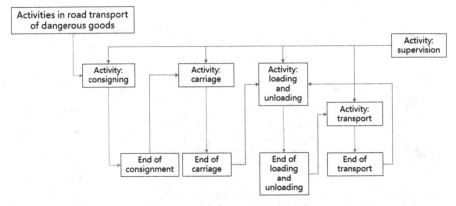

Fig. 7. Operational Activity Model

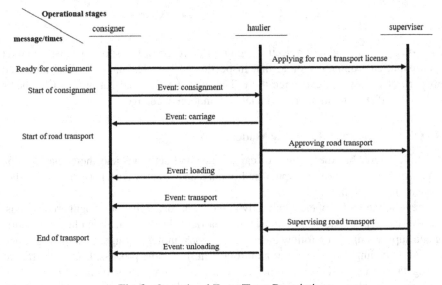

Fig. 8. Operational Event/Trace Descriptions

3.9 DIV-1 [13]Conceptual Data Model

The following is the conceptual data model. It provides a reference for managing ideas, methods, models and systems of urban road freight transport of dangerous goods. This model describes events emerging from episodes, staff involved in each episode, equipment/system monitoring, alarming, accidents and consumable resources during accident treatment. It also describes the standards needed in urban road freight transport of dangerous goods (Fig. 9).

In this model, events involved in road transport of dangerous goods mainly include production, storage, transport, utilization, disposal of waste, etc. These events mainly

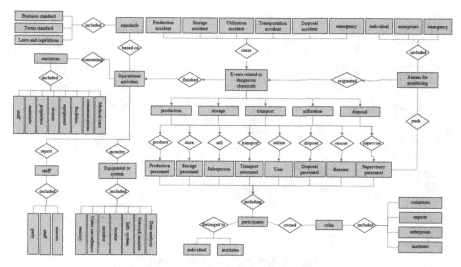

Fig. 9. DIV-1 Conceptual Data Model

emerge from the process of production, storage, operation, transport, utilization, disposal, rescue and supervision. Thus, accidents occur at corresponding stages.

In this model, participants involved are listed, from individuals to institutes and enterprises, including volunteers, experts, enterprises/institutes of dangerous chemicals.

Alarm monitoring information is given in the model. It mainly comes from equipment/systems (including sensors, video monitors, monitoring facilities, locators, information systems, network monitoring, data analysis, etc.) which collect data automatically and staff who reports.

Consumable resources are given as staff, materials, properties, money, equipment, facilities, communications and medical care, etc.

Standards/systems included in urban road freight transport of dangerous goods are given as business, terms, laws and regulations, etc.

3.10   DIV-2 Logical Data Model

The DIV-2 [14] allows analysis of an architecture's data definition aspect without consideration of implementation or product-specific issues. The other purpose is to provide a common dictionary [18] of data definitions to consistently express models wherever logical-level data elements are included in the descriptions.

The following is the logical data model. It focuses on the logical data model of the urban road freight transport of dangerous goods. Requirements of consignment, carriage, loading and unloading, transporting and relevant supervisory bodies are involved. The activities and requirements of the enterprises and supervisory bodies concerned are given. (In the following Fig. 10, info. equals information.)

As a logical data model, it can provide not only a reference for the urban road freight transport of dangerous goods but also guidance for the physical data model of relevant platforms.

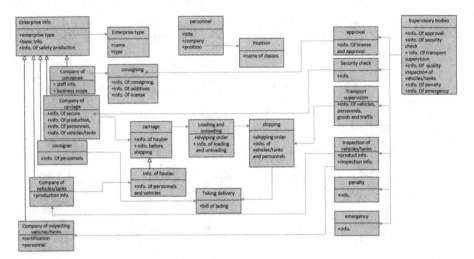

Fig. 10. DIV-2 Logical Data Model

It describes the logical relationships among the five stages -- consignment, carriage, loading and unloading, transporting, and supervising. Therefore, it can provide guidance for the business logical implementation of relevant platforms.

It also describes the logical relationships among enterprises and the supervisory bodies concerned. The enterprises in production, storage, consignment, carriage, operation, production and inspection of vehicles/tanks are involved. Therefore, it provides guidance for the architectural design of relevant platforms.

4 Conclusion

The architecture framework of urban road freight transport of dangerous goods based on DoDAF is designed at the top level from the aspects of CV, DIV and OV. Viewpoints or models such as capabilities vision are proposed. Some viewpoints describe the correlation and transformation of capabilities, activities, information and data. That offers a method of systems modelling and realization for the platform of the urban road freight transport of dangerous goods to supervise, monitor/alarm, analyse its tendency and support its policy-decision. Thus, it has a good value of research and reference.

References

1. Measures for the administration of road transport safety of dangerous goods, China transport newspaper. Accessed 20 Jan 2020
2. Peng, X.U.: Research on the construction of road transportation safety supervision system of dangerous goods in Ningxia. Chongqing Jiaotong University, Chongqing, China(2020)
3. Zhang, F.: Governmental supervisory strategies for road transport of dangerous chemicals in the background of internet plus. China Stor. Transp. (05), 82–83 (2022)

4. Bing, S.U.I.: Study on safety risk analysis and management countermeasures of dangerous chemicals logistics transportation enterprises in Dongying. Logist. Eng. Manage. **44**(02), 165–167 (2022)
5. Zhao, M.: Research on top-level design of regional health information based on DoDAF. Tianjin University, Tianjin (2014)
6. Shao, B.: The top-level design of emergency system based on the DODAF. Tianjin University, Tianjin (2014)
7. Huang, X.: Modelling design of UAS based on SoSE. J. Telemetry, Track. Command **39**(03), 21–28 (2018)
8. Tao, Z., Luo, Y., Chen, C., Wang, M. Ni, F.: Enterprise application architecture development based on DoDAF and TOGAF. Enterp. Inf. Syst. **11**(5) (2015)
9. Yang, W., Hou, J., Liu, M.: Research on demand analysis method of military civilian integration medical equipment based on DoDAF. Basic Clin. Pharmacol. Toxicol. **128** (2021)
10. Zhang, C., Xu, T., Zhang, H.: Naval combined operation architecture framework in Island-Reef area based on DoDAF. Command Inf. Syst. Technol. **8**(05), 20–24 (2017)
11. Yang, W., Yuan, C., Zhao, J., He, Y., Li, R.: Research on weapon and equipment requirement analysis method based on DODAF. In: Proceedings of 2019 International Conference on Virtual Reality and Intelligent Systems (ICVRIS 2019), Hunan, China, vol. II, pp. 102–104 (2019)
12. Feng, W., Qiancong, Q.: Research on military logistics system of theater based on DoDAF. Ship Electr. Eng. **41**(12), 119–125 (2021)
13. Wang, Y., Chen, J., Na, C., Li, Z., Gao, S.: Modelling of reef distributed reconnaissance and early warning system based on DoDAF. J. Phys.: Conf. Ser. (1), 1646 (2020)
14. Wei, P., Xiong, L., Zhongxuan, L., Guijun, X.: Research on high-level operational concept graphic of cyberspace-based equipment support at tactical level. J. Equipm. Aca. **28**(01), 20–26 (2017)
15. Wang, W., Yang, P., Dong, C.: Study and application of emergency case ontology model. J. Comput. Appl. **29**(05), 1437–1440+1445 (2009)
16. Yueheng, S., Weiyi, Y., Wenjun, W.: Research on the sentiment discrimination of network public opinion for government departments. J. Intell. **39**(08), 88–93 (2020)
17. Xu, Y.: Research on aviation medical rescue standard system based on DoDAF. J. Changchun Inst. Tech. (Nat. Sci. Edi.) **22**(04), 73–77 (2021)
18. Ma, H.: Emergency Management of a megacity taken the example of Shenzhen City. China Emerg. Manage. (10), 36–39 (2021)

Statistal Methods of Bus Passenger Flow Based on Improved YOLOv5s and DeepSORT Algorithms

Jinfan Yang[✉] and Xiaoqiang Wang

Inner Mongolia University of Technology, Hohhot, China
1848886840@qq.com

Abstract. Aiming at the problem of low tracking accuracy in the statistics of bus passengers getting on and off, an improved passenger flow statistics algorithm based on YOLOv5s combined with DeepSORT is proposed. The GAM integrated into Group Convolution and ChannelShuffle is integrated with the backbone and neck parts of the YOLOv5s network structure to enhance the network feature extraction capability. The Decoupled Head is replaced by the YOLOv5s detection head to improve the detection accuracy of passengers in crowded situations. Alpha-IoU is used as the target frame regression loss to further improve the positioning accuracy. The improved YOLOv5s is connected with DeepSORT, and detection lines are set up in the monitoring video of the front and rear doors of the bus to count the flow of passengers getting on and off. The experimental results show that our algorithm in this paper is 1.1% and 8.5% higher than the YOLOv5s algorithm in mAP0.5 and mAP.5:.95, respectively. After connecting DeepSORT, the passenger flow statistics in the scene of getting on and off the bus, the accuracy rate reached 96.8% and 98.1% .

Keywords: Passenger Flow Statistics Algorithm · YOLOv5s · DeepSORT

1 Introduction

With the continuous advancement of urbanization and the rapid development of urban bus construction, bus passenger flow statistics have become an indispensable basis for station distribution and bus route adjustment. The use of video surveillance in buses to obtain passenger flow data has become a means of feeding back important information such as peak and low-peak intervals of passenger flow and crowded stations. Therefore, it is very important to propose a bus passenger flow statistical algorithm with low computational cost and high detection accuracy.

The bus passenger flow statistics based on surveillance video include two parts: passenger target detection and tracking. Traditional passenger target detection extracts artificially designed head or head and shoulders features, such as HOG1, and LBP2. to input classifiers SVM3, Adaboost 4, etc. for feature classification to obtain passenger targets. These traditional passenger target detection algorithms based on sliding window selection have high time complexity, and the robustness of the passenger's head or head and shoulders features is designed under the change of light intensity and complex interior background cannot be obtained, which affects the detection accuracy. With the development of deep learning algorithms, research on passenger target detection algorithms has gradually turned to target detection based on deep learning. Multilevel passenger features are extracted through convolutional neural networks, which are more robust and are mainly divided into one-stage methods and two-stage methods. The two-stage method based on the candidate frame generates the candidate region containing the target, and performs classification and position regression through the convolutional neural network. Representative algorithms include the R-CNN series [5–7]. The one-stage method based on regression does not need to generate candidate regions, and the detection speed is greatly improved, but the detection accuracy is lower than that of the two-stage algorithms. Representative algorithms include the YOLO series7–10, and SSD series1112–16. Traditional passenger target tracking algorithms are mainly used to model the target or track the target feature. The representative algorithms include the Kalman filter17, Meanshift18, Camshift19 algorithm, etc. They search for targets by extracting target features and locating targets in subsequent frames or adding prediction algorithms. The algorithms ignore background information, which can easily lead to tracking failure in the case of motion occlusion and light changes. With the development of deep learning, the detection-based tracking(DBT) mode is the mainstream of the current deep learning passenger target tracking algorithms. Due to the combination with deep learning target detection algorithms, the tracking efficiency is greatly affected by the detection model. The superposition of various deep learning modules makes the model more complex, and the detection speed needs to be improved.

Due to the limited computing resources in practical application scenarios, passenger detection based on deep learning is widely used due to its advantages in detection speed and accuracy. However, the target tracking model based on deep learning is complex, and passenger tracking still uses traditional tracking algorithms. Liu et al. 20 proposed a bus passenger flow statistics algorithm based on YOLOv2 combined with the MIL tracker, and determined the tracking target of the next frame by setting the IoU threshold of the detection frame and the tracking frame. However, the MIL algorithm has a high tracking failure rate in the case of occlusion and passenger morphological changes. The author only tracks the passengers in the video stream of the front door of the bus also. Another point worth noting is that the target angle of the passengers in the dataset is relatively single. You et al. [21] used the Faster-RCNN target detection model to extract the head area of target passengers, the Kalman filter algorithm to carry out correlation estimation and then used the data association to track the target. Due to the limitations of the Kalman filter itself, the occlusion and deformation problems caused by passengers in the process of moving will lead to a high tracking failure rate and unstable tracking.

At present, research on bus passenger flow statistics focuses on lightweight target detection models and optimized tracking algorithms. Although the complexity of traditional target tracking model is low, the tracking failure rate is high in crowded scenes, resulting in low counting accuracy. Therefore, it is a research hotspot in the field of bus passenger flow statistics in the future to explore a high-precision and lightweight target detection model with an efficient target tracking algorithm based on DBT mode.

In this paper, we propose to use the lightweight target detection model YOLOv5s combined with the multitarget tracking algorithm DeepSORT to realize the statistics of bus passenger flow. The proposed method consists of three major steps: (1) passenger object detection; (2) passenger object tracking; and (3) counting. In the passenger object detection step, the GAM is introduced to integrate with the backbone and neck parts of the YOLOv5s network structure; Decoupled Head is replaced with the YOLOv5s detection head; and the Alpha-IoU is used as the target frame regression loss to further improve the positioning accuracy. In the passenger object tracking step, we combined the improved YOLOv5s with DeepSORT. In the count step, the cross-line counting method is used to realize bus passenger flow statistics. Our main contributions are as follows:

1. To the best of our knowledge, the DeepSORT algorithm is applied to the field of bus passenger flow statistics for the first time.
2. Compared with the original YOLOv5s, an improved GAM module is proposed, which introduces ChannelShuffle and Group Convolution. Meanwhile, integrate it with the backbone and neck parts of YOLOv5s.
3. YOLOX is used to introduce the Decouple Head to avoid conflicts between classification and regression tasks and speed up network convergence.
4. We try using Alpha-IoU loss instead of CIoU loss to obtain more accurate bounding box regression, and finally achieve an improvement in detection accuracy.
5. Designing a bidirectional cross-line counting method suitable for getting on and off the bus scene.

The paper is organized as follows: Sect. 2 reviews the related preliminaries with YOLOv5s and DeepSORT models, while Sect. 3 shows the details of the proposed model. In Sect. 4, ablation experiments and comparative experiments are designed to validate the strengths of the proposed model. Finally, Sect. 5 presents a brief summary of this paper.

2 Preliminaries

2.1 A YOLOv5s Passenger Detection Algorithm

As shown in Fig. 1, YOLOv5s uses the CSPDarket53 structure and designs two CSP structures for reference from CSPNet. The CSP1_X structure is applied to the backbone network, and the residual structure is used to build a deep network to obtain more feature information. The CSP2_X structure is used in the neck to reduce the amount of computation while ensuring accuracy. The backbone of YOLOv5s is mainly composed of CBS, BottleneckCSP and SSPF. To obtain the feature information extracted by the backbone network more effectively, the network structure in Neck uses the FPN + PAN structure to construct a high-level semantic feature map from top to bottom, combined with bottom-up compensation to strengthen the positioning information. The head part obtains the feature map extracted by the backbone network and neck for prediction, generates a bounding box and predicts the category. When the input is an image of 640 × 640, feature maps at three scales of 80 × 80, 40 × 40, and 20 × 20 are obtained.

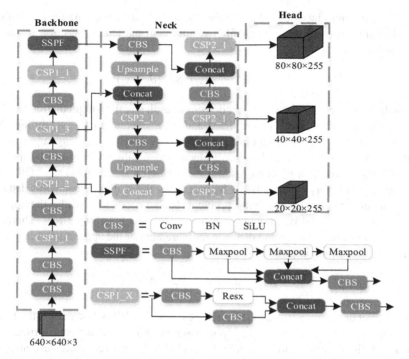

Fig. 1. Structure of YOLOv5s.

2.2 DeepSORT Passenger Tracking Algorithm

Aiming at the problem of tracking failure caused by the one-frame mismatch deletion mechanism and the matching mechanism of the IoU cost matrix of the SORT algorithm, DeepSORT introduces deep appearance information and uses cascade matching combined with the IoU matching mechanism, which greatly reduces ID switching.

DeepSORT defines the tracking scene in an eight-dimensional state space $(u, v, \gamma, h, \dot{x}, \dot{y}, \dot{\gamma} h)$, where (u, v) is the center point coordinate of the bounding box(BBox), γ, and h are the aspect ratio and height of the BBox, respectively, and $\dot{x}, \dot{y}, \dot{\gamma}, \dot{h}$ are the relative velocities of the corresponding parameters mentioned above in the image coordinates. DeepSORT uses eight parameters to describe the motion state, predicts the motion state of the target through the Kalman filter, initializes the counter for each tracked target in combination with the detection results of the target detector, and calculates the number of frames since the last successful correlation of the target. If the predicted moving target is successfully matched with the detected target, the counter is reset to 0, and a new trajectory assumption will be made for the moving target that fails to match successfully, If the tracker fails to successfully associate and detect the target within three consecutive frames, it is considered that the target leaves the moving scene and is deleted in the track set.

DeepSORT introduces the Mahalanobis distance based on the traditional Kalman filter algorithm to correlate Kalman filter results with the target detection results, as shown in formula (1):

$$d^{(1)}(i,j) = (d_j - y_i)^T S_i^{-1} (d_j - y_i) \qquad (1)$$

d_j, y_i is the state vector of the j-th target detection result and the i-th prediction result, S_i is the covariance matrix between the BBox and the tracker, and $(d_j - y_i)$ through S_i is normalized to obtain the Mahalanobis distance between the i-th tracking target and the j-th detection target. If the Mahalanobis distance of association is less than the specified threshold, the association of motion states is considered successful. DeepSORT only measures the proximity between BBox by measuring the spatial Mahalanobis distance, which cannot solve the ID switching problem. It also needs to consider the apparent characteristics in the BBox, to obtain a better association matching effect. Therefore, DeepSORT introduces the cosine distance measurement of the apparent characteristics on this basis, as shown in formula (2):

$$d^{(2)}(i,j) = min\left(1 - r_j^T r_k^{(i)} | r_k^{(i)} \in R_i\right) \qquad (2)$$

The target detection BBox and the tracking prediction BBox first extract the feature vector through the neural network. Using a series of residual network structures to extract 128 dimensional feature vectors, l_2 regularization is used for feature mapping. r_j corresponds to the j-th target detection eigenvector, $r_k^{(i)}$ corresponds to the tracked feature vector, which is a set that retains the features successfully tracked k times in the past, and $1 - r_j^T r_k^{(i)}$ is the cosine distance between the two feature vectors. The formula calculates the minimum cosine distance between all feature vectors tracked by the i-th object and the j-th target detection. According to formulas (1) and (2), there are two costs in DeepSORT data association: the Mahalanobis distance and cosine distance. Therefore, the linear weighting of the two measures is used as the final measure, as shown in formula (3):

$$c_{i,j} = \lambda d^{(1)}(i,j) + (1 - \lambda) d^{(2)}(i,j) \qquad (3)$$

3 Proposed Algorithm

In this section, we propose an improved YOLOv5s model for passenger detection by adding an attention module, changing the detection head and improving the loss function. The model mainly consists of three improvements:

(1) GAM [22] integrated into the Group Convolution and ChannelShuffle is integrated with the Backbone and Neck parts of the YOLOv5s network structure.
(2) Replace the detection head of the original YOLOv5s with the Dcoupled Head.
(3) Improve the original CIoU loss with Alpha-IoU loss.

3.1   Group Convolution and ChannelShuffle

ShuffleNet [23] affords us lessons that using Group Convolution and ChannelShuffle can lighten the model, so we integrate this architecture into the GAM module to reduce the number of parameters. Group Convolution uses a channel sparse connection method, by grouping different characteristic maps of the input layer and convoluting each group with different convolution kernels. As shown in Fig. 2, (a) is a common group convolution, which processes the information in a single group only by connecting simple channels in series. The output of each channel comes from the corresponding small part of the channel input. Each convolution group cannot realize information flow, which reduces the ability of information representation. Therefore, ChannelShuffle is introduced to obtain the input of different groups. (b) is the implementation process of ChannelShuffle. For a convolution layer divided into k groups, the number of output channels is $k \times n$, and then it is reorganized into a (k, n) matrix and transposed. Next, the transposed matrix (n, K) is redivided into k groups according to rows and input to the next layer. As shown in figure (c), the convolution layer obtained by transposing and repacking is output.

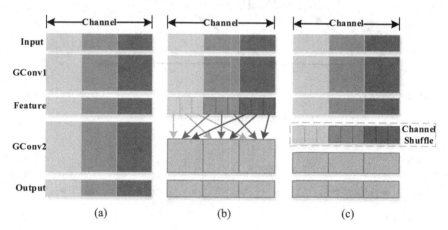

Fig. 2.   Structure of YOLOv5s.

3.2   Improved GAM Module

Liu et al. [22] proposed GAM, an attention mechanism that can capture the important characteristics of the three dimensions of channel, spatial width and height, aiming at the problem that the current attention mechanism generally ignores the channel spatial attention interaction and easily loses cross dimensional information. As shown in formulas (4), and (5) and Fig. 3, the channel attention submodule uses 3D arrangement to maintain a 3D information, and uses a multilayer perceptron (MLP) to amplify the cross channel spatial dependence to obtain the channel attention map M_C. Multiply element by element and activate through sigmoid to obtain intermediate state F_2. The spatial attention submodule uses group convolutions to replace the ordinary convolution for spatial information fusion to reduce the number of parameters. Deleting the maximum pooling layer ensures feature mapping, and the spatial attention map M_S is obtained after sigmoid. The final output status is F_3. In this paper, group convolution combined with the ChannelShuffle framework is integrated into the 7×7 convolution of the spatial attention submodule of GAM. On the premise of not weakening the ability of spatial information acquisition, the number of parameters is reduced. Figure 4 shows the structure of the improved spatial attention submodule.

Given input feature mapping $F_1 \in R^{C \times H \times W}$

$$F_2 = M_C(F_1) \otimes F_1 \tag{4}$$

$$F_3 = M_S(F_2) \otimes F_2 \tag{5}$$

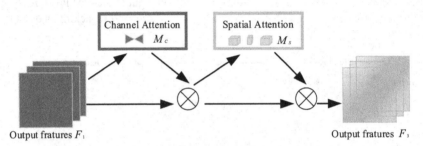

Fig. 3. Structure of GAM.

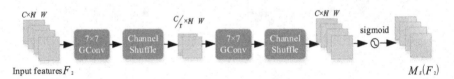

Fig. 4. Structure of improved spatial attention submodule.

GAM further reduces the loss of feature information by improving the global feature interaction, and improves the performance of the deep neural network. The backbone of YOLOv5s is the most critical part of model feature extraction, in which the SSPF module extracts and fuses high-level semantic features to the greatest extent through multiple maximum pooling layers, and the neck further fuses feature maps of different sizes to obtain feature information. Therefore, this paper integrates GAM before the SSPF module of the backbone network and after the neck to further enhance the effect of feature extraction. The network structure is shown in Fig. 5. Figure 6 is the scatter diagram of the detection BBox distribution of the passenger target detection dataset in this paper. It can be seen that the dataset has the problems of uneven distribution and large size change of detection BBox. By introducing GAM to expand the network receptive field, we can achieve accurate target positioning.

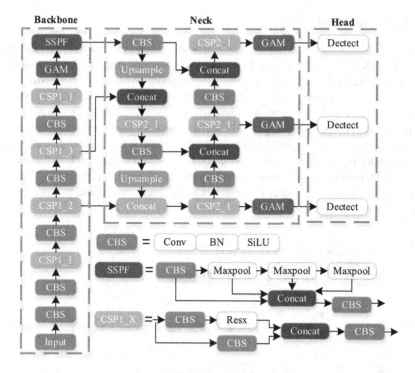

Fig. 5. New structure after introducing GAM.

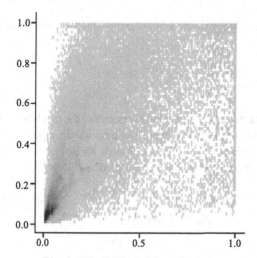

Fig. 6. Distribution of detection box.

3.3 Decoupled Head

Decoupled Head is used in many one-stage networks, such as RetinaNet [24], and FCOS [25]. YOLOX [26] considers that YOLO series detection heads ignore the conflict of classification and regression tasks, resulting in the reduction of feature expression ability, and then replace them to further improve the detection accuracy. Figure 7 shows the network structure of this paper after integrating the Decoupled Head. Get three branches before concat operation: cls_output indicates the category prediction score of the target box; obj_output is used to judge whether the target box is foreground or background; reg_output predicts the coordinate information (x, y, w, h) of the target box. Concatenate its three branch outputs to obtain feature information, concatenate the outputs of the three Decoupled Head branches after the reshaping operation, and obtain two-dimensional vector information after transposition.

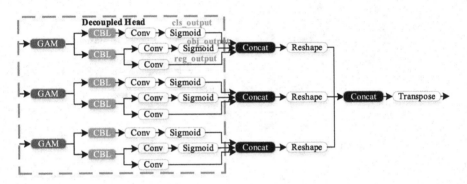

Fig. 7. New structure of integrating into Decoupled Head.

3.4 Alpha-IoU

When both prediction boxes are located in the center of the real box, it is better to consider the coordinate effect to reduce the influence of gradient disappearance. Therefore, CIoU further improves on the basis of DIoU and adds the aspect ratio. The corresponding mathematical definition of CIoU can be described as follows:

$$\begin{cases} L_{CIoU} = 1 - IoU(A, B) + \ell^2(A_{ctr}, B_{ctr}) \big/ c^2 + \beta v \\ v = \frac{4}{\pi^2} \left(arctan \frac{w^{gt}}{h^{gt}} - arctan \frac{w}{h} \right)^2 \\ \beta = \frac{v}{(1-IoU)+v} \end{cases} \quad (6)$$

where A also B are two prediction boxes, A_{ctr}, B_{ctr} are the center points of A and B, respectively, $\ell^2(A_{ctr}, B_{ctr})$ is the Euclidean distance between the center point of the prediction bounding box and the real bounding box, c is the diagonal distance of the smallest enclosed area containing both the prediction BBox and the real BBox, and v is used to measure the similarity of aspect ratio and introduce the weight value. When

IoU is larger, β will give priority to v, otherwise, β will give priority to the distance ratio. Alpha-IoU adopts power transformation on this basis, as shown in formula (7). When IoU is greater than 0.5, the gradient of loss is greater than -1, and the convergence speed is faster. In this paper, Alpha-IoU is used to accelerate the convergence speed of the model and improve the positioning accuracy.

$$L_{CIoU} = 1 - IoU(A, B) + \ell^2(A_{ctr}, B_{ctr}) / c^2 + \alpha v \Rightarrow L_{\alpha-CIoU} = 1 - IoU^\alpha + \ell^{2\alpha}(A_{ctr}, B_{ctr}) / c^2 + (\beta v)^\alpha \qquad (7)$$

4   Experiments and Results

In this section, the pedestrian categories in COCO2017, VOC2007 and the real monitoring video data in the bus are extracted to form the passenger detection dataset. The images in the bus contain different shooting angles, including the angles of passengers getting on, getting off and inside the bus, including different lighting conditions during the day and at night, as shown in Fig. 8. The passenger detection dataset in this paper is composed of 26187 images extracted from the three datasets mentioned above, 21031 images were randomly assigned as the training set, and 5156 images were assigned the verification set. Experiments 1–2 (Sect. 4.1.1–4.1.2) use the passenger detection dataset as the research object. The person reidentification dataset- Market1501 is used to train DeepSORT. This dataset is captured by 6 cameras on the campus of Tsinghua University, including 32,217 images of 1,501 identities.

Fig. 8. Partial dataset display.

The experimental environment of this paper is shown in Table 1. We use Recall, mAP@0.5, and mAP@.5:.95 to evaluate the performance of the improved model, and the number of identity switching IDs and tracking frames per second are used as the evaluation indicators of the target tracking model.

Table 1. Table captions should be placed above the tables.

Heading level	Software
CPU processor: Intel(R) Core(TM) i7-10750H CPU @ 2.60 GHz 2.59 GHz	Python3.7
GPU processor: Nvidia Tesla P100 Memory: 12GiB	Pytorch1.10.0 PaddlePaddle2.2

4.1 Detection Results on the Passenger Detection Dataset

To analyse the performance of the improved YOLOv5s, we use Experiments 1–2 for analysis and validation on the passenger detection dataset.

4.1.1 Experiment 1: YOLOv5s Ablation Experiments

In this section, we set up ablation experiments for the three improvement strategies on the passenger detection dataset to verify the effectiveness of each improvement. The input image size is 640 × 640, and the model training uses the default hyperparameter configuration. Table 2. The results of the ablation experiments.

Table 2. YOLOv5s ablation experiments.

GAM	Alpha-IoU	Dcoupled Head	Recall(%)	mAP@0.5(%)	mAP@.5:.95(%)
—	—	—	73.3	83.7	56.2
√	—	—	74.9	84.4	61.6
—	√	—	74	83.7	62.3
—	—	√	73.9	84.1	62.1
√	√	—	74.9	84.4	63.9
—	√	√	74.1	84.4	63.5
√	√	√	73.4	84.8	64.7

Through the analysis of the experiment results in Table 2, it can be seen that after the introduction of GAM module, the model is increased in Recall, mAP@0.5, mAP@.5:.95 by 1.6%, 0.7% and 5.4%, respectively; Although the improvement effect of Alpha-IoU in Recall and mAP@0.5 is weak, a significant increase is achieved in mAP@.5:.95 by 6.1%, and the introduction of Alpha-IoU is better than using GAM module and Decoupled Head alone in mAP@.5:.95, increased by 2.3% and 1.4% respectively, confirming the advantages of Alpha-IoU in high-precision level and without increasing the amount of model parameters, it can alleviate the problems of missing and wrong detection of passengers caused by occlusion; By comparing the detection results of introducing GAM + Alpha IoU and Dcoupled Head + Alpha IoU, it can be seen that the effect of introducing Dcoupled Head on single target detection is weak. After introducing the Decoupled Head, GAM module and Alpha-IoU at the same time, the mAP@0.5, and mAP@.5:.95 increased by 1.1% and 8.5% respectively compared with the original YOLOv5s.

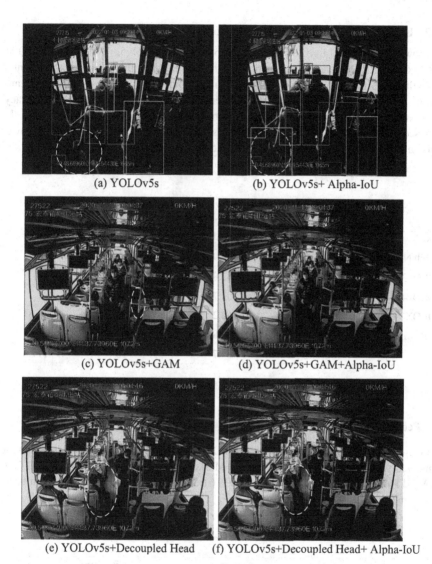

(a) YOLOv5s   (b) YOLOv5s+ Alpha-IoU

(c) YOLOv5s+GAM   (d) YOLOv5s+GAM+Alpha-IoU

(e) YOLOv5s+Decoupled Head   (f) YOLOv5s+Decoupled Head+ Alpha-IoU

Fig. 9. The results.

To further analyse the influence of Alpha-IoU on the positioning accuracy of the model, some detection results are visualized as shown in Fig. 9. (a), (c), and (e) show the detection effect of the original YOLOv5s, YOLOv5s + GAM, and YOLOv5s + Decoupled Head, respectively. It can be seen that there are problems with the regression accuracy of the detection box and incorrect detection. (b), (d), and (f) all replace the

Alpha-IoU loss on the basis of the corresponding model, and the positioning of the target box is more accurate.

4.1.2 Experiment 2: Comparison with Models

As shown in Table 3, five algorithms, mobilenetv3-YOLOv5, YOLOv3, YOLOv4, YOLOX and PP-PicoDet27, are compared horizontally in this paper. Experiment 2 shows that the algorithm proposed in this paper has obvious advantages in mAP@0.5 and mAP@.5:.95. Although YOLOv4 is equivalent to the algorithm in detection accuracy, its parameter quantity is 64.3 M and detection speed is 34.3 FPS, which is far from the proposed algorithm. Although the detection speed of the proposed algorithm is lower than that of the original YOLOv5s, it still meets the needs of real-time detection, and the comprehensive performance of the compared model is the best.

Table 3. Comparison with different models.

Model	mAP@0.5	mAP@.5:.95(%)	Params(M)	FPS
MobileNetv3-YOLOv5	77.5	48.9	3.5	243
YOLOv3	81.8	62.8	61.9	30
YOLOv4	84.5	63.7	64.3	22.7
YOLOX	80.6	62.2	9	39.3
PP-PicoDet	71.2	56.8	1.18	—
ours	84.8	64.7	18	117.6

4.2 Pedestrain Tracking Experiment

The original YOLO5s and the improved YOLOv5s model proposed in this paper are connected with DeepSORT trained by the Market1501 dataset and tested on MOT16–09, MOT16–10 and MOT16–11 in the MOT16 training set. The experimental results are shown in Table 4.

Table 4. The pedestrain tracking results.

Model	IDs/times	Speed/Hz
YOLOv5s + DeepSORT	98	32
Ours + DeepSORT	65	30

The YOLOv5s connected with DeepSORT has 98 identity switches in three test videos, while our algorithm has 65 identity switches, the IDs are reduced by 34%, and the detection speed reaches 30 Hz, which meets the real-time detection requirements.

4.3 Passenger Flow Statistics Experiment

In this paper, the passengers are counted by setting detection lines. Two horizontal detection lines with different colors of yellow and blue are set at the door for two-way detection. Whether getting on and off behavior occurs is determined by the line collision point set on the target detection box. Suppose that when the line collision point first passes the yellow line, it is considered that the alighting action is in progress, and then when it passes the blue detection line, it is considered that the passengers have alighted, and the number of passengers getting off accumulates. Bidirectional counting is realized by judging the color of the detection line that passes successively. In this paper, the statistical data of passengers boarding and deboarding the bus collected by the front and rear door monitoring video are counted manually, YOLOv5s and then the algorithm proposed in this paper, and the algorithm proposed in reference [21] are compared. Table 5 shows the results. Each line of data represents the number of passengers getting on and off the bus counted by manual, YOLOv5s, the proposed algorithm in this paper and the algorithm proposed in [21]. The results show that the statistical accuracy of the algorithm proposed in this paper is higher than that of YOLOv5s and the algorithm proposed in [21] in the two scenes of up and down, which are 95.5% and 97.4% respectively. Due to the large deformation of passengers caused by the angle of the front door camera and the repeated counting problem caused by passenger aggregation, the statistical accuracy of passengers getting on decreases. Figure 10(a), and 10(b) show the number of passengers getting on and off counted by the original YOLOv5s combined with DeepSORT, and our algorithm combined with DeepSORT.

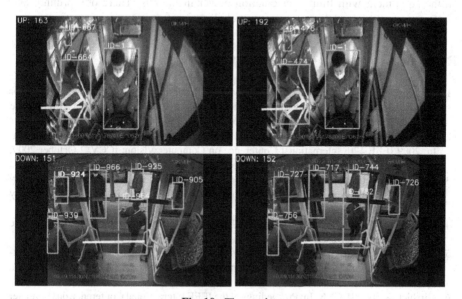

Fig. 10. The results.

Table 5. The counting results.

Model	Up	Down
Manual	186	155
YOLOv5s- DeepSORT	163	151
Model [21]	175	148
Ours	192	152

5 Discussion and Conclusion

Our algorithm based on YOLOv5s combined with DeepSORT realizes the statistics of bus passenger on-off flow. The GAM module combined with Group Convolution and ChannelShuffle is fused with YOLOv5s to reduce the parameters of the model and improve the detection accuracy. Decoupled Head and Alpha-IoU are introduced to replace the original detection head and CIoU loss, so as to further improve the positioning accuracy and reduce the missed detection situation under crowded conditions. Then we connct our model with DeepSORT, and the passenger flow statistics experiment is carried out on the video images of passengers of public transport vehicles in operation. The results show that the algorithm proposed in this paper has high statistical accuracy in both the getting on and off scenarios, reaching 96.8%, and 98.1%, respectively. Although the parameters of our model are sufficiently small, there is still considerable pressure on the equipment with limited calculation power in the bus. Therefore, pruning and compression of the model is a future research direction.

References

1. Cao, X., Wu, C., Yan, P., et al.: Linear SVM classification using boosting HOG features for vehicle detection in low-altitude airborne videos. In: 2011 18th IEEE International Conference on Image Processing, ICIP, 29 December, 2011, pp. 2421–2424. IEEE, Piscataway (2011)
2. Wang, X., Han, T.X., Yan, S.: An HOG-LBP human detector with partial occlusion handling. In: 2009 IEEE 12th International Conference on Computer Vision, ICCV, 2 October 2009, pp. 32–39. IEEE, Piscataway (2009)
3. kazemi, F.M., et al.: Vehicle recognition using curvelet transform and SVM. In: Fourth International Conference on Information Technology (ITNG'07), ITNG 2007. IEEE, Piscataway (2007), pp. 516–521
4. Wu, S., Nagahashi, H.: Parameterized adaBoost: introducing a parameter to speed up the training of real AdaBoost. IEEE Sign. Proc. Lett. **21**(6), 687–691 (2014)
5. Girshick, R., et al.: Rich feature hierarchies for accurate object detection and semantic segmentation. In: Proceedings of the IEEE Conference on Computer Vision and Pattern Recognition, pp. 580–587 (2014)
6. Girshick, R.: Fast R-CNN. In: Proceedings of the IEEE International Conference on Computer Vision, pp. 1440–1448 (2015)
7. Ren, S., et al.: Faster R-CNN: towards real-time object detection with region proposal networks. In: Advances in Neural Information Processing Systems, vol. 28 (2015)

8. Redmon, J., et al.: You only look once: unified, real-time object detection. In: Proceedings of the IEEE Conference on Computer Vision and Pattern Recognition, pp. 779–788 (2016)

9. Redmon, J., Farhadi, A.: YOLO9000: better, faster, stronger. In: Proceedings of the IEEE Conference on Computer Vision and Pattern Recognition, pp. 7263–7271 (2017)

10. Redmon, J., Farhadi, A.: Yolov3: an incremental improvement. arXiv preprint: arXiv:1804.02767 (2018)

11. Bochkovskiy, A., Wang, C.Y., Liao, H.Y.M. Yolov4: optimal seed and accuracy of object detection. arXiv preprint: arXiv:2004.10934 (2020)

12. Liu, W., et al.: SSD: single shot multibox detector. arXiv:1512.02325

13. Fu, C.Y., et al.: DSSD: deconvolutional single shot detector (2017). arXiv:1701.06659

14. Jenogn, J., Park, H., Kwak, N.: Enhancement of SSD by concatenating feature maps for object detection (2017). arXiv:1705.09587

15. Shen, Z., et al.: DSOD: learning deeply supervised object detectors from scratch. In: IEEE International Conference on Computer Vision (ICCV), vol. 212, pp. 1937–1945 (2017)

16. Li, Z.X., Zhou, F.Q.: FSSD: feature fusion single shot multibox detector (2017). arXiv:1712.00960

17. Welch, G., Bishop, G.: An Introduction to the Kalman Filter. University of North Carolina at Chapel Hill, Chapel Hill, NC, USA (2001)

18. Comaniciu, D., Meer, P.: Mean shift: a robust approach toward feature space analysis. IEEE Trans. Pattern Anal. Mach. Intell. 24(5), 603–619 (2002)

19. Bradski, G.R.: Computer vision face tracking for use in a perceptual user interface. Intel Technol. J. (1998)

20. Liu, L., et al.: A technology for automatically counting bus passenger based on YOLOv2 and MIL algorithm. In: 2020 IEEE 5th International Conference on Image, Vision and Computing (ICIVC) pp. 166–170 (2020)

21. You, X., et al.: Research on bus passenger flow statistics based on video images. In: 2021 2nd International Conference on Electronics, Communications and Information Technology (CECIT), pp. 937–942. IEEE (2021)

22. Liu, Y., Shao, Z., Hoffmann, N.: Global attention mechanism: retain information to enhance channel-spatial interactions. arXiv preprint: arXiv:2112.05561 (2021)

23. Zhang, X., et al.: ShuffleNet: an extremely efficient convolutional neural network for mobile devices. In: Proceedings of the IEEE Conference on Computer Vision and Pattern Recognition, pp. 6848–6856 (2018)

24. Lin, T.Y., et al.: Focal loss for dense object detection. In: Proceedings of the IEEE International Conference on Computer Vision, pp. 2980–2988 (2017)

25. Tian, Z., et al.: FCOS: fully convolutional one-stage object detection. In: Proceedings of the IEEE/CVF International Conference on Computer Vision, pp. 9627–9636 (2019)

26. Ge, Z., et al.: Yolox: exceeding Yolo series in 2021. arXiv preprint: arXiv:2107.08430 (2021)

27. Yu, G., et al.: PP-PicoDet: a better real-time object detector on mobile devices. arXiv preprint: arXiv:2111.00902 (2021)

Correction to: A Survey of Control Flow Graph Recovery for Binary Code

Qianjin Wang, Xiangdong Li, Chong Yue, and Yuchen He

Correction to:
Chapter 16 in: M. Zhang et al. (Eds.): *Computer Applications,*
CCIS 1960, https://doi.org/10.1007/978-981-99-8761-0_16

A spelling error in the word "Survey" in the title of this chapter has been corrected after the initial publication.

The updated version of this chapter can be found at
https://doi.org/10.1007/978-981-99-8761-0_16

Author Index

Printed in the United States
by Baker & Taylor Publisher Services